How Americans

Can

Buy American

How Americans Can

Buy American

The Power of Consumer Patriotism
Second Edition

by

Roger Simmermaker

RIVERCROSS PUBLISHING, INC.
Orlando

Printed in the United States of America. No part of this book may be used or reproduced in any manner whatsoever without written permission, except in the case of brief quotations embodied in critical articles and reviews. For information address RIVERCROSS PUBLISHING, INC. 6214 Wynfield Court, Orlando, Florida 32819 or editor@rivercross.com

ISBN: 1-58141-080-8

Library of Congress Catalog Card Number: 2002068202

Third Printing

Library of Congress Cataloging-in-Publication Data

Simmermaker, Roger.
    How Americans can buy American / by Roger Simmermaker—2nd ed.
      p. cm
    Includes bibliographical references.
    ISBN 1-58141-080-8
      1. Brand name products—United States. 2. Brand choice—United States.
3. Buy national policy—United States. I. Title.

HD69.B7 S56 2002
658.8′343—dc21

                                    2002068202

Contents

Acknowledgements

I thank God Almighty for giving me the idea for this book and for the strength to complete it.

A very special thank you goes to my loving wife Linda. Without her help and enduring patience and trust in me, this second edition would not be possible.

Thanks to my father and mother Loren and Bernice Simmermaker, Josh Furman at Rivercross Publishing and book cover designers Kim and Allen D'Angelo at Archer-Ellison Design. Thanks also to Charles Mercer of the Union Label & Service Trades Department of the AFL-CIO for providing me with the union database information.

Thanks also to Pat Buchanan, Gus Stelzer, Charley Reese, Pat Choate, James McMillion, Linda Muller and Nancy Greystone.

Criteria

The criteria used in this book for determining if a brand is American owned or foreign owned is the same criteria used by the Directory of Corporate Affiliations, which was my main source of information.

A brand is considered to be American owned only if it is at least 50% owned by an American company. Otherwise, it is considered to be foreign owned. For example, 7-Eleven Stores are owned by 7-Eleven, Inc. based in Dallas, TX. However, 7-Eleven, Inc. is 64% owned by Ito-Yokado Co., Ltd. of Japan. Therefore, 7-Eleven Stores are considered to be foreign owned.

Disclaimer

The information contained in this book is the result of years of exhaustive research by the author. It is not always possible to be 100% accurate because of erroneous information from references and sources used or human error. However, this book is accurate to the extent that exhaustive research and investigation has been able to create.

Correspondence

How Americans Can Buy American
PO Box 780839
Orlando, FL 32878-0839
Email: buyamerican@howtobuyamerican.com
Phone: 1-888-US OWNED (876-9633)
http://www.howtobuyamerican.com

PART I

Chapter 1

Buying American in the Purest Sense of the Term

Buy American! It is sometimes more easily said than done. Many patriotic Americans have the best of intentions, but buying American made products these days can be an especially difficult task. Even though American consumers still buy about half of the goods produced by other Americans, it seems that the made in China label is increasingly more prevalent.

But before we enter into a discussion of "Buying American" and how to do it, we must first establish the term as used in this chapter and define exactly what it really means.

First of all, the term "Buy American" is not synonymous with the term "Made in USA." If it was, we would all be happy patriotic consumers if the only brands we ever bought were Mitsubishi, Toshiba, Hitachi and Sony products as long as the Japanese, in this example, decided to employ Americans to manufacture or assemble the product for us. I don't believe that any consumer who seriously intends to buy American would subscribe to such a scenario. Also, many of the bigger-ticket items such as automobiles have calculated percentages of domestic parts content, so it is likely that even an American made product could be assembled with a high percentage of imported parts.

So it follows then that buying American is a term that goes much deeper than looking for the "Made in USA" label. Buying an American made product is part of the larger "Buy American" picture, of which there are three distinct parts. Two have already been mentioned—which I will from this point forward refer to as "made" and "parts" or "parts content."

The part of the "Buy American" picture that is most often overlooked, but is actually the most important, is ownership. Ownership equals control, and control equals independence. America simply is not independent to control its own destiny if its factories are owned by foreign companies and their overseas investors. When we buy products from foreign owned companies such as Honda, Toyota, Hyundai, etc., we may support some jobs here in the United States, but we lose in the long run since the profits are siphoned out of the country, and the taxes on those profits are paid to foreign governments—not the American government. So next time you hear about the fact that there isn't enough money for social security, the health care system is in crisis, or that we are now running a national deficit to increase military spending to fund the war on terrorism, part of the reason is that we have failed to fund the necessary costs of government by making our nation poorer as a result of our everyday consumer purchases.

Current U.S. Treasury Secretary Paul O'Neill has publicly stated that the Social Security Trust Fund he is responsible for managing has "no assets," and politicians now publicly admit that only unacceptable tax hikes on voters can allow them to keep social security pension promises to future retirees of the baby boomer generation and their children.

Regardless of our good intentions to buy American made products, we often contribute to the demise of our own financial well-being by buying them from foreign-owned companies. So if we look to buy not only American made products, but also those made by American owned companies, not only do we support more American jobs, but we also fund such important programs and benefits such as educating our children, paying the salaries of our policemen and firemen, and of the members of our military who are fighting to keep America free. We also support our veterans who gave us the freedom we now enjoy and who may be disabled and unable to work or need medical assistance from our government through Medicare or Medicaid. All these programs are funded only by tax dollars paid by American workers and American companies. Foreign workers, and to a large extent, foreign companies, don't pay a dime towards funding the cost of government. Foreign companies pay *less than* 1% of their total profits in taxes to America, where U.S.-based companies pay *over* 3%. Corporate taxes represent 10.1% of all government receipts.

Also, U.S. companies' earnings and profits are distributed to American stockholders. The shares of these companies make up many of our retirement funds, and American companies are more likely to donate to charities for the benefit of this country. The most recent example of this was the large donations made by American companies in the wake of the September 11 tragedy. American companies Ford and General Motors gave millions of dollars and donated several of their trucks for the rescue effort. Of the several hundred companies that donated to September 11-related funds, the overwhelming majority of them were American owned.

According to Gus Stelzer, retired Senior Executive of General Motors and author of *The Nightmare of Camelot,* there are many other features obtained only by buying American made products from American owned companies.

Mr. Stelzer commented that ''These quality features are made possible only by taxes paid by American companies and American workers. Foreign companies and foreign workers don't pay taxes in America.''

Real Deficit Reduction	Aid to Disadvantaged
Public Colleges	Food Stamps
Public Libraries	Parks and Recreation
Public Hospitals	Grants to the Arts and
NASA Space Program	Humanities
Sanitation Services	Construction and Maintenance
Aid to Minorities	of Roads, Streets and Bridges

The fact that American companies are taxed to support these obligations and foreign companies are not also means that foreign producers usually have enormous production cost advantages over American producers. For example, we spend over $1,000 per American citizen for military defense, where China spends about $30 per Chinese citizen.

Congress has imposed literally thousands of government mandates and regulations on domestic producers while at the same time offering to exempt those same producers if they will fire their American workers and reopen new factories in China where they would be exempt from such costly mandates and regulations. These production cost burdens include but are certainly not limited to a mandated minimum wage, unemployment compensation, workmen's compensation, health and safety regulations (OSHA), environmental protection regulations (EPA), the Food and Drug Administration (FDA), civil rights laws, and other labor laws and tax laws. American companies often have no choice but to gradually move some of their factories overseas, given the lack of support from their own government that often prevents them from employing their own people. It is unfair to penalize domestic producers if they are required to charge higher prices than foreign producers simply because of the laws that ''We, The People'' have advocated that they be taxed to pay for.

The most recent reality check on the importance of American ownership surfaced when Stanley Tools Co. announced they were moving their headquarters from Connecticut, where they have been for over 150 years, to Bermuda. The reason: To avoid paying U.S. taxes. Stanley has shown their true colors, and they are obviously not red, white and blue. Fruit of the Loom, formerly based in Chicago, had the same tax-evasion scheme in mind when they reincorporated in the Cayman Islands in 1999. This paperwork scheme is further brought to light when we realize that many of the foreign companies we have been supporting for years, such as Michelin, Firestone, Holiday Inn, Dunkin' Donuts, Citgo and 7-Eleven have also enjoyed this nearly tax-free status since they are not American-based companies either.

By changing just a few simple buying habits, usually at little or no cost or inconvenience to the consumer, we can re-direct literally thousands of dollars out of hands of foreigners and into the hands of Americans. Allow me to give one simple example.

After the release of the first edition of *How Americans Can Buy American* in 1996, I gave a speech to a local Machinist Union during which I mentioned that Citgo was not an American company, but based in Venezuela. After the speech, the president of that union told me that both he and his wife had Citgo credit cards and spent about $25 each week in gas. Simple math tells us that one family changing just one buying habit can represent taking hundreds of dollars a month and thousands of dollars a year out of the hands of foreign companies and putting it into the hands of American companies. Think of the powerful, positive potential you hold in your hands with the 15,000+ listings in this book. We as consumers wield far more control over our own economy than we ever imagined. If every American would change just three simple buying habits from foreign to American, the positive impact on the U.S. economy would be nothing short of enormous. Buying American is more than about borders and NAFTA or the Democrats and Republicans. It's really about us and who we are as a people and how we are able to steer the global economy. So let's step up to the wheel and steer the economy in a direction that best benefits America and her people!

Citgo of Venezuela was also responsible for forcing President Clinton to change our clean air laws as a result of losing a World Trade Organization (WTO) decision initiated by Citgo. In my home state of Florida, 7-Eleven stores almost exclusively offer Citgo gasoline at the pump. By avoiding Japanese-owned 7-Eleven and Venezuelan-owned Citgo gasoline altogether, we keep even more money out of the hands of foreign companies and their investors since 7-Eleven is 64% owned by Ito-Yokado Co., Ltd. The largest and most successful convenience-store chain in America isn't even American.

In detail in Part II, Chapter 3 I discuss what foreign companies and their investors often do with the dollars that we send them. Many use the money that used to be ours to buy financially struggling or bankrupt American companies and their assets, which further transfers wealth out of the country. When we buy the products of or patronize the services of foreign companies, we many times end up unknowingly subsidizing foreign purchases of our own American factories and businesses. We then become employees of distant foreign bosses who have little or no connection or regard for the American communities where their workers are employed.

I also discuss in detail in Part II, Chapter 3 how when two companies "merge," the ownership of the newly merged company is determined by which company is bigger or stronger financially. For instance, one example I used in the first edition of this book was that of Pillsbury and General Mills. Both companies were popular makers of flour, both made their flour in the USA, and both claimed Minneapolis, MN was their home. The difference was that Pillsbury was foreign owned and General Mills was American owned. Profits reaped by Pillsbury were sent to England to their corporate parent Grand Metropolitan PLC, which was later bought by Diageo PLC of England. Taxes on Pillsbury's profits were paid to the British government, while taxes on General Mills' profits were paid to the U.S. government. Another argument made in the first edition was that if we supported foreign companies more than similar American companies and these two companies merged, the new larger company would be foreign owned instead of American owned and siphon even more wealth and tax dollars out of the country.

In October 2001, General Mills bought its foreign rival Pillsbury. Profits reaped by Pillsbury will be now be taxed by the U.S. government to pay for the ever-increasing cost of government in America instead of England.

Other little-known uses of our tax dollars, made possible only by American workers and American companies, include airport renovations and beach-rehabilitation projects. In May of 2001, President Bush proposed to cut the percentage of federal tax dollars used to fix America's water pollution problems and eroding coastlines. This was a particularly startling proposal since beach closings increased nearly two-fold from 1999 to 2000 according to the Natural Resources Defense Council, because of sewage pollution. Such proposals are evidence that there aren't enough tax dollars to go around for the benefits Americans have come to take for granted.

In August 2001, just weeks before the September 11 tragedy, Bush proposed charging an additional tax on airline carriers that offered flights at peak travel hours as a way to help pay for upgrades to an outdated air traffic control system. And of course we all know that as a result of September 11, even more government funds (tax dollars) are being used to subsidize airport renovations and increased security. The point here is that we can help fund the war on terrorism and all other government expenditures, in many cases, without spending an extra dime by making more intelligent consumer purchases.

Our government also subsidizes housing in several ways with our tax dollars. The most popular, of course, is the interest deduction on mortgage loans. This subsidy alone costs the government $55 billion a year. The government also sponsors low-cost loans through Fannie Mae and Freddie Mac, and allows these two companies to borrow at lower rates so that mortgage interest rates for those who want a piece of the American dream can also borrow at lower rates.

Knowing about the billions of dollars of taxpayer funds that are used to benefit Americans, who would buy foreign-owned Lysol disinfectant instead of Kmart's American Fare disinfectant knowing that less tax dollars would go to pay for funding the cost of Social Security, Medicare, Medicaid, our children's education, the military, and funding the war on terrorism as a result? Kmart's American Fare even costs less than Lysol. Why not buy American-owned and made Zest soap instead of Japanese-owned, American-made Jergens soap? Why not buy American-owned and made Cooper tires instead of Japanese-owned, American made Firestone tires? How about an American-owned and made Kodak disposable camera instead of a foreign owned, American-made Fuji disposable camera.

Your tax dollars funded the United States to represent Kodak in a 1995 WTO dispute against Fuji—a dispute that Kodak lost. In the filing, it was claimed that the Japanese government conspired with Fuji to prevent wider distribution of American-made Kodak film in Japanese retail outlets (Kodak only enjoys a 10% share of the Japanese market). Are we to fund the U.S. government to defend American owned companies like Kodak with our tax dollars and simultaneously fund foreign-owned companies like Fuji with our consumer dollars? Such a scenario speaks to double standards.

Exactly how much in tax revenue do we lose each year as a result of buying foreign owned products instead of American owned products? Economist Pat Choate has estimated that the figure is at least $30 billion annually. As our economy has recently slipped from a national surplus to a national deficit, your preferences in consumer purchases could actually keep us in the black and speed up the recovery from the recent recession. American taxpayers often fail to realize that any revenue shortfall in our government will be compensated by an increase in income taxes. The rate at which U.S. citizens are taxed is a direct result of the amount of funds, or lack thereof, the government is able to collect by other means. One such potential source of revenue is import tariffs, but our governmental trade policies have replaced tariffs on imports (an indirect tax) with direct taxes on income.

There really is so much more that can be done than by contacting your representatives in congress. Voicing your concerns to your elected officials is an important part in creating a better America, but we have a much louder voice and can speak much more often with our wallet, checkbook or credit card. The power we have as consumers is many times bigger than politics and partisanism. We only vote as citizens at the polls every two or four years, but we vote as consumers at the stores *every day*! If we decide as consumers to support only American companies, to the extent possible, that make things in the USA and leave foreign owned, foreign made products to rot on the shelves, there isn't a trade policy any government can devise to reverse such a united consumer strategy.

Sometimes because of government policies, it makes actually makes sense for American companies to manufacture overseas, and there is often very little we can do about that individually. But what we *can* do as Americans collectively is learn which American companies are employing the most American workers and support them so that more American workers can stay employed and not become victims of bad government trade policies. As of March 1999, The United Auto Workers (UAW) represented 220,000 employees who work for General Motors and 101,000 employees who work for Ford. German-owned DaimlerChrysler has about 75,000 UAW-represented employees.

As Americans see some of our companies gradually close factories here and move them overseas, many have the opinion that American companies "don't give a hoot" about American workers. But to make that point stick, you would also need to somehow make a convincing argument that foreign companies care about American workers more. American companies don't need to be motivated by American patriotism for American citizens to reap the benefits of their repatriated profits and the taxes paid to America on those profits.

After Honda decided to shut down one of its five automobile assembly lines in Japan in 1999, they were quick to announce that their roots will surely remain in Japan. And although the United States is seen as increasingly contributing to the growth of the company, Japan will be the main source for ideas, technology and "creative" manufacturing.

Many have argued that we should stress corporate responsibility, but efforts to stress such obligations can only be directed at American companies. Foreign companies owe no allegiance to the United States, so corporate responsibility speeches and ploys do not affect foreign companies. If we are to convince any company to return more of their production to America, it must be an American company since they are based here and owned primarily by American investors. And since American companies benefit America by paying more tax dollars to our government, we need to ensure they get our consumer dollars with which to remain profitable so they can move back to our shores and pay the higher wages required for operating here.

"Ownership entails obligations. Its use should also serve the public interest."
The German Constitution

Another benefit of American ownership is that it provides jobs for more Americans than foreign owned companies. For example, if two similar companies—one American owned and the other foreign owned—make similar products in America, the American owned company will generally support more American jobs in two different ways.

First, since American companies have their headquarters based in the United States, they generally employ American workers in such positions as research and development, design, engineering, administration, testing and advertising. Foreign companies, since their headquarters are based overseas, generally employ workers in their home country for these jobs.

For example, in August 1999, American-based disk drive maker Komag, Inc. announced it was laying off 480 manufacturing workers, but the 350 workers in research and development remained employed at the San Jose, California headquarters. No American should be happy to see these manufacturing jobs be sent overseas, but the point here is that there is a difference we can make even in the most unfortunate of circumstances. The difference here between supporting an American-based disk drive maker and a foreign-based disk drive maker is at least 350 jobs. An emphasis should definitely be placed on keeping manufacturing jobs in the United States whenever possible, but there are other American jobs in other professions that can be saved just by buying an American owned company's product, even when none of the products in a given category are American made.

Second, just by supporting an American company, we generally support more American jobs in the parts or parts content sector. Some Japanese cars are manufactured here, and it would seem like buying an American-made Japanese car is a good thing since they have hired American factory workers to assemble their automobiles.

But the reality is that American automobile companies employ more Americans in the parts or parts sector industry than comparable foreign-owned firms. Harley-Davidson, for example, makes all of their motocycles in the United States with a 95% domestic parts content. Honda makes some of their motorcycles in the United States too, but they import more of their parts from Japan.

What most Americans don't realize, however, is that same foreign company that manufactures their cars here is causing a lot of other American workers to lose their jobs because they import more of their parts compared to American automobile companies. As a result, many of the American workers who used to make automobile parts for American companies are now being laid off. The problem is that there are a lot more parts workers being laid off than there are manufacturing workers being hired. This means that buying a foreign car made in the USA is a job destroyer rather than a job creator, and is one reason why foreign investment does not reduce imports. The UAW estimated that by the mid-1990's, at least 500,000 American jobs had been eliminated because of foreign owned automobile manufacturers operating in the United States. So by simply buying an American-owned company's product, we often help keep more Americans employed in the parts industry.

American companies also need profits to continue to boost spending for research and development in an increasingly competitive world marketplace. In 1999, for example, U.S. corporations increased spending on research and development over the previous year's level by 9.3%. American companies further increased research and development spending again in 2000 by 10.6%. Such spending makes keeping jobs for American workers at American companies like Komag possible, even if the manufacturing jobs gravitate overseas.

Also, prosperous American companies appear to have a ripple effect for other American companies as well. In January 1999, Ford selected IBM to develop nearly all of the auto maker's software. A new campus for integrating 1,000 employees from each firm to develop the new information-technology was scheduled to be built in Michigan.

New technology today is increasingly more expensive to develop. We need to know whose pockets we are lining so our consumer dollars end up in the hands of American companies so they can be on the cutting-edge of research and development technology, which in this case supported 2,000 American jobs between Ford and IBM. The jobs for both of these companies were off the radar screen as far as manufacturing was concerned, but they are American jobs nonetheless.

It is amazing that upon talking to many American engineers, the depth of their understanding of buying American is limited to advocating the support of American manufacturing jobs. Many fail to realize that their own jobs are made possible by the American company they work for and the fact that American-based companies generally hire American engineers. Chances are they would be out looking for another job if the American company that employs them happened to be foreign owned.

In March 2001, Sony recruited IBM to develop *and produce* their next generation "Cell" microprocessor to be used in Sony's PlayStation 3. In June 2001, IBM announced they had created the world's fastest silicon transistor. In October 2001, IBM announced plans to invest $3 billion in East Fishkill, N.Y. to construct a new semiconductor manufacturing facility. It is clear that without significant profits, IBM would not be able to constantly develop the world's fastest communications devices, invest billions of dollars in development and production facilities to employ Americans, and fund the cost of government with their tax dollars that provide the benefits we enjoy as American citizens.

There has been much speculation and disagreement about exactly how to define an "American product." For the purposes of this chapter, an American product will be defined as any product made or produced by an American owned company, regardless of the point of manufacture.

For example, a Mercury Grand Marquis made in Canada is to be considered an American product, and a Toyota Camry made in the United States is to be considered a foreign product. A Mercury Grand Marquis can properly be called an import, but it is certainly not a foreign product since car was designed by American engineers employed by an American company. Assembly workers in Canada may have a stake in Ford as shareholders, but the percentage is certainly not enough to classify the automobile they assemble a Canadian product. An automobile takes several months to design, yet only several hours to assemble. In today's more sophisticated economy, an increasing percentage of the value of products such as automobiles are imbedded in the brand name, intellectual property and design. The brand name is American, and therefore the finished product, regardless of manufacturing location, is American as well.

Again, there are other jobs to be considered besides manufacturing or assembly jobs. Since manufacturing now represents less than 20% of the jobs in the United States, that means we have over 80% of other jobs to consider when we make our everyday purchases. If we buy products based upon "Made in USA" only, we make 100% of the decision based on less that 20% of the information. The jobs in such areas discussed earlier are in testing, administration, design, research and development and advertising. Since Mercury is an American company, these jobs reside in America. As Friedrich List was quoted as saying, "The power of producing wealth is . . . infinitely more important than wealth itself." Since Mercury is owned by American-based Ford, it is an American company that retains the power to create wealth. Also American companies are more subject to the laws and mandates of the American government than foreign companies. Corporate responsibility can also be demanded by the American people or their government. It was the sentiment of corporate responsibility that prompted so many American companies to donate to the September 11th Fund, for example.

In his review of the first edition of *How Americans Can Buy American*, syndicated columnist Charley Reese stated that it is correct to assert that "it is easier to persuade American companies to bring back jobs than it is to persuade foreign companies to keep jobs here."

Still, many buy American-conscious consumers direct their dissatisfaction that certain American cars are built in Canada, but they are misguided in placing the blame at the feet of American companies. The majority of the blame deserves to be laid at the feet of the U.S. government and their trade policies. Consider that during the Lyndon B. Johnson administration, the U.S. negotiated an auto pact with Canada that stipulated for every car America sells to Canada, one would be built in Canada, which basically tied the hands of American auto manufacturers. It is therefore blatantly unfair to fault American companies for producing so many of their cars and trucks across our northern border. The U.S. government can only make this guarantee on behalf of American companies, not foreign companies.

Part of the problem with our government's trade policies is that it has too often forced us to become too preoccupied in convincing other countries to buy American instead of our own. Washington is repeatedly angered by China for advocating the purchase of their own domestic goods, and specifically for granting tax breaks to their own companies to minimize the damage of the Asian Crisis of 1997. It is quite possible that what angers Washington the most is that China is benefiting from a protectionist trade policy from which America herself used to benefit. As is mentioned in Part II, Chapter 2, we would be wise to read up on U.S. trade history and revisit our own protectionist past which proved to be so prosperous. It seems that Washington too often tries to get citizens of every country to buy American except its own citizens, who are most likely motivated to do so.

In early 2000, more than 50 U.S. Senators wrote Beijing to convince China to buy more American wheat, meat and citrus. We have sacrificed our own market to predatory foreign forces to such an extent that we must now resort to getting on bended knee to beg foreign countries to buy our goods. We clearly have no right to ask other countries to surrender their markets to America just because we have foolishly surrendered ours.

Even as the U.S. Senate writes Beijing to convince China to buy American agriculture, the Made in America Information Act (HR 725) is being ignored. Passed by the House of Representatives in every congressional session since the 103rd congress, this bill would establish a toll-free number Americans could call to locate American made products. Yet every year, the bill goes to the Senate where it gets stuck in committee and dies. To sign the petition to get the Senate to take up the bill, which passed the House by an overwhelming margin of 407-3, go to www.howtobuyamerican.com. The toll-free number would be funded by the domestic producers that chose to participate in the program at no cost to the U.S. government or the American taxpayer.

We must also understand that because of unfair trade agreements, it is sometimes necessary for American companies to produce offshore. It is unrealistic, for example, to expect American electronics companies to employ all their workers in high-wage America, when similar foreign companies like Sony employ 60% of their workforce in low-wage Asian countries.

So when faced with a decision to buy a foreign-made clock radio, since none are made in the United States, it is more beneficial to America to buy an American-owned General Electric or Emerson radio, for instance, instead of a foreign-owned Sony radio. The U.S. government will reap more tax revenue, and more American jobs in areas other than manufacturing will be supported as a result. More American stockholders will also reap the gains of a more profitable American company.

In the first edition of this book, it was stated that by the end of 1996 that VF Corporation, maker of Lee and Wrangler jeans, planned to have 30-35% of their apparel made offshore and the situation was likely to get worse. By the end of 2000, about 70% of VF Corp.'s apparel was made offshore. Wake Forest University Economist Gary Shoesmith maintains that this does not mean that the apparel or textile industry is doomed because "American companies are going to be profitable, they're just going to employ a lot of foreigners, and their profits will be repatriated."

If we can't supply our own needs, then we are not an independent country. Buying products from foreign companies making things in the USA is contrary to such American virtues as independence, self-reliance and self-sufficiency, and we forfeit the independence that our founding father's fought and died to preserve by buying American made products from foreign owned companies. Only by supporting the home team, even when their products are made elsewhere, can we truly remain an independent nation.

The strategies being described in this book are about more than borders and NAFTA or Mexico and Canada. It's more about us as individuals and who we are and the power we have as consumers that matters. Buying American empowers us to regain some of the power many Americans feel they have lost in reforming their own government. And it just so happens that we can do something to help our country and ultimately help ourselves at the same time.

So if you care about your child's education, then you need to care about buying American. If you care about your own retirement, then you need to care about buying American. Associating buying American with items like funding our social security or children's education and fire and police protection isn't a connection we would normally make, but the relationship is there whether we choose to realize it or not.

Much like in the way citizens of a small town enjoy patronizing their locally-owned business to keep profits and jobs within their community instead of patronizing the chain stores which will send profits outside their communities, we need to patronize American companies to keep profits within our national borders instead of foreign companies which will send profits outside our national borders. It really comes down to the question of "whose pockets are we lining?" Why not line our own?

Even in times of perceived national prosperity and increased consumerism, we need to shake the feeling of invulnerability which may lead us to believe that the good times will always last and we will always have prosperity. During times like these, there is often less regard for where and how we spend our money and for who gets the benefit of our increased consumerism. To assure that we receive the benefits and reap the returns on our own investments, we need to buy American in the purest sense of the term so we leave ourselves and our country in good financial shape for when the inevitable economic downturn arrives.

If we don't patronize American products and services, we aren't adding to the pool of funds we all draw from for the social services and programs mentioned in this chapter.

For an example on a more personal level, since I work for one of America's largest defense contractors, my wages are derived completely from American tax dollars. It would be therefore blatantly hypocritical for me to not support American companies that pay the most taxes from which I draw my income. Even if your wages are not derived directly from the government, it is still hypocritical to rely on and expect tax-payer-subsidized services from the government and not simultaneously support American companies, where possible, who pay the most tax dollars to the funds you draw from. So, when you support foreign companies with your purchases, you are not only shortchanging America, but you are also shortchanging yourself.

Buying American can be easier than we initially imagine if we focus not so much on the bigger-ticket items like automobiles that we buy less often and more on smaller-ticket items that we buy more often. A good place to start is in your local grocery store. Buying American here is made easy since almost all products in supermarkets are American made, and since there is usually no parts content to consider, we can focus almost strictly on ownership as our guide to buying American. The examples below are also in Part II, but I have listed them again here for quick reference.

American Owned/American Made	Foreign Owned/American Made
White House	Mott's
Grey Poupon	French's
Swiss Miss	Carnation
Johnson & Johnson	Q-Tips
Yoplait	Dannon
Prego	Ragu
Campbell's	Libby's
Iams	Purina
Sprite	7-Up

What is interestingly evident from the listing above is that it is nearly impossible to determine whether a brand is American by its familiarity or by how it sounds. Both Grey Poupon (American-owned) and French's (British-owned) sound foreign, but both are not. Swiss Miss is American, but Carnation is owned by the Swiss. Purina was bought by Swiss-owned Nestle this year and 7-Up, along with Dr. Pepper, has been British-owned since 1995.

It is easy to change habits to buy American in the food store where most consumers are indifferent as to which product to buy. If there is brand loyalty to a foreign product in some area, then focus your attention where there is no brand loyalty and where an American alternative will suffice.

Even with brand names with the word "American" in them aren't always American owned. French-owned Dannon bought bottled-water brands Great American and Pure American Natural Spring Water in 1998. Reading labels can be very misleading as well, since all the foreign-owned products listed above will list the address of their U.S. subsidiaries on the package. This tricks us into thinking we are buying American when we clearly are not.

Besides patronizing American owned products, we can also patronize American-owned services. In this area, ownership is again our only guide since services don't have product labels or parts content.

Below is another quick-reference guide to some common and popular services we often patronize.

American Owned	Foreign Owned
Circle K	7-Eleven
Vitamin World	GNC
Best Buy	CompUSA
Days Inn	Holiday Inn
Krispy Kreme	Dunkin' Donuts
Chevron	Shell

In the listing of services, like the previous listing of products, we find some familiar brand names that are foreign owned and other American-sounding names that aren't American at all. GNC was acquired by a European company in 1999. Holiday Inn and Dunkin' Donuts have both been foreign owned for several years and CompUSA was bought by Mexican investors in 1999. Shell, who recently bought Pennzoil-Quaker State after their recent merger, is based in The Netherlands. So we see there are other ways to easily buy American where the cost or inconvenience, if any, is negligible.

When we are faced with buying two similar products where parts content is not a factor, such as in the supermarket, I have listed the order that will best benefit the U.S. economy below.

1. American owned/American made
2. American owned/Foreign made
3. Foreign owned/American made
4. Foreign owned/Foreign made

Even when parts content is a factor, the above listing still applies since American companies generally have higher domestic parts contents in their products compared to similar foreign owned companies. This means, for example, it is more beneficial for America to buy a Ford made overseas than it is a Toyota made in America. There are more American jobs involved in producing a Ford to be exported to the U.S. than there are American jobs involved in producing a domestically built Toyota.

The only exception to the above listing concerns communist China. American companies operating in China are not fully-owned American companies since they are required to enter joint-ventures with Chinese companies as a condition for doing business there, so in many cases the fact that their products have an American brand name on them is misleading. Also, contrary to those who would advocate increased trade engagement with China even in light of our huge trade deficit, China is more of an adversary to be dealt with more than they are a "trading partner." Profits sent to China, since most are not repatriated to the United States, are used for building up the Chinese war machine that America may well confront directly someday. If this confrontation occurs, it will not be any consolation that we were able to supposedly take advantage of the cost benefits of cheap imports. In fact, if we spent less of our money on cheap Chinese imports that we really don't need in the first place, we would have more money to spend on American products.

Prosperity is great, but it also commands attention to keep our prosperity here so that we may extend the ripple effect of the gains into not-so prosperous times. Increased consumerism in times of prosperity can work against us since we tend to loosen our belts a little and tend to forget about who is benefiting from our increased consumerism. We need to ensure that as we prosper as individuals that we also prosper as a nation. Buying American during a time when it really doesn't seem to matter will ensure that we, as General Motors recently put it, "Keep America Rolling."

THE WALL STREET JOURNAL

"Actually, son, whether the glass is half full
or empty isn't important –
it's who *owns* the glass."

Guide to Abbreviations for Foreign Countries

ARG	Argentina
AST	Austria
AUS	Australia
BG	Belgium
BMD	Bermuda
BZL	Brazil
C	Canada
CH	China
CHL	Chile
CI	Cayman Islands
DEN	Denmark
FIN	Finland
FR	France
G	Germany
HK	Hong Kong
ICE	Iceland
IND	India
IRE	Ireland
ISR	Israel
ITL	Italy
J	Japan
JAM	Jamaica
K	Korea
MAL	Malaysia
MEX	Mexico
N	Netherlands
NOR	Norway
NZ	New Zealand
PHI	Philippines
POR	Portugal
RUS	Russia
SAF	South Africa
SNG	Singapore
SP	Spain
SWE	Sweden
SWI	Switzerland
THAI	Thailand
TUR	Turkey
TWN	Taiwan
UK	England
UKN	Unilever*
V	Venezuela

*Unilever is a joint venture between England and The Netherlands

Chapter 2

Transportation/Automotive

AIRLINES

American owned

Alaska		TWA	
American Airlines		United Airlines	
Delta		US Airways	
Southwest			

Foreign owned

Aer Lingus	IRE	KLM	N
Air New Zealand	NZ	Lan Chile	CHL
Air-India	IND	Mexicana Airlines	MEX
Air-Jamaica	JAM	Phillipine Airlines	PHI
Alitalia	ITL	Quantas	AUS
Cathay Pacific	HK	Singapore Airlines	SNG
Icelandair	ICE	Swissair	SWI
Japan Airlines	J		

ANTI-FREEZE

American owned

Havoline	STP
Peak	Streetguard
Polar	Zerex
Prestone	

Foreign owned

Car And Driver	FR	Firestone Frigitone	J

AUTO PARTS

American owned

AC Delco	Dayco
Batco	FAG
Brake Technology	Filko
Brakeware	Gabriel
Cherry Bomb Mufflers	Holley
Cooper	J/Wax
Cragar Wheels	NAPA

Foreign owned

Bosch	G	Gates Belts & Hoses	UK
Fix-A-Flat	N	Robert Bosch	G

AUTOMOBILES

American owned

Aston Martin	Lincoln
Buick	Mercury
Cadillac	Oldsmobile
Chevrolet	Opel
Ford	Pontiac
Geo	Saab
GMC	Saturn
Jaguar	Volvo

Foreign owned

Acura	J	Lamborghini	G
Alfa Romeo	ITL	Lexus	J
Audi	G	Lotus	MAL
Bentley	G	Maserati	ITL
BMW	G	Mazda	J
Chrysler	G	Mercedes	G
Daewoo	K	Mitsubishi	J
Daihatsu	J	Nissan	J
Datsun	J	Peugot	FR
Dodge	G	Plymouth	G
Eagle	G	Porsche	G
Ferrari	ITL	Renault	FR
Fiat	ITL	Rolls Royce	G
Honda	J	Subaru	J
Hyundai	K	Suzuki	J
Isuzu	J	Toyota	J
Jeep	G	Volkswagen	G
Kia	K		

CAR POLISH

American owned

Armor All	PolyShell
Blue Coral	Raindance
Finish 2001	Rally
Kit	Turtle Wax
Liquid Crystal	Zip Wax
Minute Wax	

Foreign owned
No foreign brands could be located for this category.

CAR RENTAL

American owned

Alamo	National
Avis	Sears
Budget	Thrifty
Dollar	Ugly Ducking
Enterprise	Wallwork
Hertz	

Foreign owned
No foreign brands could be located for this category.

GASOLINE

American owned

Chevron	Petro
Coastal	Phillips 66
Conoco	Sergaz
Esso	Sinclair
Exxon	Sonoco
Gas Express	Spur
Getty	Star Kleen
Gulf	STP Fuel Centers
Hess	Sunoco
Kerr-McGee	Tenneco
Marathon	Texaco
Martin	Ultramar
Mobil	Union 76
Murphy USA	Zephyr
Pate	

Foreign owned

Amoco	UK	Futura	FIN
Arco	UK	Red Rooster	C
Boron	UK	Shell	N
BP	UK	Sohio	UK
Citgo	V	Standard	UK
Fina	FR	Total	FR

MOTORCYCLES

Harley-Davidson, Buell and Polaris motorcycles are made in USA. Ninety-five percent of Harley-Davidson motorcycle parts are made in the United States.

American owned

Buell		Polaris	
Harley-Davidson			

Foreign owned

BMW	G	Magna	J
Gold Wing	J	Suzuki	J
Honda	J	Yamaha	J
Katana	J	Husky/Husqvarna	SWE
Kawasaki	J		

MOTOR OIL

Royal Dutch Shell made an offer to acquire Pennzoil-Quaker State in March 2002. Since it is doubtful that there will be any significant regulatory opposition to the acquisition, I have listed Pennzoil and Quaker State as foreign brands.

American owned

76 Motor Oil	Phillips 66
AMS Oil	Proforce
Cardinal	Proline
Chevron	Slick 50
Coastal	Sonoco
Havoline	STP
Mobil	Sunoco
Mobil 1	Trop-Artic
Motorcraft	Valvoline
Pate	

Foreign owned

Amoco	UK	Pennzoil	N
Castrol	UK	Permalube	UK
Citgo	V	Primas	MAL
Fire & Ice 2000	N	Quaker State	N
LDO	UK	Shell	N
Oilzum	UK	Truck Guard	N

OUTBOARD MOTORS

American owned

Force Outboard Motor   MerCruiser
Johnson   Mercury Outboards
Mariner

Foreign owned

No foreign brands could be located for this category.

TIRES

Every automobile tire Cooper sells to the U.S. market is made in USA. Cooper exports American-made tires to over more than 100 countries and has resisted the popular practice of shipping factories overseas to become a more-global company. Cooper CEO Thomas A. Dattilo insists that becoming one of the largest tire manufacturers globally "doesn't give you any inherent advantage."

American owned

Cooper   Metric
Dean   Sears Roadhandler
Goodyear   Starfire
Kelly Springfield   Unocal 76
Mastercraft

Foreign owned

ANS FARM	J	General	G
BF Goodrich	FR	Michelin	FR
Bridgestone	J	Mohawk	J
Continental	G	Pirelli	ITL
Dayton	J	Toyo	J
Dunlop	AUS	Uniroyal	FR
Firestone	J	Yokohoma	J

Chapter 3

Retail Stores

AUTO PARTS STORES

American owned

AutoZone
Big O Tires
CarQuest
Discount Auto Parts
Hahn Automotive

Hi/Lo Automotive
O'Reilly
Pep Boys
R & S Strauss
Trak Auto

Foreign owned

Auto 5   BG

BOOKSTORES

American owned

B. Dalton
Barnes & Noble
Bookland
Books & Co.

Books-A-Million
Borders
The Bookend
Waldenbooks

Foreign owned

Chapters   C

CONVENIENCE STORES

7-Eleven Stores, Inc. is 64% owned by Ito-Yokado Co., Ltd. of Japan.

American owned

Beacon
Bonded
Breakplace
Budget
Casey's General Stores
Cash Mart
Checker
Circle K
Coastal Mart
Convenient Food Mart
Country Cupboard
Crown
Dairy Mart
Dandy Mini Marts
Diamond Shamrock
Economy Food Stores
Enmark
Express 1 Stop

E-Z Serve
Farm Stores
Fast Fare
Fiesta Mart
Flying J Travel Plazas
Food-N-Fuel
Gastown
Happy Dan's
Harper's
Hess Mart
Huck's
Jif-E Mart
Krauszer's
Kwik Pantry
Kwik Sak
Lil' Champ
Majik Markets
Marathon

Maverik
Mini Mart
Minitman
Mr. Cut-Rate
Murphy-Select Market
Nu-Way Oil
Petro Stopping Centers
Pilot
Presto Food Stores
Quiktrip
Racetrac
Raceway
Road Runner
Sergaz
Speedway
Speedway SuperAmerica
Speedway/Starvin' Marvin
Stewart's Shops

Stop N Go
Sunshine Travel Center
SuperAmerica
Swifty Mart
Taylor Food Mart
Timesaver
Total
Uni Marts
United
United Dairy Farmers
Vickers
Village Pantry
Vista
Wareco
White Hen Pantry
Whiting
Williams Express

Foreign owned

7-Eleven	J	Mac's	C
Becker's	C	Mapco Express	ISR
Daisy Mart	C	Red Rooster	C
Fast & Fresh	AUS	Servus	SWE
Getty Mart	RUS	Split Second	UK
High's	J	Wilson's Farms	N

DEPARTMENT STORES

American owned

Alexander's
Ames
Ann Taylor
Beall's
Belk Stores
Bergdorf Goodman
Bergner's
Big Lots
Bloomingdale's
Boscov's
Boston Store
Burdines
Carson Pirie Scott
Catherines

Dayton Hudson
Dayton's
Dillard's
Elder-Beerman
Family Bargain Centers
Famous-Barr
Filene's Basement
Foley's Department Store
Fred Meyer
Fred's
Goldsmith
Gottschalks
Hart's
Hecht's

Herberger's
Hudson's
J.C. Penney
Jacobson
Kaufmann's
Kline's
Kmart
Kohl's
L.S. Ayries
Lazarus
Lord & Taylor
Mac Frugals Bargains Closeouts
Macy's
Marshall Field's
Marshalls
Masters
McRae's
Meier & Frank
Meijer
Mervyn's
Nordstrom
Nordstrom Rack
Odd Lots
Odd N Ends
Odd-Job
Odd's-n-End's
Pamida
Parisian

Pic 'N' Save
Proffitt's
Rich's
Rich's/Lazarus
Robinsons-May
Ross Stores
Saks Direct
Saks Fifth Avenue
Saks Off Fifth
Schottenstein Stores
Sears
Service Merchandise
Shepler's
Shopko
Stein Mart
Stern's
Strawbridge
Strawbridge's
T.J. Maxx
Target
The Bon
The Bon Marche
The Jones Store
Troutman's
Value City
Wal-Mart
Younkers
Zion's

Foreign owned

Lotte   J

Myer Direct   AUS

DRUG STORES

American owned

Astrup
Drug Emporium
Duane Reade
Eckerd's
Edgehill Drugs
Erickson's
Genovese
Longs
Osco
Pathmark

Pharmaprix
Pharmhouse
Phar-Mor
Rite Aid
Rx America
Savon Drugs
Smith's
Thriftway
Walgreen

Foreign owned

Pay Less   UK

FURNITURE STORES

American owned

Aaron Rents and Sells Furniture	Krause's
Aaron's Plus	La-Z-Boy Galleries
ABC Carpet & Home	Levitz
Accentrics	Mattress Discounters
Arbek Furniture	Paine Furniture
Bedroom Superstore	R.C. Willey
Big Lots	Rhodes
Cargo	Rooms To Go
Crossroads	RoomStore
Ethan Allen	Seaman
Farmers Furniture Company	Sears Homelife
Furniture Mart	Star Furniture
Gallery Furniture	Storehouse
Heilig-Meyers	The Bedroom Store
Home Elements	The Bombay Company
Huffman Koos	Thomasville
Jennifer Convertibles	Welcome Home
Jordan's	

Foreign owned

Famsa   MEX   Ikea   N

GENERAL RETAIL

"The Body Shop" is a foreign-owned chain that specializes in hair and skin care products. "Body Shop" is an American-owned chain that specializes in apparel.

American owned

4Day Tire Stores	AfterThoughts
84 Lumber	American Eagle Outfitters
99 Cents Only Stores	American Hair Force
A & N Stores	Ann Taylor
A&E Stores	Annie Sez
Adray Appliance & Photo	Appleseed's
Afaze	Appliance $Mart

Arcadia Shops
Arden B.
Ashley Avery Collectables
Athletic Attic
Atlanta Apparel Mart
August Max
August Max Woman
Babbage's
Babies ''R'' Us
Baby Gap
Baldwin
Banana Republic
Barneys New York
Bass Pro Shops
Bath & Body Works
Bed, Bath & Beyond
Belk
Bentley's Luggage
Best Buy
Big Lots
Big O Tires
Bijoux One
Bill's Dollar Stores
Blockbuster Video
Blooming Basket Floral Shop
Body Shop
Bon Appetit
Boston Traders
Brookstone
Burlington Coat Factory
Buten The Paint & Paper People
Cache
Calico Corners
Casual Corner
Casual Male
Caswell/Massey
Catherines
Cato
Cato Fashions
Cato Plus
Champs Sports
Chico's
Christopher & Banks
Circuit City

Clairborne Menswear
Claire's Boutiques
Clothestime
Coldwater Creek
Computer Renaissance
Contempo Casuals
CookieTree Cookies
Cork & Cap Liquor Shops
Cost Plus
Country General Stores
Country Seat
County Post Stores
Crate & Barrel
CVS
Dara Michelle
David's Bridal
Deb Shops
Deck The Walls
Delia's
Designs
Dollar Express
Dollar General
Dollar Tree
Dress Barn
Duckwall-Alco
Eddie Bauer
Einstein Moomjy
Electronics Boutique
Elisabeth
Encore Recycled Appliances
Factory 2-U Stores
Family Dollar
Fannie May Candy Shops
Fanny Farmer Candy Shops
Fantastic Sams
Fashion Bar
Fashion Bug
Fashion Bug Plus
Fast Max
Fiesta Mart
Filene's Basement
Foot Locker
Frames Unlimited
Frank's Nursery & Crafts

Frederick's Of Hollywood
Fry's Electronics
Funco
G&G
G.C. Murphy
Gadzooks
Gantos
GapKids
Garden Ridge
Gateway Country
Genesco Factory To You
Gingiss Formal Wear
Good Guys
Goody's Family Clothing
Great Earth
Guess Home Stores
Guitar Center
Gump's
Gymboree
Haircuts Plus
Hallmark
Hamilton
Hammacher, Schlemmer
Hancock Fabrics
Harold's Stores
Harris Teeter
Hit Or Miss
Holiday RV Superstore
Hollywood Video
Hot Topic
J.J. Newberry
Jacobson
Jarman/Flagg
Jay Jacobs
Jo-Ann Fabric & Crafts
K&G Men's Center
K-B Toys
Kids "R" Us
King Koil Bedquarters
Kinko's
Kleinsleep
Kuppenheimer
Land's End
Lane Bryant

Laura Ashley
Laura Secord
Leather Warehouse
Lechters
Lerner New York
Levi's Outlets
Liberty House
Life Uniform & Shoe Shops
Limbo Lounge
Limited Too
Linda Karen
Linens 'N Things
Loehmann's
Longs Drug Stores
Luggage Gallery
Magnolia HiFi
Mandee
Mardi Gras Liquor Stores
Marshalls
Mattress Discounters
McCrory
Memory Lane (Card & Gifts)
Men's Wearhouse
Michaels Stores
MicroAge
Mothers Work
Moto Photo
Movie Star Factory Outlet
Movies & More
Noodle Kidoodle
NordicTrack
Nordstrom
Northern Reflections
Northwest Fabrics
NPD
Off 5th
Office Depot
Officemax
Old Navy
Once Upon A Child
One Price
Pacific Sunwear of California
Paper Plus
Paper Warehouse

Party City
Paul Harris
Paul Stuart
Payless Cashways
Perfumania
Petite Sophisticate
Petsmart
Pic 'N' Save
Picture People
Pier 1 Imports
Piercing Pagoda
Pizazz
Play It Again Sports
Popcorn's
Pottery Barn
Pottery Barn Kids
Price Costco
Pro-Cuts
Quality Farm & Fleet
Radio Shack
Rag Shops
Rainbow Apparel Distribution
Rand McNally
Rapid American
Repp Big & Tall
Rex
Richman Brothers
Right Start
Rose's
Ross Stores
S & K
S&K Famous Brands
Saks Fifth Avenue
San Francisco Music Box
Saturday Matinee
Sav-On Inc.
Sax Arts & Crafts
Scribbles & Giggles
See's Candy Shops
Service Merchandise
Simply For Sports
Smith & Hawken
Software Etc
Sound Advice

Sound Warehouse
Sporting Dog
Stage
Staples
Star Flooring
Stars Stuff
Strawberry
Stride Rite
Strouds
Strouds Home Compass
Strouds Linen Outlet
Strouds, The Linen Experts
Structure
SuperPetz
Swiss Colony
Syms
T.G.&Y
T.J. Maxx
Table & Vine
The Children's Place
The Dress Barn
The Gap
The Good Guys
The Limited
The One Stop Movie Shop
The Original Levi's Store
The Paper Shop
The Place
The Popcorn Factory
The Rag Shop
The RX Place
The Sharper Image
The Water's Edge
Things Remembered
Tiffany & Co
Tire Kingdom
Today's Man
Topkapi
Tops Appliance City
Toys "R" Us
Tuesday Morning
Urban Outfitters
Victoria's Secret
Vitamin World

Wallpapers-To-Go
Welcome Home
Wet Seal
Wherehouse
Wicks 'N' Sticks
Widmann

Willoughby's
Wilsons-The Leather Experts
Wolohan Lumber
Woolrich
Zany Brainy

Foreign owned

Benetton	ITL	MVC Entertainment	UK
Britches Great Outdoors	C	PC World	UK
Brooks Brothers	UK	Reno-Depot	UK
Cara Shop	C	Spencer Gifts	FR
CompUSA	MEX	Sunglass Hut	ITL
Currys	UK	Talbots	J
Dixons	UK	The Body Shop	UK
Early Learning Center	UK	The Body Shop For Men	UK
F.A.O. Schwarz	N	The Discovery Channel	C
General Nutrition Center (GNC)	N	The Nature Company	C
Ikea	N	The Olympic Store Direct	AUS
Jaeger Sportswear	UK	Tire Centers	FR

GROCERY STORES

American owned

Acme Markets
Albertson's
Aldi
Alfalfa's Markets (Nutritional)
Appletree Markets
Baker's Supermarkets
Beans, Grains & Things (Nutritional)
Big Bear
Big M
Big V
Big Y
Bi-Lo Foods (Penn Traffic Co.)
Bozzuto's
Bread & Circus
Butera
C & K Market
Capers Markets (Nutritional)
Carr Gottstein
Cash Mart
Charles & Co.
Country Cupboard Food Stores

Cub Foods
DelChamps
Dick's
Dominick's
Eagle Country Market
Easters
Econofoods
Economart
Erickson's
Family Thrift Center
Fareway Stores
Farm Fresh
Food 4 Less
Food Bonanza
Food City
Food Fair
Food Folks
Food For Thought Markets
Food Giant
Food Pavillion
Food Pride

Food Town
Foodland
Fresh Fields
Furr's
Gator Food Stores
Gelson's
Genuardi's Family Markets
Grand Union
Gristedes
Gruber's Food Town
Harp's Food Stores
Harris Teeter
Harvest Foods
Homeland
IGA
Ingles
Jack & Jill
Jay C. Food Stores
Jewel
Jewel/Osco
Jitney Jungle
Jr. Food Stores
Kessell Food Markets
King Kullen
Kroger
Lucky
Mars Super Markets
Marsh
Mayfair
Megamarket
Minitman
Minyard Food Stores
More 4
National
Nature's Northwest
P & C Food Markets
Pak 'N Save
Pathmark
Pavilions
Pay Less
Pick 'N Save
Piggly Wiggly
Prairie Market
Presto Food Stores

Price Chopper
Publix
Pueblo
QFC
Quality Food Centers
Quality Markets
Ralph's
Ray's Food Place
Rays Food Warehouse
Ray's Price Less Foods
Ray's Shop Smart Food Warehouse
Red Apple
Red Apple Store
Rini-Rego Marketplace
Rini-Rego Stop-N-Shop
Riverside Markets
Rosauer's
Sam's Club
Sav-U Foods
Schnuck's
Seaway Food Town
Sentry
Shoprite
ShopRite
Sloans
Smith's Food & Drug
Spencer
Sun Mart
Sunshine Grocery
Super H
Supersaver
Supervalu
Sure Save
Thrift
Thriftway
Tolland
True Value
Ukrop's
United
Uptown Whole Foods
URM Stores
Valumarket
Village
Vons

Warehouse Market
Wegmans
Weis Markets
Whole Foods Market

Wild Oats Community Markets
Wild Oats Markets (Nutritional)
Winn-Dixie
Xtra Super Food Centers

Foreign owned

A & P	G	Igloo	UK
Bi-Lo (Royal Ahold NV)	N	Kaiser's Grocery Store	G
Bruno's	N	Kash N' Karry	BG
Coles	AUS	Kings Super Markets	UK
Dominion	G	Kohl's	G
Family Choice	UK	Martin's Food Centers	BG
Farmer Jack	G	Sav-A-Centers	G
Finast	N	Save-A-Lot	N
Food Emporium	G	Shaw's	UK
Food Lion	BG	Shop 'N Save	BG
Food World	N	Star Market	UK
FoodMax	N	Stop & Shop	N
Giant Food Stores	N	Super Discount Markets	BG
Giant Markets	N	Super Fresh	G
Golden Gallon	N	Super G	N
Hannaford	BG	Tops Markets	N
Holyoke Food Mart	G	Waldbaum	G
Iceland	UK		

HARDWARE STORES

American owned

Ace Hardware
Coast to Coast
Do It Center
Eagle Hardware & Garden
Fastenal
Hardware Hank
Home Depot
Lowe's
N-E Thing Supply Co.
Orchard Hardware & Garden

Orchard Supply Hardware
Restoration Hardware
Seigle's
Servistar
Star Lumber & Supply Co.
True Value Hardware
Trustworthy
Trustworthy Howe
Villager's Hardware
Wickes Lumber

Foreign owned

B&Q	UK

JEWELRY STORES

American owned

A. Hirsch & Son	Lundstrom
Bailey Banks & Biddle	Marks & Morgan
Barclay	Marks Bros.
Carlyle	Mayor's
De Vons	Melart
Diamond Park	Merksamer
Dobbins	Michael Anthony
Finlay	Mills
Fred Meyer	Mission
Friedman's Jewelers	Reeds
G.M. Pollack & Sons	Samuels
Gordon's	Schubach
Hatfield	Tiffany
Helzberg	Tiffany & Co.
Jewelry Land	Whitehall Co.
Littman	Zales

Foreign owned

Beldens	UK	Luigi Lucardi	N
Friedlander's	UK	Osterman's	UK
Goodman	UK	Shaw's	UK
H. Samuel	UK	Siebel	N
J.B. Robinson	UK	Sterling	UK
Jared—The Gallery of Jewelry	UK	The Westhall Co.	UK
Kay	UK	Weisfield	UK
Leroy's	UK		

MUSIC STORES

American owned

Blockbuster	Record Town
Camelot Music	Sam Goody
Coconuts Music & Movies	Spec's
Disc Jockey	Strawberries
J&R Music World	Tape World
Music Oasis	The Wall
Music X	Tower Records
Music-Go-Round	Trans World Entertainment
Musicland	Vibes Music
National Record Mart	Waxie Maxie's
On Cue	Wherehouse Entertainment
Planet Music	

Foreign owned

MVC Entertainment   UK

OPTICAL CENTERS

In May 2000, a division of Switzerland's Novartis AG agreed to purchase Wesley Jessen VisionCare, outbidding U.S.-owned Bausch & Lomb.

American owned

American Vision Centers	Pearle Vision
Binyons Optical	Royal Optical
BJ's Wholesale Club	Sam's Club
Costco Wholesale	Sears Optical
D.O.C. Eyeworld	Shawnee Optical
Emerging Vision	Shopko
Eye Care Centers of America	Sterling Optical
Eye Masters	Vision Plaza
Eyeglass Emporium	Vision Works
Horner Rausch	Vision World
Hour Eye	Vista Eyecare
J.C. Penney	Vizer
Nuvision	Wal-Mart

Foreign owned

Eye Masters	ITL	Optiworld	ITL
Eye World	ITL	Specttica	ITL
Laser Vision Centers	C	TLC Laser Eye Centers	C
LensCrafters	ITL	Wesley-Jessen	SWI

RENTAL STORES

American owned

Aaron Direct	Rent-A-Center
Aaron Plus	RentaVision
Aaron Rents and Sells Furniture	Ryder
Colortyme	Selix Formal Wear
Grantree	U-Haul
Rainbow	

Foreign owned

No foreign brands could be located for this category.

SHOE STORES

American owned

Altier Shoe Annex
Athletic Attic
Athletic Lady
Baker's
Butler
El-Bee
Famous Footwear
Finish Line
Florsheim
Foot Locker
FootAction USA
Jarman
Johnston & Murphy
Journeys
Just For Feet
Keds
Kids Foot Locker
Kinney

Lady Foot Locker
Mathers
Mil-Mar Shoe
Naturalizer
Nike Town
Parade of Shoes
Payless Kids
Payless Shoe Source
Pic 'N Pay
Shoe Pavilion
Shoe World
The General Shoe Warehouse
Tony Lama
Tradehome
Underground Station
Wee Foot Fashions
Williams The Shoemen

Foreign owned

Athlete's Foot	FR	Clark	UK
Bostonian	UK	Hanover	UK
C & J Clark	UK		

SPORTING GOODS STORES

American owned

Big 5
Champs
G.I. Joe's
Galyans
Gart Sports
Hibbett

Modell's
Oshman's
Play It Again Sports
Sport Chalet
Sports Authority

Foreign owned

No foreign brands could be located for this category.

Chapter 4

Food Products

ARTIFICIAL SWEETENER

American owned

Canderel	Sugar Twin
Equal	Sweet 'N Low
Nutrasweet	Sweet One
Splenda	Sweetmate

Foreign owned
No foreign brands could be located for this category.

BABY FOOD/FORMULA

Heinz and Beech-Nut are No. 2 and No. 3 respectively in the prepared baby food market. Gerber is owned by Switzerland's Novartis AG, and has a 70% share of the U.S. baby food market. American-owned Heinz and Beech Nut both trail the Swiss company with a combined market share of only 28%.

American owned

Advance	Isomil
Alactamil	Lofenalac
Baby's First	Nutramigen
Beech-Nut	Pedialite
Bonamil	Plasmon
Earth's Best (organic)	Pregestimil
Enfalac	Prosobee
Enfamil	Similac
Enfapro	SMA, Nursoy
Farley's	Stages
Heinz	Tabletime

Foreign owned

1st Foods	SWI	Chil-Mil	J
2nd Foods	SWI	Gerber	SWI
Alete	SWI	Lait Guigoz	SWI
Alprem	SWI	Mellin	FR
Baby Head	SWI	Nativa	SWI
Bean Stalk Organic	J	Nestum	SWI
Bledina	FR	Tender Harvest	SWI
Carnation	SWI		

BAGELS

American owned

Bagel Delight		Food Club	
Big 'N Crusty		Lender's	
Earth Grains		Sara Lee	

Foreign owned

Thomas'	C	Weston	C

BAKED GOODS

When Unilever made an offer to acquire American-based Bestfoods in 2000, they were required to sell-off Bestfoods' Baking Co., which included the brands Entenmann's baked goods and Thomas' English muffins and bagels among others. Unilever found a buyer in Canada's George Weston Ltd., outbidding American-based Sara Lee.

American owned

Charlotte Charles	Mrs. Wrights
Chef David	Ovenfresh
Cottage Hearth	Parisian
Egekvist	Pepperidge Farm
Flavor-Kist	Rainbo
Flowers	Rich Traditions
Hilltop Hearth	Sara Lee
Lumberjack	Snak N' Fresh
Mackinaw Milling Co.	Stella D'oro

Foreign owned

Country Harvest	C	Levy's	UKN
Entenmann's	C	Montmartre	J
Fibre Goodness	C	Old London	UKN
Fielders	AUS	Vogel's	AUS
Fleur De Lait	FR	Wheat 'N Bran	C
Interbake Foods	C		

BAKING GOODS

American owned

4C Bread Crumbs	Aunt Sweeties
4C Crumb 'N Bake	Baker Brand
Amapola	Baker's
Arm & Hammer	Bakers Chocolate
Armix Shortening	Baker's Joy
Aunt Jemima	Beattie Corn Meal

Betty Crocker
Cake Mate
Calumet Baking Powder
Chipits
Clabber Girl
Country Hearth
Crisco Shortening
Dakota Maid
Davis
Del Destino Olive Oil
Drinkwater Flour
Duncan Hines
Early Harvest
Fearn
Fluffo Shortening
Indian Head Corn Meal
Jiffy Mixes
KC
Magic

Mini Chips
Mrs. Crutchfield's
Olean Cooking Oil
Pam Cooking Spray
Puritan Oil
Red Hill Corn Syrup
Satin Fry Shortening
Smart Size
Sunflower Cornmeal
Swift'ning Shortening
Washington Cake Mixes
Washington Frosting Mix
Washington Muffin Mixes
Washington Self Rising Corn Meal
Wesson Oil
White Lily
Wilderness Pie Fillings
Win You Pie Fillings

Foreign owned

American Ingredients Co.	N
Argo	UKN
Arrozina Corn Starch	UKN
Bakemark	N
Benchmate	AUS
Benson's Corn Starch	UKN
Bertolli Olive Oil	ITL
Brown & Polson	UKN
Cremogema	UKN
Defiance	AUS
Dover Flour	C
Duryeas	UKN
Fleischmann's Yeast	AUS
Karp's	N
Kre-mel	UKN

Lady's Choice	UKN
Maizena	UKN
Majala	UKN
Malile	UKN
Mazola Cooking Oil	UKN
Montemps	J
Poti	UKN
QA Products	N
Rafhan Corn Oil	UKN
Serrol	AUS
Smith's Flour Mills	UK
Spry Shortening	UKN
St. Lawrence Corn Oil	UKN
Toll House	SWI
Yabon	UKN

BEANS

American owned

Allen's
B&M
Bean Cuisine
Big Johns
Brooks

Bush's
Campbell's
Casa Fiesta
Colonna
Del Monte

el-Rio
Freshlike
Green Giant
Heinz
Jack Rabbit
Kuner's Southwestern
La Preferida
Luck's Inc
Mexene
Old El Paso

Progresso
Ranch Style
Rosarita
Seaside
Showboat
Stokely's
Sun Vista
Trappey's
Van Camp
Wagon Master

Foreign owned

Iberia	UKN	Ortega	SWI

BREAD

American owned

Beefsteak
Betsy Ross
Betterway
Bread Du Jour
Bridgford
Bunny
Butter Krust
Buttermaid
Butternut
Cable Car
Castle
Cobblestone Mill
Colonial
Cotton's Bread
Country Hearth
Dandee
Earth Grains
Eddy's
Emrich
European Bakers
Evangeline Maid
Flowers
Franklin
Franz
Gardner
Golden Hearth
Gonnella
Grant's Farm

Harvest Recipe
Hillbilly
Holland Rusk Toast
Holsum
Home Pride
Hometown
Honeybran
Hudson Bay Milling Co.
Iron Kids
Jaeger
Kilpatrick's
Manor
Maryann Rosen
Master
Merico
Merita
Millbrook
Mother's
Mrs. Karl's
National
Natures Harvest
Nature's Own
New York
Newly Weds
Nutri-Bran
Oatmeal Goodness
Old Home
Old San Francisco Style

Our Special Touch
Palagonia
Pepperidge Farm
Power Kids
Rainbo
Rich Grain
Roman Light
Roman Meal
Snyder

Sun Grain
Sunbeam
Sunbeam Lite
Sweetheart
Toast 4
Torino
Weber's
Wonder

Foreign owned

Arnold	C	Levys	UKN
Bimbo	MEX	Light N Natural	C
Bran'nola	UKN	Molenberg	AUS
Brick Oven	UKN	Mother's Pride	UK
Buttercup	AUS	Nimble	UK
California Gold Miner	C	Old London	UKN
Country Bake	AUS	Orowheat	C
Country Split	AUS	Pasco	J
Duroi	FR	Pataks	AUS
Earth Harvest	C	Sahara	UKN
Francisco	C	Stroehmann	C
Freihofer's	C	Sunicrust	AUS
Granary	UK	Sunset Harvest	MEX
Grissol	J	Tender Touch	C
Hearth Farms	C	Thomas'	C
Home Style	AUS	Vogel	AUS
Hovis	UK	Weston	C
Jacquet	FR	Windmill	UK

BUTTER/MARGARINE

Unilever (UKN) is the world's largest maker of margarine.

American owned

Benacol
Blue Bonnet
Country Churn
Country Morning
Farm Fresh

Fleischmann's
Land O' Lakes
Nucoa
Parkay
Simon Fischer

Foreign owned

Becal	UKN	Country Crock	UKN
Belolive	G	Dawn Butter	IRE
Brummel & Brown	UKN	Dawn Light Butter	IRE

ETA	AUS	Mrs. Filbert's	UKN
Fama	G	Mrs. McGregors	AUS
Hotel Bar	FR	Planta	POR
I Can't Believe It's Not Butter	UKN	Praise	AUS
Imperial Margarine	UKN	Promise	UKN
Keller's	FR	Rama	UKN
Kerrymaid	IRE	Roda	G
Lady's Choice	UKN	Royal	UKN
Linea	POR	Saffola	J
Luna	TUR	Sanella	UKN
Masmix	FIN	Savory	J
Mazola	UKN	Savourin	C
Meadow Lee	AUS	Shedd's Country Crock	UKN
Minelma	G	Soyola	TUR
Mom's	UKN	Sunnyland	J
Monarch	UKN	Take Control	UKN
Mother's Choice	AUS	Utterly Butterly	UK
		Vaqueiro	POR

CANDY

American owned

3 Musketeers	Bolster
5th Avenue	Bounty
Abba-Zaba	Brach
Almond Coconut Delight	Brach's
Almond Joy	Breath Savers
Almond Roca	Brock
Altoids	Brown & Haley Selections
Amazin' Fruit	Bug City
Andes	Buterlets
Ann Raskas	Cadbury's (Hershey)
Archibald	Cadbury's Fruit & Nut
Astro Pops	Cadbury's Krisp
Balisto	Cadbury's Roast Almond
Bar None	Callard & Bowser
Barringer's	Canada Mints
Bartons Candy	Candy Cupboard
Bayer Candy	Candy Dish
Belle Camp	Canterbury
Big Block	Casanova Chocolates
Big Hunk	Cella's
Blommer	Certs
Blue Razz-Berry	Charleston Chew

Charms
Charms Blow Pops
Cherry Blossom
Chew-ets
Chipaway
Chuckles
Clara Stover
Clorets
Cookies 'N' Mint
Cool Blasts
Cordially Yours Cherries
Cote D'Or
Crows
Crunch & Munch
Cyberspeak
D & P Rock Candy
Dots
Double Fudge 'N Caramel
Dove Chocolate
Dovebar
Dream Candy
Dum-Dum Suckers
Elana Chocolates
Fannie May
Fanny Farmer
Farley
Fiesta
Flavor Rolls
Foxes
Glosette Peanuts & Raisins
Godiva
Golden Almond
Goldenburg Peanut Chews
Good & Fruity
Good & Plenty
Goodies
Gummi Savers
Gurley's
Hall's
Harmony Foods
Haviland
Heath Bar
Hershey's
Hershey's Classic Caramels

Hershey's Cookies 'N' Créme
Hershey's Hugs
Hershey's Kisses
Hershey's Miniatures
Holidays
Hot Tamales
Hugs
Ice Breakers
Imperial Cherries
Jet-Puffed
Jolly Rancher
Judson-Atkinson
Jujyfruits
Jungle Jollies
Junior Mints
King Leo
Kiss Cool
Kisses
Kit Kat
Krackel
Krema
Kron Chocolatier
Kudo's
La Vosgienne
Life Savers
Lila Pause
Lockets
Look
Lowney
Luden's Elite
M&M's
Mallo Cup
Marabou
Marathon
Mars
Mars Bar
Mary Jane
Mason
Mason Dots
Masterpieces
Mello Mint
Memory
Mexican Hats
Mike & Ike

Milk Duds
Milky Way
Mintlets
Mounds
Mr. Goodbar
Mrs. Stover's Candies
Munch
My Buddy
Necco
Nibs
Ovation
P.B. Max
Park Avenue
Payday
Peanut Butter Cup
Peanut Butter Log
Peanut Roll
Peeps/Bunnies
Pepperidge Farm
Peter Paul Mounds
Planters
Pot Of Gold
Priama
Pucker Hustle
Push Pop Lollipops
Queen Anne
Queen Anne's Best
Queen of My Hearts
Reed
Reese's
Reese's Nutrageous
Reese's Peanut Butter Cups
Reese's Pieces
Reesesticks
Ring Pop Lollipops
Roca
Roca Bits
Rocky Mountain Chocolate Factory
Rocky Road
Rolo
Rondos
Royals Mint Chocolate
Russell Stover Candies
Saf-T-Pops

Sathers
Schraff's Candy
See's
Sherwood Cows
Signature
Sixlets
Skittles
Skor
Sky Bar
Slap Stix
Smoothie Peanut Butter Cup
Snickers
Sour Dudes
Sour Fruit Burst
Sour Jacks
Spearmintlets
Special Crisp
Special Dark
Squareshooter
Squeeze Pop
Squirms
Star Brites
Starburst
Stark Gummi Fruits
Suchard
Sugar Babies
Sugar Daddies
Sugus
Summit
Summit Cookie Bars
Super Twizzlers
Sweet Choice
Sweethearts
Sweetworld Lollies
Symphony
Tastetations
Teenee Beanee
Thumb Fun Lollipops
Thumb Suckers
Tobler
Toblerone
Toggi Wagers
Tootsie Pop
Tootsie Roll

Toyals
Traditions
Trolli Gummi
Twix
Twizzelators
Twizzlers
U-No-Bar
Vitafreze
Wacky Frootz
Whatchamacallit
Whitman
Whitman Chocolates

Whitman's Samper
Whoppers
Winters Chocolates
World's Finest
Wunderbeans
Y&S
York Peppermint Patties
Zagnut
Zero
Zip-A-Dee-Doo-Da
Zours

Foreign owned

100 Grand Bar	SWI	Chunky	SWI
Aero	SWI	Connaisseurs	SWI
After Eight	SWI	Continental	UK
Airheads	N	Creola	SWI
Allan	UK	Crispy Crunch	C
Alpine White	SWI	Crunchie	C
Baby Ruth	SWI	Crystal Mints	UK
Baci	SWI	Demet's	SWI
Barratt	UK	Drifter	SWI
Bassett	UK	Duciora	UK
Beich	SWI	Dweebs	SWI
Bit-O-Honey	SWI	FAAM Licorice	UK
Black Magic	SWI	Ferraro Rocher	ITL
Bouquet D'Or	UK	Frigor	SWI
Buncha Crunch	SWI	Frisia	UK
Butterfinger	SWI	Fruit-Tella	N
Buttermint	UK	Fry's	UK
Cadbury (Cadbury Schweppes)	UK	Fun Dip	SWI
Cadbury (George Weston)	C	Galak	SWI
Caffarel	SWI	Ghirardelli	SWI
Cailler	SWI	Gobstoppers	SWI
Candy Time	N	Goobers	SWI
Candytops	SWI	Halba	SWI
Caramac	SWI	Heavenly Truffle	UK
Caramello	UK	Hofbauer	SWI
Caramilk	C	Hueso	UK
Chelsea	J	Kinder	ITL
Chewy Runts	SWI	Kohler	SWI
Chewy Spree	SWI	Krem-Top	SWI
Chocolate Koka	J	Laffy Taffy	SWI

Lapiequi Chante	FR	Runts	SWI
Lingots	SWI	Sarotti	SWI
Lion	UK	Sharps Toffee	UK
Lion Bar	SWI	Shock Tarts	SWI
Look-O-Look	N	Smith's Flour Mills	UK
Lucky Eggs	ITL	Snapple Beans	UK
Macrobertson	UK	Snapple Fruits	UK
Mamba Soft	G	Snapple Snapplets	UK
Matchmakers	SWI	Snapple Whirls	UK
Maynards	UK	Sno-Caps	SWI
Meller	N	Special Toffee	UK
Meltykiss	J	Spree	SWI
Mentos	N	Stophoest	N
Mon Cheri	ITL	Storck	G
Montego	SWI	Sundy	SWI
Mr. Big	C	Sunmark	SWI
Nerds	SWI	Sweet Marie	C
Nestle	SWI	Sweetarts	SWI
Nestle Crunch	SWI	Swiss Thins	SWI
Nestle Quik Bar	SWI	Swiss Tradition	SWI
Nestle-Beich	SWI	Texan	SWI
Oh Henry!	SWI	Tic Tac	ITL
P.S. Chocolate	UK	Tikkels	N
Pascall	UK	Timeout	UK
Pearson's Nips	SWI	Toffee Crisp	SWI
Perk	UK	Toffifay	G
Perugina	SWI	Toffo	SWI
Peter	SWI	Tomtom	UK
Piasten	UK	Treasures	SWI
Picnic	UK	Trebor	UK
Pixy Stix	SWI	Truffon	SWI
Polo	SWI	Turtles	SWI
Poulain	UK	Twirl	UK
Premior	UK	Van Melle	N
Prince Noir	SWI	Verduyn	N
Quik	SWI	Walnut Whip	SWI
Raisinets	SWI	Werther's Original	G
Red Tulip	UK	Willy Wonka	SWI
Riesen	G	Yan Yan	J
Rowntree	SWI	Yorkie	SWI

CANNED FRUITS & VEGETABLES

American owned

Allen's	Musselman's
Butter Kernel	Ocean Spray
Campbell's	Orchard County
Catalina	Princella
Comstock	Rotel
Del Monte	Royal Prince
Dole	S&W
Frank's	Showboat
Fresh Juice	Southern Gem
Freshlike	Stokely's
Green Giant	Sunshine
Hunt's	Tendersweet
Ideal	Thank You
Kuner	Veg-All
Kuner-Empson	White House
Market Basket	Wilderness Foods

Foreign owned

Contadina	SWI	Mott's	UK
Libby's	SWI		

CEREAL

American owned

100% Bran	Blueberry Morning
100% Natural Cereal	Blueberry Squares
40% Bran Flakes	Body Buddies
All Bran Extra Fiber	Boo-Berry
All-Bran	Bran Buds
Almond Delight	Breadshop's
Alpha-Bits	Cap'N Crunch
Apple Cinnamon Cheerios	Cheerios
Apple Cinnamon Rice Krispies	Chex
Apple Cinnamon Squares	Choco Crunch
Apple Cinnamon Toasty O's	Cinnamon Mini Buns
Apple Jacks	Cinnamon Toast Crunch
Apple Raisin Crisp	Cocoa Krispies
Arrowhead Mills (organic)	Cocoa Pebbles
Banana Nut Krunch	Cocoa Puffs
Basic 4	Colossal Crunch
Berry Berry Kix	Common Sense Oat Bran
Berry Colossal Crunch	Common Sense With Raisins

Complete Bran Flakes
Cookie Blast
Cookie Crisp
Corn Bursts
Corn Pops
Count Chocula
Country Corn Flakes
Cracklin' Oat Bran
Cream of Rice
Cream of Wheat
Creusli
Crispix
Crispy Rice
Crispy Wheaties 'N Raisins
Day Dawn
Debbie's Famous Granola
Double Dip Crunch
Fiber One
Franken Berry
Froot Loops
Frosted Bran
Frosted Krispies
Frosted Mini-Wheats
Frosted Toasty O's
Fruit Flavored Toasty O's
Fruit N Fibre
Fruitful Bran
Fruity Marshmallow Krispies
Fruity Pebbles
Golden Crisp
Golden Grahams
Golden Puffs
Grape Nuts
Great Grains
Harmony
Harvest Crunch
H-O
Honey Bunches of Oats
Honey Nut Cheerios
Honey Nut Clusters
Honey Nut Crunch
Honey Nut Toasty O's
Honeycomb
Hot Wheat Cereal

Just Right
Just Right Fruit & Nut
Just Right With Crunchy Nuggets
Kaboom
Kashi
Kellogg's Corn Flakes
Kellogg's Frosted Flakes
Kellogg's Just Right
Kellogg's Raisin Bran
Kellogg's Rice Krispies
King Vitamin
Kix
Life
Lucky Charms
Maltex
Malt-O-Meal
Marshmallow Matey's
Maypo
Mother's
Mueslix Crispy Blend
Mueslix Golden Crunch
Multi Grain Cheerios
Nabisco Shredded Wheat
Natural Bran Flakes
Nature Valley Granola
Nature Valley Granola
Nut & Honey Crunch
Nut & Honey Crunch O's
Nutri-Grain Almond Raisin
Nutri-Grain Golden Wheat
Nutri-Grain Golden Wheat & Raisins
Nutri-Grain Nuggets
Oatmeal Crisp
Oatmeal Crisp Raisin
Oatmeal Crunch
Oatmeal Raisin Crisp
Oats 'N Fiber
Oh's
Old Mill Oatmeal
Pebbles
Pillsbury
Pop-Tarts Crunch
Post
Post Raisin Bran

Post Toasties
Post-Tens
Product 19
Puffed Wheat & Rice
Purity
Quaker
Quaker Instant Grits
Quaker Oat Bran
Quaker Oat Squares
Quaker Oatmeal
Quaker Puffed Rice
Quaker Puffed Wheat
Quick 'N Hearty
Quisp
Raisin Bran
Raisin Life
Raisin Nut Bran
Raisin Squares
Red River
Reese's Peanut Butter Puffs
Rice Chex
Rice Krispies
Rice Krispies Treats
Shredded Wheat
Shredded Wheat 'N Bran
Shreddies

Smacks
S'mores Grahams
Smurf-Berry
Special K
Spoon Size Shredded Wheat
Strawberry Squares
Sugar Frosted Flakes
Sugar Puffs
Sun Country
Sunbelt
Super Golden Crisp
Team Cheerios
Toasted Oat
Toasties
Toasty O's
Tootie Fruitie's
Total
Total Corn Flakes
Total Raisin Bran
Trix
U.S. Soccer Golden Goals
Waffle Crisp
Wheat Hearts
Wheatena
Wheaties

Foreign owned

Alpen	UK	Grainfields	UK
Chocapic	SWI	Prairie Maid	UKN
Dunkin' Donuts	UK	Sportis	SWI
Familia	SWI	Telma	UKN
Flemings Oaten Products	AUS	Weetabix	UK

CHEESE

American owned

4-Quart
AC
American Heritage
Anco
Astrian Alps
Athenos
Babybel
Bar-S

Bonbel
Borden
Borden Lite-Line
Cache Valley
Cheese Whiz
Cheez Whiz
Churny
Clearfield

Cloverbloom
Colonna Romano
Country Line
Cracker Barell
Di Giorno
Fieldgate
Friendship
Galbani
Golden Velvet
Harvest Moon
Healthy Choice
Hoffman
Hoffman's
Il Primo
Kaukauna
Kraft
La Diva
Laughing Cow
Light N' Lively
Merkt
Merkt's
Mini Bonbel
Miss Winconsin
Mootown Snacks
Old English
Old Wisconsin

Patuxent Farms
Paul J. Barnett
Pier Franco
Polly-O
Premium Bristol Gold
President Pride
Prices Home-Style Spreads
Provincia
Red Rooster
Rondele
Roselli
Sargento
Soy-A-Melt
Soymage
Star Valley
Thiel
Tiger
Tillamook
Treasure Cave
Twin Falls
Ultimo!
Velveeta
Vitalait
Wispride
Woody's

Foreign owned

Arpin	FR	Geramont	FR
Balderson	ITL	Gerard	FR
Bayernland	G	Gervais	FR
Bel Paese	FR	Heluva Good	N
Belle Des Champs	FR	Jockey	FR
Black Diamond	ITL	Lepetit	FR
Boisange	FR	Malthe	AUS
Bresso	UKN	Milkana	UKN
Buko	AUS	Montagnard	FR
Chamois D'or	FR	Montracher	FR
Cheesestrings	ITL	Mountain Farms	FR
Country Crock	UKN	Mr. Wilson	UK
Entremont	FR	New Holland	FR
Etorki	FR	Precious	FR
Fine Bouche	FR	Puck	AUS
Fromageries Riches Monts	FR	Rosenborg	AUS

Rowntree's	SWI	St. Albray	FR
San Regim	ARG	Taillefine	FR
Santa Lucia	FR	Tasmanian	FR
Sorrento	FR	Tourtrain	FR

CHEWING GUM

American owned

AAAHH! Real Monsters	Fruit Tape
Bazooka	Green Slime
Beech-Nut	Hollywood
Big League Chew	Hubba Bubba
Big Red	Jolly Rancher
Bubbaloo	Juicy Fruit
Bubble Beeper	Malabar
Bubble Jug	Mint-A-Burst
Bubble Locker	Neon Bubble Strips
Bubble Tape	Ouch
Bubble Yum	Popeye
Bubblicious	Quench Gum
Cash	Rain-Blo
Chiclets	Soft Bubble
Cinn-A-Burst	Stimoral
Clorets	Striped
Dentyne	Super Bubble
Dentyne Ice	Tape Twisters
Doublemint	Tongue Dippers
Eclipse	Tonigum
Excel	Trident
Extra	Triple Blasts
Freedent	Tropical Twists
Freshen-Up	Tubble Gum
Fruit Stripe Gum	Wrigley's

Foreign owned

Beldent	UK	Chappie	UK
Blueberry Gum	J	Xylifresh	N
Bubbl-eez	J	Xylish	J

CHILI

American owned

Armour Star	Chili Man
Carroll Shelby	Chilli Man
Chili Makin's	Cincinnati Recipe

Dennison's

Gebhardt

Hormel

Nalley's

Stenger

Van Camp's

Wolf Brand

Foreign owned

No foreign brands could be located for this category.

COFFEE CREAMER

American owned

Coffee Rich

Cremora

Farm Rich

Mocha Mix

Poly Rich

Foreign owned

Carnation	SWI	Creap	J
Coffee-Mate	SWI	Krem-Top	SWI

COOKIES

American owned

Albert's

Anselmi

Apple Newtons

Austin

Bakers Bonus

Bakery Wagon

Barnum's Animal Crackers

Biscos

Brown Edge

Bugs Bunny

Cameo

Charlies

Chip-A-Roos

Chipaway

Chips Ahoy!

Chips Deluxe

Chocolate Chip Snaps

Christie

Cookie Jar Classic

Cookie Tree

Cookies 'N Fudge

Deluxe Grahams

Demitasse Biscuits

Dixie Vanilla

Droxxies

Dunkaroos

E.L. Fudge

Effin Delights

Family Favorites

Famosa

Famous Amos

Farm Chunk

Fig Newtons

Fudge Sticks

Fudge Stripes

Grandma's Cookies

Greg's

Gurley's

Harnois

Homestyle Soft Batch

Hydrox

Jack's

Jackson's

Keebler

Krisp Kreem

Mallomars

McCann's

Mrs. Field's

Murray
Mystic Mint Sandwich Cookies
Nabisco
Newtons
Nilla Wafers
Nutter Butter
Old Fashioned Ginger Snaps
Oreo
Pecan Sandies
Pecan Supreme
Pepperidge Farm
Pride O' The Farm
Rainbow Chips Deluxe

Rainbow Cookie Stix
Ruger Wafers
SGD Cookie Express
Snackwells
Social Tea Biscuits
Soft Batch
Stella D'oro
Sunny
Sunshine
Teddy Grahams
Tru Blu
Vienna Fingers
West Brae Natural

Foreign owned

America's Finest	ITL	Lido	J
Archway	ITL	Lu	ITL
Bertolli	ITL	Mandolin	UK
Colonial	ITL	Maxifruit	J
Dad's	ITL	McCormick's	J
Fleetwood Snacks	J	Mother's Cookies	ITL
Koala Yummies	J	Mrs. Alison's	ITL

CRACKERS

American owned

American Classic
Anselmi
Austin
Barnum's Animal
Better Cheddars
Cheese Nips
Cheese Tid-Bit
Cheez-it
Chicken in a Biscuit
Christie
Club
Crown Pilot
Flavor-Kist
Harvest Crisps
Hi-Ho
Honey Grahams
Honey Maid Graham Crackers
Nips
Oat Thins

Premium
Quackers
Ritz
Ritz Bits
Royal Lunch
Smackers
Snackwells
Snorkel's
Sociables
Sunshine
Swiss Cheese
Tam Tam
Town House
Town House & Cheddar
Triscuit
Vegetable Thins
Waverly
Wheat & Cheddar
Wheat Thins

| Wheatables | | Zesta | |
| Wheatsworth | | Zwieback | |

Foreign owned

Belin	FR	Jacob's	FR
Bitelife	J	Paulins	J
Fleetwood Snacks	J	San-J	J
Greenhill	UK	Tom's	SWI

DAIRY PRODUCTS

American owned

Albertson's
Allen
Alta-Dena
Armour Star
Barber
Biltmore Farms
Borden
Breakstone's
Cabot
Cloverleaf
Coburg
Coleman
Crystal
Dairi-Fresh
Dairy Belle
Dean
Eggland's Best
Farm Rich Non Dairy Creamer
Festival
Fresh 'N Light
Knudsen
Kohler
Lakeview Farms
Land-O-Sun
Lite Time
Lucerne
McColls
Melody Farms
Midnite Sun
Milk Mate

Mountain Dairy
National Champion
Natural Select
Natural Select Organics
Naturally Yours
Naturally Yours Sour Crème
Pastry Pride
Patuxent Farms
Pennsylvania Dutch Egg Nog
Pet
Pevely
Philadelphia Cream Cheese
Polly-O
Sealtest
Slim N' Trim
Sokreem
Sokreem Sour Cream
Sour Treat Sour Cream
State Brand
Sysco
Temp-Tee Cream Cheese
Thiel Cheese
Turkey Hill
Vita-Lite
Vitamilk
Viva
Westsoy Light
Westview
Yocream Pure

Foreign owned

Ambrosia	UKN	MD	AUS
Atlanta Dairies	ITL	Milkmaid	SWI
Axelrod	N	Neilson	c
Beatrice	ITL	Nespray	SWI
Bridel	FR	Nido	SWI
Bridelice	FR	Pauls	ITL
Carnation	SWI	Penn Maid	N
Copper Cliff	BG	Pensupreme	N
Cracka Dip	ITL	President	FR
Crowley	N	Royal Oak	BG
Curtis Farm	ITL	Sancor	ARG
Dale Farm	UK	Sandhurst Farms	ITL
Eggstro'dnaire	SWI	Silverwood	BG
Glenfarms	N	Societe	FR
Greens	N	Soy-Life	ITL
Ice Break	ITL	St. Ivel & Shape	UK
Ideal	SWI	Suncoast	ITL
Kemps Dairy Products	N	Tres Ninas	ARG
Lactel	FR	Trim	ITL
Marigold/Kemp	N		

EGG SUBSTITUTE

American owned

All Whites	Egg Whites
Better'N Eggs	Mac Scramble Eez
Egg Beaters	Second Nature

Foreign owned

Eggstro'dnaire	SWI

FLOUR

In October 2001, Britain's Diageo PLC agreed to sell Pillsbury to American-based General Mills.

American owned

Amapola	Payara
Arrowhead Mills	Pillsbury
Crutchfield's	Red Band
Gold Medal	Robin Hood
Heckers	Softasilk
La Pina	Sunflour
Pathfinder	Washington

White Lily   Wondra
White Rose
    Foreign owned

Allied	AUS	Smith's Flour Mills	UK
Champion	AUS	Soyafluff	ITL
Duryeas	UKN	Soyarich	ITL
Highloaf	C	Tia Rosa	MEX
Polly	UKN	Vitamilho	UKN
Sensation	C		

FROZEN FOOD

    American owned

Arden International Kitchens
Armour
Aunt Jemima
Aunt Jemima Homestyle
Award
Bagel Bites
Bak-A-Fry
Banquet
Battergold
Battersweet
Birds Eye
Blue Ribbon French Fries
Blue Star
Brighton's
Budget Gourmet
Butterball
Café Mexico
Calypso
Casa Maid
Catch of the Day
Charlies
Chicken By George
Chillripe
Chun King
ConAgra
Country Skillet
Covington Farms Chicken
Crispers
Crispy Crowns
Cross Valley Farms

Dakota Hearth
Di Giorno
Dutch Farms
Edwards Frozen Pies
Eggo Waffles
El Charrito
El Monterey
Flav-R-Pac Vegetables
Fresh Juice
Freshlike
Frostar
Frosting Pride
Frozen Rite
Frozfruit
Global
Gold King
Golddiggers
Golden Valley
Gourmet Selection
Green Giant
Hanover
Harbor Banks
Healthy Balance
Healthy Choice
Honey Stung Poultry
Hormel
Hot Pockets
Hungry Man
Icelandic Seafood
Idaho Naturally

Jack's
Janet Davis
Jell-O
Jiffy
Jon Donaire
Kid Cuisine
Kineret
King Kold
Kingston
Kitchen Treat
Kraft Fresh Creations
La Choy
Lady Aster
Lean Pockets
Looney Tunes
Mama Tisch's
Mary Kitchen
McKenzie Vegetables & Fruits
McKenzie's
Michelina's
Morton
Morton's
Mountain Top
Mr. Freeze
Mrs. Paul's
Mrs. Smith's Desserts
Myers
Natural Touch
Naturally Good Fruit
New Traditions
New York
Ocoma
Oh Boy
Okray's
Old American
Old El Paso
On-Cor
Onion Ringers
Oregon Farms Frozen Desserts
Ore-Ida
Oronoque Orchard
Oven Express
Papa's Piroshki
Pasta Perfect

Pastry Pride
Patio
Patterson Fruits & Vegetables
Patti Jean
Pepperidge Farm
Perfection
Pet-Ritz Frozen Pies
Pictsweet
Pierre
Pillsbury
Pop-Ice
Portlock
Pour-A-Quiche
Rainbow
Red Baron Pockets
Rhodes
Rosita-Si
Ruiz
Ruiz Mexican
Sanderson Farms
Sara Lee
Schwan's
Sea Star
Seapak
Shape-Ups
Ship Ahoy
Simplot Classics
Singleton
Smart Ones
Soup Supreme
Southern Farms
Springfield
Steak-Umms
Stealth Natural Cut Fries
Stilwell Vegetables & Pies
Swanson
Swoopee Pops
Sysco
Taste O'Sea
Tater O's
TGI Friday's
The Sensible Chef
The Wide Body Burger
Tombstone Frozen Pizza

Tony's Pizza
Top Frost
Trade Winds
Tropic Isle
Twister Fries
Tyson

United Food
Van de Kamps
Vitafreze
Weaver
Weight Watchers
Yocream

Foreign owned

Akebono	J	La Cocinera	FR
Aldons	UKN	Lean Cuisine	SWI
Arctic Cape	NOR	Maplehurst	C
Big Bomb Posicle	J	Mette Munk	DEN
Big C Popsicle	J	North Cape	NOR
Bluewater	NOR	Pataks	AUS
Booth	C	Port Clyde	C
Bunch O Crunch Fish Sticks	NOR	Ready Bake	C
Caterpac French Fries	C	Right Course	SWI
Chef Francisco	BG	SeaFresh	C
Dorset Foods	UK	Smart Cuisine	IRE
F.P.I. Seafood	C	Stouffer's	SWI
Findus	SWI	Stouffer's Lean Cuisine	SWI
Fine Cuisine	SWI	Supercrisps French Fries	C
Fisher Boy	C	Superfries	C
Fisherings	C	Superstar French Fries	C
Floresta	C	Tina's Burritos	J
Food Club	C	Top Hat	FR
Freezer Queen	IRE	Topsicle	J
Frigodan	DEN	Tropic Popsicle	J
Frionor	NOR	Unisea	J
Frisco	SWI	Valley Farms	C
Frozen Queen	IRE	Vienetta	UKN
Gina Italian Village	C	Viscount	NOR
Gorton's	UKN	Weston	C
Groko	DEN	Yogen Fruz	C
High Liner	C	Yopa	SWI
Italian Village	C		

GENERAL FOOD PRODUCTS

American owned

4C
A-1 Steak Sauce
AC Seasoning
Ac'cent Seasoning

Adolphus Rice
Aim
Alamo Fruit
Alex

Algood
Allen
Always Fresh
Always Tender
Amapola
Amberex Yeast
Amish Kitchen
Andrews Dried Beef
Antiones
Aristocrat Sauces
Armour
Armour Star
Arnott's Biscuits
Arrezio
Arrowhead Mills
Ashley's of Texas
Aunt Jemima
Azteca Tortillas
B&G
Bacos
Bag N Season
Bagel Dogs
Baker's Chocolate
Bakit
Balance Bar
Bama
Bandito Diavolo
Bar-K
Bar-S
Bayfield County
Beardsley
Bearitos
Beatrice (non-dairy products)
Beaver Falls
Bel Aria
Bell & Evans Chicken
Bell's
Bell's Seasoning
Benenuts
Bennett's Sauces
Benson's Old Home Kitchens
Berkshire Hills
Best's Kosher
Better Batter

Betty Crocker
B-Family
Big Chunk
Big Mama
Big Valley
Bil-Mar
Biltmore Farms
Bishop
Bisto (Campbell's)
Blossom Brand
Blue Bird
Blue Ribbon Rice
Blueberry Squares
Bob Evans Sausage
Boca Burger
Bon Appetit
Boone County
Bradshaw's Honey
Bran N' Honey
Bran Thins
Bravo
Brer Rabbit
Brown & Serve
Brown Cow
Bruce's
Brunswick Canned Seafood
Buena Vida Tortillas
Bull's Eye B-B-Q Sauce
Bunker Hill Brand
Bureleson's Honey
Bush's Best
Butter Buds
Butter Charm
Butter Kernel
Butterball
Buttercup Farms
Butterfield
Buy 'N Save
By George
Café Pierre
Cajun King
Calavo
Calavo Avocados
Calavo Mangos

Calavo Papaya
Campbell's Soup
Cap'N Pride Seafood
Carolina Rice
Casa Fiesta
Casa Solana
Castelberry's
Catalina
Certified Red Label
Charlotte Charles
Cheese Whiz
Cheez Whiz
Chef Magic Hot Sauce
Chef Pleaser Bacon
Chef-Boy-Ar-Dee
Chef's Classic Seasonings
Cherry Central Produce
Chesapeake Seasoning
Chestnut Hills Farms
Chicken By George
Chick'N Easy
Chili Makin's Chili Mix
China Pride Duck Sauce
Christopher Edwards Pies
Chun King
Classic American Foods
Clearsoy
Clements
Clover Maid Honey
Cloverleaf
Colavita
Colonna
Comet Rice
Comstock Pie Fillings
ConAgra
Consul Fruits
Cool Whip
Coral Seafood
Country Best Potatoes
Country Delight
Country Inn
Country Manor
Country's Delight
Crispura

Crispy Bakes
Crisscut Fries
Cross Valley Farms
Crown Prince
Cub Foods
Custom Foods
Dai Day
Dairy Sweet
Davinci
Del Monte
Delmonico
Delseys
Delta
Delta Molasses
Dennisons
Diamond Crystal
Dillons
Diner
Dinty Moore
Dip Classics
Dip N Crisp Seafood
Dole
Dolly Madison
Dolmio Italian
Don Miguel Mexican
Douville
Doxsee Clam Products
Dream Whip
Dubon
Duck Trap
Duncan Hines
Dutch Mill
Duyvis
Eagle Canyon
East Texas Fair Peas
Eckrich
El Charrito
El Dorado Avacados
El Pasado
El Toro
Elan Foods
Eli's Cheesecake
el-Rio
Enrico's

Enzio
Equal
Excel
Excell
Famous Flavor Sausages
Fancy Condiments
Fantasia Bakery Products
Farm Foods
Farm Rich Vegetables
Farman's
Farmens
Farmhouse Foods
Fast Choice
Fast 'N Easy
Fastbites
Fiesta Seasonings
Finest
Fini
Fisher Nuts
Flavacol Seasoning Salt
Flavor Charm Non-Dairy Creamer
Flavor-Cap Flavorings & Spices
Flav-R-Pac
Fluffy
Flyers Spicy Chicken Wings
Food Club
Franco American
Frank 'N Stuff
Frank's Canned Foods
Fred Bear
Fresh Gourmet
Fresh 'N Ready Desserts
Freshlike
Friendship
Fruit Naturals
Fruit Patch Produce
Fun Feast
Funyuns Onion Rings
Furmano's Processed Vegetables
Furman's Processed Vegetables
F-V-M
Galaxy
Garden Club
Gardenfare

Garlic Plus
Gattuso
Gebhardt Mexican
General Mills
Georgia Mustard BBQ Sauce
Gibbs
Gilroy Farms
Gingham
Global
Global Grill
Glosette
Golden Grain Rice
Golden Shore
Golden Star
Golden State Almonds
Gooch
Good-N-Fast
Gourmet Baker
Goya
Grand Duke
Grandma's Seasonings
Gravy Master
Great Impressions
Great Lakes Blueberries
Great Ocean Canned Hams
Green Giant
Green Tree Canned Hams
Guest Ready
Gulfstream Seafood
Habitant
Happy Kids
Harbor Banks
Harrington Ham
Harvest Moon
Hauser
Health Valley
Hearthside Select
Hebrew National
Heinz
Herbal Bouquet
Herb-Ox
Hershey's Syrup
Hickory Farms
Hickory Hill Sausage

Hoffman
Hoffman House
Holiday Harvest Cranberry Sauce
Hollywood
Homefolks
Homestyle Gravy
Honey Bear Poultry
Honeysoy
Hook & Ladder
Hormel
Hot Digity Subs
Hot Shot Seasoning
Hot-Rageous Sausages
House of Tsang
Hungry-Man
Hunt's
Hunt-Wesson
Icicle Seafood
Icy Point
Idaho Naturally
Idaho Supreme
Ideal
IGA
Il Primo
Imo Food Dressings
Imperial Gardens
Imperial Sampan
Indian Trail
Indo
Inn Maid Noodles
Jack Rabbit
Jell-O
Jenny's Cuisine
Jimmy Dean Sausage
Johnsonville
Jones Dairy Farm
Just Pikt
K.C. Masterpiece
Kai Guava Fruit
Kan Tong Fried Rice
K-Blazer
Kellogg's Breadia
Kellogg's Croutettes
Kern

Kerr
King Soopers
Kingston
Knauss Dried Beef
Knott's Berry Farm
Kohler
Kosher King
Kowality
Kowalski
Kozy Kitten
Kraft
Krispy Kreme Doughnuts
Kuner
Kuner-Empson
La Casa Salsa
La Chedda Cheese Sauce
La Choy
La Preferida
La Primera Sausages
La Restaurante Salsa
Lady Lee
Lakeside
Lamb's Supreme
Lamisoy
Lance
Land O' Lakes
Las Palmas Mexican
Lassie
Lazy Maple Bacon
Le Bisquit
Le Gourmet Rice
Lean Cream
Lean Magic
Libby
Like Mom's
Lil-Salt
Link-N-Dog
Lite-Line
Little Pig Barbeque Sauce
Little Sizzlers
Log Cabin
Loma Linda
London Pub
Longmont

Louis Kemp Seafood
Louisiana Hot Sauce
Lucca Italian
Lucky Leaf
Lunch and More
Lunchables
Lustersoy
Luzianne
Lynn Wilson's Mexican
Mac Scramble Eez
Magic Valley
Magic Valley Instant Potatoes
Mahatma Rice
Makin Cajun Spices & Sauces
Mama Tish Ices
Mandalay Rice
Manischewitz Kosher Foods
Manwich
Market Basket
Martel Canned Seafood
Marval
Mary Kitchen
Maryland Chief
Marzetti
McCormick/Schilling
Menu Maker
Mexene
Mexican Original
Micromagic
Microrave Cake Mix
Minute Rice
Miracoli
Mitia
Miyako
Monica Rice
Monterey Mushrooms
Moon Palace
Morningstar Farms
Morrison & Schiff
Morton House Canned Meat
Morton Table Salt
Mountain House
Mozzarella Crisps
Mr. Spud

Mr. Turkey
Mrs. Butterworth's
Mrs. Cubbison's
Mrs. Dash
Mrs. Difillippo's Meatballs
Mrs. Grass Soups & Dry Mixes
Mrs. Grimes
Mrs. Paterson's Aussie Pie
Mrs. Weiss Noodles
MTC Japanese Food
Musselman's
My-T-Fine Puddings
Nalley's
National Brands
Nature's Recipe
Naturfresh
Near East Flavored Rice
New Traditions
New Vegit
Newman's Own
Nomis Processed Vegetables
Noodle Roni
North Bay Produce
Northland Queen
Not So Sloppy Joe
Oasis Fine Foods
Oberti Olives
Ocean Beauty Salmon
Ocean Prince
Ocean Prize
Oceanway
Ohse
Old Bay Seafood
Old Dutch
Old Mill
Old South Log Rolls
Old Time
Old Wisconsin
On Top Non-Dairy Topping
Onion Crisps
Onion Magic
Onion Ringers
Open Pit Barbeque Sauce
Orchard Boy

Orchard County
Ore-Ida
Original Deluxe Fruit Cakes
Oscar Mayer
Our Classic
Our Deluxe
Our Family
Our Premium
Pace Picante Sauce
Panni Imported
Papa Lynn Mexican
Parade
Paramount Pickles
Parker 1/2 Runner
Pastry Pride Topping
Patak's Ethnic Foods
Pauly Desserts
Peloponnese
Pemmican Meat Snacks
Pennant
Pepperidge Farm
Pesta Pickles
Phillips
Pictsweet
Pie Piper
Pierre
Pierre Classics
Pillarrock
Pillsbury
Pinata
Plush Pippin Pies
Point View Vegetables
Polynesian Sauces
Popeye Leaf Spinach
Pop-Tarts
Potato Buds
Powerbar Harvest Fitness Bars
Powerbar Performance Fitness Bars
Prairie Farms
Preformers Potato Products
Prego
Premium Bristol Gold
Presidents Pride
Price Saver

Pride Canned Vegetables
Pride of Alaska
Pride Of The Fram
Prima Porta Sausages
Produce Partners
Progresso
Pudding Plus
Purity
Quaker Rice Cakes
Queen Anne
Raga Muffins
Rainbow
Read Salads
Real Cream
Realemon
Reames Egg Noodles
Red Cross Vegetables
Reddi Whip
Regal Crown Canned Hams
Reputation
Rib Nibblers
Rib-B-Q
Rice-A-Roni
Riceland Rice
Richfood
River Rice
Robin Hood
Rockin' Burger
Rod's Salad Dressing & Dips
Roegelein
Rokeach Kosher Foods
Romanoff Cavier
Rosarita Mexican Food
Rotel
Rotel Canned Tomatoes
Royal
Royal Fruits & Vegetables
Royal Kerry
Royal Reef Seafood
Royalty Pineapple
Rudy's Farm
Rymer
S&W Fine Foods
Sadano's

Salad Crispins
Salad Crunchies
Salad Shoppe
Salmon Chef
Salsa Naturala
San Remo Genoa Sausage
Sanderson Farms
Santay
Sara Lee
Sauceworks
Sau-Sea
Saver's Choice
Savory Classics
Schilling
Schwan's
Schweigert
Scott's Rolled Oats
Sea Alaska
Sea Greens
Sea Maid
Sea-Best
Sea-Est
Seas'n Easy
Season 'n Fry
Seaway
Select Recipes
Seneca
Sensitive Eyes
Serano Pickled Peppers
Shake 'N Bake
Shake 'N Pour Pancake Mix
Shenandoah
Ship Ahoy
Shoestrings
Shogun Seafood
Short Orders
Showboat Canned Vegetables
Shur Valu
Shurfine
Shurfresh
Sig
Silver Floss Sauerkraut
Silver Medal
Simplesse

Simplot
Simplou
Simply Potatoes
Simply Superior
Singleton Seafood
Sizzlean
Skincredibles
Skyland
Smart Beat
Smart Start
Smart Temptations
Smithfield Meats
Smuckers Pockets
Snack Pack
Snackin' Fruits
Snokist
Snow-Floss Canned Food
Snow's
Snow's Clam Products
Solo
Soup Starter
Soup Supreme
Southern Foods
Southern Gen
Spaghettio's
Sparta Foods
Springfield
St. Luc
State Brand
State Fair Foods
Steak-Umms
Steakwich
Steer
Steerburger
Steero
Stella D'oro
Stenger
Stew Starter
Stir 'N Bake
Stir-N-Serv
Stock Yards Chicago
Stove Top
Strawberry Squares
Stuart (Imported)

Stuffables
Success Rice
Suddenly Salad
Sue Bee Honey
Sugar Baby Vegetables
Sugardale Meat Products
Sundae Syrup
Sun-Maid
Sun-Maid Raisins
Sunny Fresh
Sunny Square
Sunshine Vegetables
Superfine
Swanson
Sweet Sue
Swift Meat Products
Swift Water Seafood
Swiss Miss
Sysco
Taco Bell
Tac-Ole Mexican
Taste of Paradise
Tasty Wings
TastyKake
Temperno
Tendersweet Vegetables
Texas AA Instant Rice
Thank You Brand
Three Bees Honey
Thrift King
Tico Avocados
Time Savor Line
Tip Top
Toast'em Pop-up
Toastettes
Tony's
Top Quality
Torrido
Totino's
Touch O' Gold Peanut Oil
Trade Winds
Trappey's
Tree Top Apple Sauce
Turkey By George

Turrorosso Tomatoes
Tuxedo
UF
Ultimate Choice
Uncle Ben's Rice
Underwood Canned Meats
Underwood Meat Spreads
Valley Chef
Valu-Time
Van Camp's
Van de Kamps
Van Wagenen Schickhaus
Vanity Vegetable
Veg-All
Vegetable Crisps
Vegetables N' Pastry
Veribest Canned Meats
Vienna Beef
Vita
Wacky Mac
Wagon Master
Water Maid Rice
Weaver
Weight Watchers
Weinstein Seafood
Welch's Totally Fruit
Wesson Vegetable Oil
West Brae Natural
Western Family
Western Steer
Westin
White House
White River Farms
White Rose
Wholesome Foods
Williams-Sonoma
Wolco
Wonder Rice
Wonderbites
Woodman's
Woodman's Sauces
Woody's BBQ Sauce
World Classics
Worthington

Wyler's		Zappetites	
Yeoman		Zeda	
Yoshida			

Foreign owned

Adolph's Seasoning	UKN	Chirat	UKN
Agnesi	FR	Colonial Biscuits	ITL
Akebono	J	Coltina	J
Aldons	UKN	Conimex	UKN
Alpro	G	Connaisseur Seafood	C
Ambrosia	UKN	Contadina Tomato Paste	SWI
American Original Seafoods	C	Crosse & Blackwell	SWI
America's Choice	G	Cup Noodles	J
Amora	FR	Curry-O	J
Amoy Chinese Sauces	FR	Danepak Bacon	DEN
Aoluette	FR	Delacre Biscuits	UK
Aromat Food Seasoning	UKN	Delta Rice	UKN
Atora	UK	Deming's	J
Ault	BG	Deming's Canned Salmon	J
Batchelors	UK	Denny	UKN
Beatrice (dairy products)	ITL	Double Q Canned Salmon	J
Belin	FR	Du Chef Syl	UKN
Benson's	UKN	Durkee	AUS
Bertolli	ITL	Dutch Harbor	J
Best Foods	UKN	Elders	AUS
Bisto Specialty Foods		Elke's Biscuit	UK
(Ranks Hovis)	UK	Empress	J
Blue Bay	C	Entenmann's	C
Blue Surf Seafood	C	Fazer Biscuits	UK
Boboli Pizza Crusts	UKN	Fiesta Cake	C
Brittania	FR	Five Roses	BG
Brossard	UK	Flip N' Fry	C
Brown & Polson	UKN	Florigold Citrus Fruits	BG
Brownberry	C	Fox's Biscuits	UK
Brunswick Sea Food	C	Frank's Red Hot Food Sauces	UK
Burry Biscuits	C	Freihofer's	C
Café Au Lait	J	French's	UK
California	N	Frenchs Gravy & Sauce Mixes	AUS
Captain Cook	J	French's Worcestershire Sauce	UK
Carnation	SWI	Freshworld Farms Produce	MEX
Cascade Select	J	Gayelord Hauser	FR
Cecilia Health Food	J	Germantown	AUS
Chef-Mate	SWI	Gillard's	UK
Chef's Pride	J	Gillnetters Best	J

Golden Gate	SP	No Frills	C
Goodall's	UKN	Old El Paso	UK
Grand'italia	FR	Oregon Farms	BG
Grossmann Chilled Salads	UKN	Ortega Mexican	SWI
Harvest Sausage & Weiners	C	Oxford Biscuits	UK
Heluva Good	N	Pampas Pastry	AUS
Heritage Salmon	C	Pasco Cakes	J
Hollands Pie	UK	Pasta Kauramakaroni	FIN
Holmes Sea Food	C	Paxo	UK
Humpty Dumpty Salmon	J	Peek Freans Biscuits	FR
Hungry Jack Pancake Mix	UK	Perfect Bar	J
Iberia	UKN	Peter Pan Canned Salmon	J
Indian Summer Vinegar	J	Peter Pan Seafoods	J
Iris	FR	Pfanni	UKN
Jacky	SWI	Pizza Quick	UKN
Jacob's	FR	Poundo Yam	UK
Jeffs Vegetables	UK	Puritan Canned Meats	UKN
Jimmi	UKN	Quality Fare	C
John Moir	N	Que Bueno	SWI
Kikkoman	J	Quick Whip	UKN
Knorr	UKN	Rafhan	UKN
La Lechera	SWI	Ragu	UKN
La Mariniere	C	Ramen Soup	J
La Rosa	SWI	Ramen Supreme	J
La Victoria Salsa & Sauces	MEX	Ringoes	C
Lawry's Seasonings	UKN	River Ranch	UK
Lea & Perrins	FR	Rowntree's	SWI
Libby's	SWI	Royal Jelly	J
Lidano	UKN	Saga	UK
Lord Sandwich	SWI	Sainsbury's	UK
Lucky Whip	UKN	Saltesea	C
Maple Leaf	C	Santa Rosa	UKN
Master Choice	G	Savas Health Food	J
Master's Touch Produce	MEX	Sea Fresh	C
Maxy Beef Jerky	UK	Sea Pasta	J
Mazola Corn Oil	UKN	Sea Stix	J
McCain	C	Seald-Sweet Citrus Fruits	BG
McDougall's	UK	Sensibles	C
Milkslice	ITL	Shopsy's	C
Mott's	UK	Slim-Fast	UKN
Mrs. Friday's	J	Songgai	AUS
Napolina	UKN	Spa-O	J
Nestle Toll House	SWI	Star	FR
Nissin Foods	J	Starlux	FR

Stouffer's	SWI	Valley Fresh	IRE
Table Queen	FR	Weston	C
Telma	UKN	Whipper Mix	SWI
Thomas' English Muffins	C	White Cap	J
Tia Rosa	MEX	White Wings	AUS
Toast-R-Cakes	C	Yabon	UKN
Top Ramen	J	York	C
Unisea	J		

HOT DOGS

American owned

Armour	Louis Rich
Ball Park	Lykes
Eckrich	Mr. Turkey
Healthy Choice	Nathan's
Hormel	Ohse
Hygrade's	Oscar Mayer
Jumbo Griller	Seitz

Foreign owned
No foreign brands could be located for this category.

ICE CREAM

Unilever (UKN) is the world's largest maker of ice cream.

American owned

3 Musketeers	Fosters Freeze
Baldwin	Happy Time
Blue Bell Creamery	Healthy Choice
Borden	Homemade Brand
Bridgeman	Horlucks
Brigam's	Hygeia
Calypso	Kibon
Carnival	Klondike Bar
Carvel	Knudson
Comet	Mayfield
Cookie Break	Meadow Gold
Dairi-Fresh	Mello Frozen Yogurt
Dove Ice Cream Bars	Mellobuttercup
Dreyer's	Newly Weds
Eagle	Perry's
Edy's	Pet
Fannie May	Private Label
Fanny Farmer	Queen's Choice

Reiter's

Rondos

Sani-Dairy

Schoep's

Schwan's

Sealtest

Snickers

Turner

Welcome

Foreign owned

Abbotts Old Philadelphia	BG	Ice Burg	J
Baskin-Robbins	UK	Larry's Old Fashioned	C
Beatrice	ITL	Louis Sherry	BG
Ben & Jerrys	UKN	Make-A-Wish Ice Cream Bars	C
Bon-Bons	SWI	Mr. Triple Ice Milk	J
Bresler	C	Penguin's Frozen Yogurt	FR
Breyer's	UKN	Penn Farms	N
Cascade	SWI	Pensupreme	N
Crunchy Dip Ice Milk	MAL	Peters	AUS
Drumstick	SWI	Popsicle Brand	UKN
Earle Swensen's	C	Push-Ups	SWI
Eskimo	C	Quebon	C
Eskimo Pie	C	Steve's	C
Frosty	J	Steve's Gourmet Light	C
Fruit-Line	UKN	Stouffer's	SWI
Fudgsicle	UKN	The Original Mix-In	C
Gold Bond	UKN	Valley Park	N
Good Humor	UKN	Vienetta	UKN
Haagen-Dazs	SWI	Wesley's Quaker Maid	G
Heaven	SWI	Wonderland	J

JAMS, JELLIES & PRESERVES

American owned

Algood	Ideal
Aristocrat	J.M. Smuckers
Bama	Kraft
Bell Carter	Kukui
Charlotte Charles	Lost Acres
Clements	Mary Ellen
Delicious	Polaner
Dickinson's	Regal Crown
Dutch Girl	Savory
Farley	Simply Fruit
Garden Club	Smucker's
Harvest Lane	Sorrell Ridge
Home Brands	Welch's Squeezables

Foreign owned

Berry Box	C	Robertson's	UK
Casa De Mateus	UKN	Rowntree's	SWI
Crosse & Blackwell	SWI	Santa Rosa	UKN
Frank Cooper	UKN	Triple Fruits	C
Kist	UKN	Zwaardemaker	N
Pomodorissimo	UKN		

KETCHUP

American owned

Brooks	Hunt's
Heinz	Mato Mato
Heinz Lite	Tangy

Foreign owned

Livio	UKN	Santa Rosa	UKN
Pomodorissimo	UKN		

MAYONNAISE

Both Best Foods and Hellmann's mayonnaise are now owned by Unilever (UKN.)

American owned

Blue Plate	Kraft
Cains	Nalley's
Chef's Choice	Purity
Clements	

Foreign owned

Best Foods	UKN	Hellmann's	UKN
Chirat	UKN	Lizano	UKN
ETA	AUS	Praise	AUS
Fruco	UKN	Telma	UKN
Goodall's	UKN	Vandemoortele	G

MEATS

American owned

5-Star Meats	Argal
A.C. Kissling	Armour
Abbyland	Armour Star
Alpine	Banner Brand Sausage
Aoste	Bar-S

Batcher Wagon
Bil-Mar
Block & Barrel
Blue Boar Ham
Bob Ostrow
Bridou
Bryan Foods
Buddig
Budget Wise Turkey
Bull & Hannahs
Bunker Hill Brand
Butcher's Best Poultry
Butterball
Buttercup Farms
Celebrity
Chesapeak Valley Farms
Chicken By George
Colonial
ConAgra
Cookin' Good Poultry
Country Boy Sausage
Country Cupboard
Country Pride Poultry
Country Skillet
Covington Farms Chicken
Cure/81 Ham
Curemaster Ham
Danish Crown Canned Ham
Decker
Dinner Bell
Double Diamond
Dubuque
Eckrich
Empire Kosher Poultry
Esskay
Falls Poultry
Family Pride Turkeys
Family Tradition Turkeys
Famland Pork
Farmer Boy
Farmer's Pride
Farmer's Pride Natural Chicken
Farmland Foods Pork
Galileo

Galileo Italian
Gallo Salame
Gold Label Pork
Gold Ribbon Hams
Golden Star
Golden Star Turkey
Grillmaster
Gwaltney
Hamilton Easy Karv
Hamiltons
Harker's Steaks
Harot Kosher Poultry
Harrington Ham
Hatfield
Healthy Choice
Hebrew National
Herrud
Hickory Farms
Hillshire Farms
Hillshire Lite
Holly Ridge Farms
Homeland Hard Salami
Hostess Hams
Hunter
Hygrade
Imperial Meats
James River
Jefferson County Pork
Jennie-O
John Morrell
Johnsonville Sausage
Kahn's
Kayem
King of Steaks
Kowality
Kowalski
Kraukus
Kretschmar
Krey Foods
La Italia
Lamb's Natural
Larkwood Farms Poultry
Light & Lean
Liguria

Li'l Butterball Turkey
Longmont Turkey
Louis Rich
Luter's
Lykes
Maple River
Marval Turkey
Mash's
Mayrose
McCarty Farms Poultry
McKenzie Of Vermont
Medford's
Miss Country Fair Turkey
Miss Goldy Chicken
Monfort
Morton House Canned
Mosey's
Mr. Host
Mr. Turkey
Murry's
Nathan's
National Deli
National Poultry
Norwestern Turkey
Ohse
Old Town
Old Wisconsin
Old World Sausage
Olde Smithfield
Ole Carolina
Oscar Mayer
Oven Classic
Oven Stuffers
Owens Country Sausage
Ozark Family Recipe
Ozark Fry
PA Dutch Sausages
Palm River/Grill King
Parma Brand
Partridge
Patrick Cudahy
Patuxent Farms
Perdue
Perdue Poultry

Peter Eckrich
Peyton's
Pier Franco
Pilgrim's Pride
Plantation Poultry
Pleasure Chest of Steaks
Plymouth Pride Turkey
Premium Gold Angus
President Pride
Queen Kristina
Range Brand Wranglers
Rath Blackhawk
Roast Rite Turkeys
Rockingham
Rodeo
Roegelein
Roselli
Russer
San Remo Sausage
Sandwich Maker
Schwan's
Schweigert
Scott Petersen
Seitz
Selecto
Shady Brook Farms Chicken
Shady Brook Farms Turkey
Sheboygan Deli
Sibio Pork
Simmenthal
Sinai 48
Smithfield
Spam
Stegeman
Sugardale Foods
Sugarplum Ham
Sun Land Beef
Superior Brand
Sweet Sue
Sweetheart
Swift
Swift Premium
Swift-Eckrich
Tasti-Lean Turkeys

Tasty Basted Poultry
Thorn Apple Valley
Tobin First Prize
Tom Sawyer
To-Ricos Poultry
Trim Line Poultry
Triple M
Triple MMM
Trunz
Turkey By George
Turkey Quick
Turkey Selects
Tyson
Tyson Holly Farms
Tyson's Pride

Valley Chef
Valleydale
Veribest
Vienna Beef
Wampler Foods
Watervalley
Watson
Webber Farms
West Virginia
Willowbrook Farms Poultry
Wranglers
Wright
Wunderbar
Zagreb Canned Hams

Foreign owned

Binghams	UK	Nistria	N
Bowyers	UK	Parmamec	ITL
Elders	AUS	Prime Poultry	C
Fletcher's	C	Puritan	UKN
Foodane	DEN	Schonlands	BG
Grimm's	C	Steggles Poultry	AUS
M. M. Mades	BG	Table Talk Poultry	AUS
Malton	UK	Tend-R-Fresh Poultry	C
Master Choice	G	Teriyaki Meatball	J
Meester	N		

MUSTARD

French's is the most common mustard brand in homes and restaurants across America. But it isn't French. It isn't American either. Grey Poupon sounds foreign, but is actually an American brand.

American owned

Chef's Choice
Delta
Garden Club
Great Impressions

Grey Poupon
Gulden's
Heinz
Jack Daniels

Foreign owned

Amora	FR	Hellmann's	UKN
Best Foods	UKN	Maille	FR
Dijonnaise	UKN	Savora	UKN
French's	UK		

PASTA

American owned

American Beauty
Anthony's
Antiones
Arrowhead Mills
Bean Cuisine
Bernardi
Bravo
Catelli
Classico
Colavita
Colonna
Columbia
Country Inn Pasta
Creamette
Delmonico
Di Giorno
Dutch Maid
Fiberoni
Gioia
Globe A-1
Golden Grain
Golden Grain/Mission
Ideal by San Giorgio
Light 'N Fluffy Noodles
Luxury
Merlino
Merlino's
Miracoli
Mission

Mona
Monder
Mrs. Grass
Mrs. Weiss
New Mill
P & R
Pasta Perfect
Pasta Select
Penn Dutch Noodles
Pennsylvania Dutch
Prince
R & F
Ramen Pride Noodles
Ravarino & Freschi
Red Cross
R-F
Romi
Ronco
Ronzoni
Roselli
Rosetto
San Giorgio
Santa Ninfa
Skinner
Skroodles
Trio Italiano
Vimco
West Brae Natural

Foreign owned

Anco	N	Louise's	BG
Barilla	ITL	Monte Rosa	MEX
Birkel	FR	Mueller's	UKN
Buitoni	SWI	Napolina	UKN
California	N	Olivieri	C
Diamond	AUS	Panzani	FR
Festaiola	FR	Pasta Gala	SWI
Honig	N	Ponte	FR
La Familia	FR	Record	UK
Lady's Choice	UKN	Reimassas	SWI

| Royal | UKN | Vetta | AUS |
| Vesta | ITL | Yamina | ITL |

PASTA SAUCE

American owned

Aunt Millie's	Healthy Choice
Campbell's	Hunt's
Catelli	McCormick
Classico	Medei Cuisine
Colonna	Newman's Own
Del Monte	Prego
Di Giorno	Prince
Dino's	Progresso
Enrico's	Ronzoni
Gattuso	Ultimo!
Gianni	Winsom

Foreign owned

Barilla	ITL	Napolina	UKN
Contadina	SWI	Pizza Quick	UKN
Five Brothers	UKN	Ragu	UKN

PEANUT BUTTER

American owned

Adams	Jif
Algood	Kitchen King
American	Laura Scudder's
Austin	Peter Pan
Blue Plate	Real
Capco	Reese's
Cap'N Kid	Roddenbery's
Garden Club	Savory
Happy Kids	Smucker's
Home Brands	

Foreign owned

| Best Foods | UKN | Skippy | UKN |
| Lady's Choice | UKN | Squirrel | UKN |

PET FOOD

St. Louis-based Ralston Purina was recently acquired by Swiss food giant Nestle S. A., which was already the world's largest food company prior to the acquisition. As a result, 35 brands changed from American ownership to foreign ownership.

American owned

9-Lives
Amore
Butchers Bones
Cadillac
Calo
Canigou
Canine Carry Outs
Cat Life
Cesar
Chuncks
Classy Cat
ConAgra
Country Cat
Country Kennel
Crunchy Meals
Cycle
Dad's
Dad's Chunx
Dad's Dog Foods
Dad's Econ-O-Mets
Doane
Doc Kennedy
Dog Life
Eukanuba
Figaro
Flavor Snacks
Frolic
Gainer
Gaines Burgers
Gaines Gravy Train
Gravy Train
Hearty Brand
Iams
Jazz Dog Food
Jerkey Treats
Kal Kan
Ken-L Ration

Kibbles 'N Bits
Kitekat
Kitty
Kozy Kitten
Lolli-Pups
Me & My Cat
Meaty Bone
Milk Bone
Mini Chunks
Moist 'N Beefy
Nature's Recipe
Patriot
Pedigree
Pedigree Pal
Pet Life
Pounce
Pro Energy
Professional Formula
Promark
Proud Paws
Proud Pet
Pup-peroni
Purr
Puss'N Boots
Quaker Tender Chops
Recipe
Regal
Reward
Ronron
Roscoe
Science Diet
Sheba
Skippy
Smorgasbird
Snausages
Sparkle
Sparkle Jr.

Special Cuts
Strongheart
Sun Pro
Supersweet
Techni-Cal
Tender Chops

Town & Country
Tuffy's
Twin Pet
Vets
Whiskas

Foreign owned

Alamo	SWI	Kitten Chow	SWI
Alley Cat	SWI	Lucky Dog	SWI
Alpo	SWI	Mainstay	SWI
Baron	FIN	Master's Choice	SWI
Beef Bite Treats	SWI	Matzinger	SWI
Beggin' Strips	SWI	Meow Mix	SWI
Big Mill	SWI	Mighty Dog	SWI
Bi-Ta	SWI	Moist & Meaty	SWI
Blue Mountain	SWI	Moments	SWI
Bonz	SWI	Nature's Course	SWI
Buffet	SWI	Pet Treats	SWI
Butcher's Blend	SWI	Praise	SWI
Canine/Feline	C	Pro Plan	SWI
Cheezdawgs	SWI	Pro Pup	SWI
Chuck Wagon	SWI	Puppy Chow	SWI
Come 'N Get It	SWI	Puppy Love	SWI
Deli Cat	SWI	Purina Biscuits	SWI
Deliss	FIN	Purina Cat Chow	SWI
Dr. Ballard's	SWI	Purina Chow	SWI
Fancy Feast	SWI	Purina Dog Chow	SWI
Field Formula	SWI	Purina One	SWI
Field Master	SWI	Purina Premium	SWI
Fit 'N Trim	SWI	Ribz	SWI
Friskies	SWI	Ringoos	SWI
Go-Cat	SWI	Rollitos	SWI
Gourmet	SWI	Shur-Gain	C
Grrravy	SWI	Smart Cat	SWI
Happy Cat	SWI	Special Dinners	SWI
Hearty Chews	SWI	Tabby	SWI
Hi-Pro	SWI	Tender Meaty Chunx	SWI
Hunter's Choice	SWI	Tender Moist Chunx	SWI
Jim Dandy	SWI	Tender Vittles	SWI
Katfish Pickins	SWI	Thrive	SWI
Kibbles & Cheezy Chews	SWI	Unique	SWI
Kibbles & Chunks	SWI	Wagtime Beef Basted Biscuits	SWI
Kit 'N Kaboodle	SWI		

PICKLES

American owned

Arnolds

Atkins

Aunt Jane's

B&G

Bick's

Cains

Cains/Oxford

Cairo Beauties

Capco

Cates

Chipico

Claussen

Crickles

Crispy Cuts

Daily

Daley

Del Monte

Dewkist

Extra Crisp

Farman's

Gattuso

Habitant

Happy Kids

Heifetz

Heinz

Koscuiszkowy

Lassie Jane

Ma Brown

McLarens

Mr. Kitzel

Mrs. Fanning's

Nalley's

Paramount

Pesta

Peter Piper

Pin Money

Rainbo

Roddenbery's

Rose

Schorr's

Schwartz's Pickel Barrel

Stackers

Sugar Loaf

Tree

Vlasic

Whitfield

Foreign owned

Golden Gate   SP

Pan Yan   SWI

PIZZA

American owned

Alvino

Braccacia

Celeste

Di Giorno

Don Martino

Donatos

Fresh Express

Gattuso

Healthy Choice

Jack's

Jeno's

Kroger

Little Lady Pizza

Michelina's

Natalina

Papa Lino

Papa's Piroshki

Pepe's

Pillsbury

Pizza Vita

Primerro

Red Baron

Safeway
Schwan's
Tenaro
Tombstone

Tony's
Totino's
Weight Watchers

Foreign owned

Boboli	UKN	Pizza Quick	UKN
Deep 'N Delicious	C	Stouffer's	SWI
Leaning Tower	AUS		

POPCORN

American owned

Act II
American's Best
Bachman
Blast O Butter
Chester's
Clover Club
Cracker Jack
Crunch 'n Munch
Healthy Choice
Healthy Pop Microwave
Jiffy Pop
Jolly Time
Naks-Pak
Newman's Own

O-Ke-Doke
Orville Redenbacher
Pillsbury
Pop Secret
Popeye
Pops-Rite
Popweaver
Redenbudder's
Smartfood
Super Pop
Weaver
Weight Watchers
Wise Choice

Foreign owned
No foreign brands could be located for this category.

SALAD DRESSING

American owned

Albert's Finest
Bernstein's
Cains
Cains Country
Cardini's
Charlotte Charles
Chef's Choice
Clements
Conway
Girards
Good Seasons
Great Impressions

Herb Magic
Hidden Valley
Hoffman House
Knott's Berry Farm
Kraft
La Martinique
La-Flora
Light Blend
Light Fantastic
Light Hearted
Marie's
Marzetti

Miracle Whip	Riviera
Nalley's	Rod's
Newman's Own	Roux
Old Dutch	Salad Lite and Design
Pfeiffer	Seven Seas
Purity	Simply Superior
Rancher's Choice	Spin Blend

Foreign owned

Best Foods	UKN	Lesieur	UKN
Calve	POR	Praise	AUS
Goodall's	UKN	San-J	J
Heidelberg	UKN	Western	UKN
Hellmann's	UKN	Wish-Bone	UKN
Henri's	UKN		

SAUCES

American owned

Bull Hot Sauce	Makin Cajun
Bull's-Eye Barbaque Sauce	Medei Cuisine Pasta
China Pride Duck Sauce	Mexi-Pep Hot Sauce
Country Inn Sauce	Michelini
Deerfield Tartar Sauce	Mrs. Dash
Di Giorno	Old Smokehouse Steak Sauce
Great Impressions	Pace
Heinz	Polynesian
Heinz 57 Steak Sauce	Rich & Sassy BBQ Sauce
Hoffman House	Roselli
Homepride Sauces	Saigon Sizzle Stir-Fry
Hot Stuff BBQ	Sauceworks
House of Tsang	Sysco
Hunt's Spaghetti Sauce	Texas Best
Indi-Pep Hot Sauce	Texas Pit BBQ Sauce
K.C. Masterpiece	Thai Accents
Little Pig BBQ Sauce	Woodman's
Lousiana Gold Hot Sauce	Woody's BBQ Sauce
Lousiana Hot Sauce	

Foreign owned

Buitoni	SWI	La Victoria Salsa	MEX
Chirat	UKN	Lawry's	UKN
Crosse & Blackwell	SWI	Le Gout	UKN
Kikkoman	J	Lea & Perrins	FR
Knorr	UKN	Pataks	AUS

Reddy	G	Tamari	J
San Juis Hot Sauce	MEX	Telma	UKN
San-J	J	Ubena	UKN
Santa Rosa	UKN		

SNACKS

American owned

Allen	Cheese Nips
Almond Facts	Cheese Tid-Bit
Anderson Pretzels	Chee-tos
Andy Capp's	Cheez Doodles
Anne's Nantucket	Cheez Whiz
Austin	Cheez-it
Bachman	Chip-A-Roos
Bagel Bites	Chipitos
Baked Flake	Chips Ahoy!
Baked Lays	Christie
Baked Tostitos	Clover Club
Baken-ets	Club & Cheddar
Bakers Best Pretzels	Combos
Barrel O' Fun	Confetti Almonds
Barrel O' Fun Potato Chips	CornNuts
Bearitos	Cornquistos
Beer Nuts	Cottage Fries
Better Cheddars	Country Crisp Potato Chips
Betty Lou	Cracker Jack
Bickel's	Croky (Frito Lay)
Bluebird (Flowers)	Crunch 'n Munch
Borden's	Crunch 'N Munch
Bravos	Dakota Sunflower Seeds
Break Cakes	Dan Dee
Bridgford	Devil Dogs
Britos	Ding Dongs
Brown Edge	Dipps
Bugles	Dipsy Doodles
Bullpen Chew Sunflower Seeds	Dolly Madison
Cabana	Doo Dads
California Pretzel Company	Doritos
Cape Cod	Durangos
Carson's Dried Beef	Dutchie Soft Pretzels
Cheddar Wedges	Easy Cheese Spread
Cheddar Crisps	Evon's Nuts

Fat Freddie
Fig Newtons
Fisher Nuts
Flavor House
Frito-Lay
Fritos
Fruit by the Foot
Fruit Roll Ups
Fruit Snackers
Fruit Snacks
Fruit String Thing
Funny Bones
Garden Crisps
Glosette Peanuts & Raisins
Golden Crisp Potato Chips
Golden Grahams Treats
Golden Wave Potato Chips
Grandaddy's
Granny Goose
Gushers
Guy's Foods
Harvest Crisps
Hi-Ho
Ho Hos
Honey Crunchers
Hostess Snack Cakes
Hot Knots Soft Pretzels
Husman Potato Chips
Jays Potato Chips
Jell-O
Johnson Nut
Keebler
Kidzels Pretzels
Knott's Berry Farm
Krunchers Potato Chips
Kudos Granola Bars
La Famous Tortilla Chips
La Restaurante Chips & Salsa
La Suprema Tortilla Chips
Lance
Laura Scudder's
Lay's Potato Chips
Little Bear Organic
Little Debbie

Maizetos Tortilla Chips
Mamacita Tortilla Chips
Marzetti
Mauna Loa Nuts
McKee
Mexicali
Mickey
Mickey Cakes
Mint'ees Almonds
Moore's
Moore's Potato Chips
Mootown
Mozzarella Crisps
Mr. Twister
Mrs. Goodcookie
Mrs. Ihries
Munchmates
Munchos Potato Chips
Munchrights
Nalley's
National Pretzels
New York Deli
New York Style Bagel Chips
New York Style Potato Chips
Nilla Wafers
Nut Thins
Nutri-Grain Bars
Nutzels
Oat Thins
O'Boise
Olde New England
Onion Crisps
Party Club
Pastapazazz
Pemmican
Penrose
Pepe Pork Rinds
Pepperidge Farm
Philadelphia Cheese Cake Bars
Pick O' The Grove
Pik-Nik
Pinwheels
Pizzarias
Plantation Brownies

Planters
Pocket Classics
Pop-Tarts Mini
Pow Wow
Pretzel Gourmet
Pretzel Nuts
Pretzelvania's Best
Pringle's
Quinlan Pretzels
Ranch Fries
Really Naturals
Red Seal Potato Chips
Rice Krispies Bars
Rice Krispies Treats
Ridgetts
Ridgies Potato Chips
Ring Dings
Ritz
Rold Gold Petzels
Rondos
Rough Cut
Rudolph Pork Rinds
Ruffles Potato Chips
Rustler's Meat Snacks
Santitas
Sierra Valley
Simply Kudos
Slim Jim
Smart Start Cereal Bar
Smart Temptations
Smartfoods
Smokehouse
Smokey Mountain
Smucker's Snackers
Snack Pack
Snackin' Fruits
Snapple Ice
Sno Balls
Snyder of Berlin
Snyders
Snyder's of Hanover
Southern Farms
Suddenly S'mores
Sun Chips

Sunbeam
Sunbelt
Sun-Maid Raisins
Suzy Q
Sweet Rewards
Sweet'ees Almonds
Swiss Cheese
T.G. Bearwich
Tato Skins
Teddy Grahams
Tender Delite
The Finest Gift (Nuts)
Thin 'N Light
Thin 'N Right
Tid Bits
Tim's Cascade Chips
Toggi Wafers
Tom Scott Nuts
Tom's
Tom's Great American
Tostados
Tostitos
Town House & Cheddar
Treat
Triscuits
Twigs
Twinkies
Valley Maid
Vegetable Thins
Vitners
Wavy-Lay's
Weight Watchers
Welch's Fruit Juice Bars
West Brae Natural
Wheat Thins
Wheatsworth
White Swan
Wild Bill's
Wise
Wise Choice
Wise Potato Chips
Wyandot
Yocream

Foreign owned

Belin	FR	Jane Parker	G
Bluebird (Goodman Fielder)	AUS	Karl Brand Corn Snacks	J
Bon-Bons	SWI	Kettle Chips	AUS
CC's Corn Chips	AUS	Klondike Ice Cream Bar	UKN
Cheesestrings	ITL	KP	UK
Croky (United Biscuits)	UK	Mr. Kipling	UK
Devonsheer	UKN	Mrs. Alison's	ITL
Drumsticks	SWI	Phileas Fogg	UK
ETA	FR	Poporon	J
Fiddle Faddle	SWI	Poppycock	SWI
Fiesta	ITL	Puticrape	J
Flipz	SWI	Screaming Yellow Zonkers	SWI
Fruit Scoops	SWI	Tuffy's	UKN
Frulix Snack Cakes	J	Twiglets	FR
Heinzel's	UK	Vachon	J
Heluva Good	N	Vegisnax	MEX

SOUP

American owned

AC	MBT Broth
Bean Cuisine	Mrs. Grass
Campbell's	Produce Partners
CasBah	Progresso
Colonna	Ramen
Erasco	Riviera
Habitant	Sadano's
Harris	Soup Du Jour
Harris Seafood	Soup Starter
Hilton's	Soup Supreme
LaCroix	Steero
Liebig	Stenger
Mariners Cove	Wyler's

Foreign owned

Batchelors	UK	Lipton Cup-A-Soup	UKN
California	N	Loney's	J
Country Cup	AUS	Maggi	SWI
Crosse & Blackwell	SWI	Napolina	UKN
Donald Duck	SWI	Pursoup	FR
Honig	N	Ramenyasan	J
Jokisch	UK	San-J	J
Knorr	UKN	Telma	UKN
Le Gout	UKN		

SPICES/SEASONINGS

American owned

Ac'cent
Carey Salt
Colonna
Crescent
Culinox Salt
Makin Cajun
McCormick
McCormick-Schilling
Mojave
Mongolian Fire
More For Less Seasonings
Mrs. Dash
Newly Weds
Nu-Salt
Nu-Salt Salt Substitute
Old Bay
Old Plantation
Packet Brand Salt & Pepper
Papa Dash
Pasta Prima
Peloponnese
Pop Top
Potato Toppers

Produce Partners
Red Devil Buffalo Style
Red Devil Original
Rotisserie Recipe
Salad Supreme
Salt Sense
Salt Sense Salt
Schilling
Seafood One Step
Seas'n Easy
Season 'n Fry
Season-All
Single Serv
Snider's
Snider's
Sterling Table Salt
Stock-Aid
Texas Best
Texas Pit BBQ Sauce
Vegetable Supreme
William's
Windsor Castle Table Salt

Foreign owned

Condimix	UKN	Newmenu	HK
Fruco	UKN	Perc	AUS
Jimmi	UKN	Primerba	UKN
Kitano	UKN	Ros Dee Seasonings	J
Knoor	UK	Savora	UKN
Masako Seasoning Mixes	J	Tone's	AUS
Napolina	UKN	Ubena	UKN

SUGAR

American owned

Colonial
Crystal
Diamond Crystal
Dixie Crystals
Evercane
Flosweet
Holly

Imperial Holly
Jack Frost
Maui Brand Raw
Pillsbury
Pioneer
White Satin
White Star

Foreign owned

Daddy	FR	Saint Louis	FR
Domino	UK	Taikoo	HK
Redpath	UK	Tate & Lyle	UK

SYRUP

American owned

Alaga	Knott's Berry Farm
Aunt Jemima	Log Cabin
Brer Rabbit	Maple Rich Syrup
Cane Patch	Mrs. Butterworth's
Cheryl Lyn	Nalley's
Clements	Northwoods
Country Kitchen	Oh Boy
Country Maid	Plow Boy
Delta	Pure Gold
Dewkist	Roddenbery's
Flapjack	Sunnyland
Gamecock	Tastee
Garden Club	Vermont Maid
Happy Kids	

Foreign owned

Bee Hive	UKN	Karo	UKN
Crown Brand	UKN	Old Tyme	UKN
Cusenier	FR	Spontin	BG
Golden Griddle	UKN	Staley's	UK
Hungry Jack	UK		

TUNA

American owned

Bumble Bee	Prime Catch
Celebrity	Progresso
Deep Blue	Star Kist
Greenseas	

Foreign owned

America's Choice	G	Carnation	SWI
Blue Bay	C	Chicken of the Sea	THAI

VINEGAR

American owned

Clements		Regina
Heinz		White House

Foreign owned

Bertolli	ITL	Paw Paw	J

YOGURT

American owned

Breyer's	Light N' Lively
Cal 80	Lite-Line
Columbo	Trix
Friendship	Yogurt Drinkables
Knudsen	Yogurt To Go
La Yogurt	Yoplait

Foreign owned

Beatrice	ITL	Penguin's	FR
Bifidus	J	Sprinkl'ins	FR
Dannon	FR	Trim	ITL
Delisle	FR		

Chapter 5

Home & Office Products

AIR FRESHENERS

American owned

Aero Pure	Magic Lantern
Ambi-Pur	Odor-Aire
Avon	Parry's
Banish	Renuzit
Bayberry	Round-The-Clock
Bissell	Sani-Aire
Cormatic Aire	Sani-Scent
Fresh Scents	Scent Flo
Glade	Scentsation
Hide-A-Disc	Tollet
Luxaire	Touch-of-Scent

Foreign owned

Air Wick	UK	Stick-Ups	UK
Magic Mushroom	UK	Wizard	UK
Medo	N		

ALUMINUM FOIL

American owned

Diamond	Reynolds
Capital	

Foreign owned

Alcan	C

BABY PRODUCTS/EQUIPMENT

American owned

Baby Fresh	Graco Snugride
Baby Healthflow	Johnson's
Baby Nursers	Joy Ride Car Seat
Baby Orajel	Medallion Infant Car Seat
Baby Steps Diapers	Next Step Carseat
Baby's First Year	Nexus Carseat
Century Baby Strollers	On My Way Car Seat
Century Car Seat	OshKosh B'Gosh
Diaper Genie	Playtex Baby Feeding System
Evenflo	Remco Baby
Exersaucer Baby Play Gym	Scout Car Seat
Famar	Sight Seer Booster Car Seat
Fisher-Price Carseat	Smart Fit Car Seat

Smart Move Car Seat		Travel Tandem Car Seat	
Snack & Play II		Travelite Stroller	
Sportcarrier		Zwitsal	

Foreign owned

Baby Head	SWI	Musical Toilette Plus	C
Baby's Own	UK	Roberts	UK
Baby's Target	AUS	Safety 1st	C
Babysafe	UK	TLC Car Seat	C
Cosco Carseat	C	Zorbit	UK

BAKEWARE/COOKWARE

American owned

Accent	KitchenAid
Air Bake	Magnalite
Airbake	Matrix 7
Bakers Best	Microbrowner
Bakers Secret	Mirro
Camelot	Nature's Seal
Castlewick Collection	Perfect Bake
Chefco	Performance Pans
Chef's Gallery	Princess
Chef's Ware	Priscilla
Classica	Procote
Cordon Bleu	Proglide
Corning	Pro-Grip
Coronation	Pyrex
Cuisinart	Regal Ware
Cushionaire	Revere
Dansk	Royal Diamond
Ekco	Sahara & Design
Even Bake	Saladmaster
Farberware	Saveur International
Foley	Seal-O-Matic
Graniteware II	System 7
Great Dishes	The Pampered Chef
Heat Max	Traditions by Magnalite
Honor Craft	Visions
Imperial Diamond	Vogue
KF & Design	Vogue and Design
Kitchen Factory	Wagner's 1891
Kitchen Fair	Wearever

Foreign owned

All Clad	UK	Tefal	FR
Canon	J	T-Fal	FR

BATHROOM TISSUE

American owned

Angel Soft
Banner
Bess
Big 'N Soft
Boutique
Camellia
Charmin
Chiffon
Coronet
Cottonelle
Delsey
Georgia-Pacific
Guest Ranch
Hudson
Joy
Kleenex
LYS
Marina
Mariposa
MD
Mr. Big
Neve
Nice 'N Soft
Noble
Northern
Page
Petalo
Popee
Quilted Northern
Savoy
Scott
Snow Lily
So Soft
Sof Strength
Sofpac
Soft Bloom
Softex
Soft-Ply
Splendaides
Sujay
Sunrise
Tiss
Top
Trebol
Ultima
Verigood
Viva
Warwick
White Cloud
Wondersoft

Foreign owned

Regio	MEX

BLEACH

American owned

Ace
Ayudin
Biz
Borateem
Clorox
Comet
Javex
Purex
Vibrant

Foreign owned

Parozone	UK	Vivid	UK
Snowy	UK		

CARPET

The biggest three carpet makers in the world—Shaw Industries Inc., Mohawk Industries Inc. and Beaulieu of America LLC—are based in Georgia and comprise nearly 75% of America's carpet production.

American owned

Aladdin	Howard
Alexander Smith	Lees
Bigelow	Lotus
Carriage	Milliken
Evans-Black	Mohawk
Glenoit Mills	Philadelphia
Harbinger	Salem
Harem	Schumacher
Helios	Shaw Commercial Systems
Hollytex Of California	Sutton Carpets
Horizon	Tower

Foreign owned

Genesis	UK

CEILING FANS

American owned

Casablanca	Harbor Breeze
Hampton Bay	Hunter

Foreign owned

No foreign brands could be located for this category.

CHAIN SAWS

American owned

Craftsman	Homelite

Foreign owned

Husqvarna	SWE	Stihl	G
Poulan	SWE		

CHINA

American owned

Best China	Lyrica
Buffalo	Milford
Fiesta	RCPC
Gothic	Replacements
Hall	Seville
Lenox	

Foreign owned

Franciscan	UK	Rosenthal	G
Hutschen Reuther	G	Royal Doulton	UK

CLOCKS

American owned

Baldwin	Seth Thomas
Braun	Sports Time
Elgin	Sunbeam
General Time	Timex
Great Time	Tourneau
Howard Miller	Trident
Ingraham	Welby
Lady Ben	Westclox
Ridgeway	

Foreign owned

Seiko	J

CORDLESS DRILLS

American owned

Black & Decker	Porter Cable
Craftsman	Skil
DeWalt	

Foreign owned

Makita	J	Ryobi	J
Milwaukee	SWE		

CUTLERY/SILVERWARE

American owned

1881	American Carver
All Americans	American Maple
Amcel	American Pride

Amsilco
Bio Curve
Brand Ware
Buck
Bucklite
Chefco
Cherrywood
Chicago
Chicago Blue
Connoisseur
Craft Stainless
Cub Lite
Dexter
Dexter/Russell
Duke
Dura Edge
Easy Steel
Essentials
Farberware
Folding Hunter
Ginsu
Gorham
Grillworks
Heirloom
Hoffritz
Imperial Cutlery
Lake Mate
Legacy Forged
Lenox/Kirk
Magnasharp
Magnatech
Metropolitan
Mini Buck
Ocean Mate

Odyssey
Old Hickory
Old Timer
Oneida
Palette
Premier
Profile
Quest
Quikut
Ranger
Reed & Barton
Rogers
Russell
Russell Green River
Russell International
Saladmaster
Sani Safe
Schrade
Scoutlite
Silver Sword
Sofgrip
Stanley Roberts
Stream Mate
Tech Choice
Techknife
Towle Silversmiths
Tristar
Veri-Sharp
Viking & Nordsman
Wallace Silversmiths
Walnut Tradition
Wm. Rogers & Son
World Flatware
Zipper

Foreign owned

Gerber	FIN	Regent Sheffield	AUS
Grosvenor	AUS	Rodd	AUS
Hernes	FR	Rosenthal	G
Laser	AUS	Sabatier	AUS
Montana	FIN	Silver Knights	FIN
Mundial	BZL	Staysharp	AUS

DIAPERS

American owned

Comfees

Drypers

Gards

Huggies

Kimbies

Luggi's

Luvs

Moltex

Monbebe

Monica

Pampers

Precious

Snuggems

Snugglers

Titulium

Foreign owned

No foreign brands could be located for this category.

DINNERWARE

American owned

Aartik

American Atelier

American Garden

American Royalty

Anchor Hocking

Epicure

Foreign owned

Franciscan   UK

DISHWASHER DETERGENT

American owned

American Fare

Amway

Cascade

Dial

Palmolive

Whirl

Foreign owned

All	UKN	Electrosol	UK
America's Choice	G	Jet-Dry	UK
Basic-D	J	Sunlight	UKN

DISHWASHING DETERGENT

American owned

Ayudin

Cascade

Dawn

Dermassage

Ivory Liquid

Joy

Paic Citron

Palmolive

Soila'way

Trend

Foreign owned

Coral	UK	Jet Dry	UK
Dove	UKN	Lux	UKN
Electrasol	UK	Sunlight	UKN
Finish	UK		

FABRIC SOFTENER

American owned

All Ways Soft	Fluffy
Aqua Soft	Purex
Big Value	Rinse
Bounce	Soupline
Downy	Spin Soft
Fleecy	Sta-Soft
Fluf	Sunshine

Foreign owned

Bio Gentle	SWI	Lavender Sachet	UK
Cling Free	UK	Quanto	UK
Final Touch Dryer Sheets	UKN	Snuggle	UKN
Flor	UK		

FACIAL TISSUE

American owned

Angel Soft	Northern
Boutique	Puffs
Chiffon	Sani Hanks
Coronet	Scotties Accents
Cottonelle	So Soft
Guest Ranch	Soft Bloom
Hudson	Softex
Kleenex	Softique
Klin	Soft-Ply
Little Travelers	Sujay
LYS	Tiss
Marathon	Vogue
Marcal	Wondersoft

Foreign owned
No foreign brands could be located for this category.

FURNITURE

American owned

Accent
Accent Oak
American Drew
American Legacy
American of Martinsville
Anderson Hickey
Arlington House (outdoor)
Ashley
Avon
Bahia Breeze (outdoor)
Baker
Barcalounger
Barclay
Bassett
Bedbase
Bell
Bench Craft
Berkline
Berkshire
Body System
Boyd Flotation
Brayton (office)
Brown Jordan
Broyhill
Bush (office)
Calliope
Chromcraft
Clayton-Marcus
Cochrane
Collage
Contempra
Country Court
Designer Choice Sofas
Drexel
Falcon
Founders
Gardenella
Glass Arts
Good Bedroom
Greenbriar Park
Hampton II

Harden
Henredon
Heritage
Herman Miller (office)
Hickory Chair
Highland House
Instalab
International
Jennifer Convertibles
Karges by Hand
Karpen
Kindel
Kinetics
Kling
Knob Creek
Koala Collection
Krause's
Kroeler
Lane
Largo
La-Z-Boy
Lea Industries
Lee Jofa
Lem-O-Oil
Lexington
Little Folks
Marlo
Mastercraft
Metropolitan
Mity-Lite
Mulberry
NCI
Nemschoff
O'Sullivan (office)
Pearson
Pennsylvania House
Peters-Revington
Pilliod
Reclina-Rest
Reclina-Rocker
Recollections

Relay
Rhodes
Rock-A-Lounger
Roomworks
Seaman
Signature
Signature II
Silver
Stanley
Stanton-Cooper
Steelcase (office)

Sterling Line
Stratford
Stratopedic
Techline
Thomasville
Tropitone
Tuffy
Vecta (office)
Vineyard Garden Collection
Wood Slat Collection

Foreign owned

Homeworthy	UK	O'Cedar	UK
Layezee	UK	Silentnight	UK
Natuzzi	ITL	Syroco	FIN

FURNITURE POLISH

American owned

Admire
Behold
Complete
Endust

Favor
Jubilee
Pledge
Regard

Foreign owned

| Mansion | UK | Old English | UK |
| Mr. Sheen | UK | | |

GARAGE DOOR OPENERS

American owned

Chamberlain
Craftsman

Liftmaster

Foreign owned

| Genie | J |

GLASSWARE

American owned

American Whitewall
Anchor Hocking
Complements
Confections
Elegance

Fruit Bounty
Presentations
Pyrex
Quilted Crystal

Foreign owned

Jenaer Glas	G	Spiegelau	G

HOUSEHOLD CLEANERS

Kodak sold its Lysol brand to a British company back in 1995. Formidable American alternatives to Lysol are American Fare (Kmart) and Clorox.

American owned

A World of Difference	Dri-Clean
Ajax	Fabulon
Allbrite	Fabuloso
American Fare Disinfectant	Fantastico
Amway	Fantastik
Aqua Bowl	Fine Wood
Arm & Hammer Carpet Deodorizer	First Mate
Armstrong Floor Cleaner	First Mate Disinfectant
Austin	Formula 409
Automatic Vanish	Fresh Air
Beauti-Fi	Future
Big Wally	Germ-X Disinfectant Spray
Bissell One Step	Glade
Bloo	Glass & More
Bloo Toss-Ins	Glass Brite
Blu-Water	Glass Express
Boraxo	Glo-Coat Floor Polish
Bowl Cleanse	Keeps Bowl Cleaner
Bowl Fresh	Klean 'N Shine
Bowl 'N All	Klear
Bowl Patrol	Kleen Guard
Bowlene	Like Magic
Brigade	Liquid S
Brite	Liquid-Plumr
Brite'N Shiny	Listo
Carpet Care	Lite N' Natural
Carpet Scent	Mahler Oil Soap
Carpet Science	MG Carpet Care
Cidex 7 Disinfectant	Mop & Shine
Clean 'N Clear	Mr. Blue Bowl Cleaner
Clorox	Mr. Clean
Clorox Clean-Up	Mr. Muscle Oven Cleaner
Comet	Murphy Oil
Drano	Murphy's Oil Soap

O-Cel-O
Olde Master
One Step
Panel Magic
Perfi-Clean
Pine Forest
Pine Magic
Pine Power
Pine-Sol
Playtex Rubber Gloves
Pledge
Precise
PT-4
Renuzit
Rescue
Roll-A-Wet
Room Sense
Rug Aroma Carpet Freshener
S.C. Johnson
Sani-Dex
Sanigizer
Sani-Hands
Scott's Liquid Gold
Scratchguard
Scrubbing Bubbles
Sep Saver
Shout Carpet Science
Silent Maid
Sno-Bol
Soft Scrub
Soilax

Solid Regain
Sparkle
Spic & Span
Spray 'N Wipe
Spring Scent
Stanley
Static Guard
Strip Away
Tab-Blu
Target Floor Finish
Tilex
Tob Job
Toilet/Bathroom Duck
Tri-Chem
True Pine
Tuff Stuff
Twenty Mule Team Borax
Twinkle
Ty-D-Bol
Vanish
Virex Disinfectant
Wall To Wall
Weiman
Westpine
Windex
Window Clear
Wipe 'N Clear
Wood Plus
Wood Preen
Wood Preen Floor Wax

Foreign owned

Bayclin	G	Mop & Glo	UK
Bear-Tex	FR	Penetrant	G
Bully	UK	Pine O Cleen	UK
Domestos	UKN	Regina	N
Easy-Off	UK	Resolve Carpet Cleaner	UK
Glass Plus	UK	S.O.S.	G
Glassex	UK	Sani-Flush	UK
Lime-A-Way	UK	Somat	G
Love My Carpet	UK	Steri-Det	G
Lux	SWE	Super-Croix	G
Lysol	UK	Swirl	G
Mir	G	Whitak	UK

White Disinfectants	UK	X Tra	G
Windolene	UK		

INSECT REPELLENT/INSECTICIDES

American owned

Black Flag	Muskol
Black Leaf	OFF!
Bloom	OFF! Skintastic
Combat	Pageant
Daddy Whacker	Raid
Deep Woods OFF!	Raid Max
Dursban	Raid Roach Controller
Dursbel	Repel
Fireban	Ridsect
Flit	Skin So Soft
Holiday	Stipend
Impact	Tick Stop
Lock-On	Tick Stop D-20
Lure-N'-Kill	

Foreign owned

Cutter	G	Parsec	ISR
D-Con	UK	Rimon	ISR
Gold Crest	FR	Satisfar	SWI

LAUNDRY DETERGENT/PRODUCTS

American owned

Ajax	Dynamo
Amway	Enzimax
Ariel	Era
Arm & Hammer	Fab
Axion	Fab Ultra
BDD	Fresh Start
Biotex	Gain
Biz	Gemini
Bold	Ivory
Bravo	Ivory Snow
Cheer	Klay
Cold Power	Lan-O-Sheen
Dash	Liquid-Bold 3
Dreft	Miracle White
Dryel	Octagon
Dutch	OLA

Oxydol
Punch
Purex
Rainbow
Shout
Sta Flo Liquid Starch
Stain Stick
Super Suds

Tide
Trend
Twenty Mule Team Borax
Ultra
Ultra Baby Soft
Vano Liquid Starch
Wool'N Care
Zout Stain Remover

Foreign owned

All	UKN	Lanza	UK
AVA	UK	Niagara	UKN
Breeze	UKN	Radion	UKN
Bryza	UK	Rinso	UKN
Colon	UK	Snowy Bleach	UK
Delicare	UK	Spray 'N Wash	UK
Dosia	UK	Surf	UKN
Easy-On Spray Starch	UK	Wisk	UKN
Elena	UK	Woolite	UK
Express Fine Fabric Wash	UK	Yes	UK
Final Touch	UKN		

LAWN & GARDEN

American owned

Aircap
American Made
Ames
Assault Weed Killer
Barefoot
Chemlawn
Deep Green
Emerald Edge
Fairway Green
Feed & Weed
Fert Fertilizer
Flowtron
Garden Pride
Garden Tips Garden Gloves
Greenpro
Gro-Tone

Hedge Hog
Jobe's
Knock Out
Kuron
Lawn Doctor
Lawn Restore
Lawn-Boy
Preen
Preen 'N Green
Rake-O-Vac
Right Dress
Ross
Scott's Plant Foods
True Temper
Turf-Trac
Turf-Trim

Foreign owned

Bargain Garden	NOR	Ingersoll	G
Carefree	NOR	Jiffy Miracle Peat	NOR
Enviroworks	FIN	Jiffy-7	NOR
Fiskars	FIN	Jiffy-Gro	NOR
Flymo	SWE	Jiffy-Mix	NOR
Garden Devils	FIN	Jiffy-Pots	NOR
Garden Greats	NOR	Jiffy-Strips	NOR
Gourmet	NOR	Moisture Master	FIN
Gro-Cell	NOR	Rally	SWE
Gro-Dome	NOR	Yard Pro	SWE
Husqvarna	SWE		

LAWN MOWERS

American owned

Aircap	Sabre
Atlas	Sears Craftsman
Black & Decker	Simplicity
Bolens	Snapper
Craftsman	Topflight
Cub Cadet	Toro
Dixon	Troy Built
Homelite	Turf-Trim
John Deere	Vulcan
Lawn-Boy	White
Lawnflite	Yard Machines by MTD
MTD	Yard-Man
SABO	

Foreign owned

Honda	J	Poulan	SWE
Husqvarna	SWE	Rally	SWE
Ingersoll	G	Stanley	BMD
Kubota	J	Weed Eater	SWE
Murray	UK	YardPro	SWE

MAGAZINES

American owned

Allure	American Druggist
Amazing Stories	American Girl
American City & Country	American Health
American Demographics	American Heritage

American Iron
American Printer
American Rodder
American Woodworker
Architectural Digest
Asia Week
Astronomy
Athens
Auto Racing Digest
Autoweek
Backpaker
Barron's
Baseball Digest
Basketball Digest
Beads & Bulton
Better Homes and Gardens
Better Impressions
Bicycling
Biker
Birders World
Black Enterprise
Bon Appetit
Bowling Digest
Bride's
Business Week
Catholic Digest
Child Life
Christian Reader
Christianity Today
Classic Toy
Classic Toy Trains
Colonial Homes
Conde Nast Traveler
Conde Net
Consumer Reports
Cosmopolitan
Country Gardens
Country Home
Country Living
Crafts Showcase
Crayola Kids
Crochet World
Decorative Woodcrafts
Details

Diverson
Doll World
Dollhouse Miniatures
Easy Riders
Easyriders
Ebony
Entertainment Weekly
Episodes
Esquire
Family Money
Farm Forum
Field & Stream
Fine Scale Modeler
Finescale
Flash
Flex
Food & Wine
Football Digest
Forbes
Fortune
Forum
Four Wheeler
Freeze
Gentlemen's Quarterly
Glamour
God's Word Today
Golf
Good Housekeeping
Good Old Days
Gourmet
Grays Sporting Journal
Great Possibilities
Grit
Harpers & Queen
Harper's Bazaar
Health
Hockey Digest
House & Garden
House Beautiful
How
IronWorks
Jack and Jill
Jet
Ladies' Home Journal

Life
Living Fit
Los Angeles
Mad Magazine
Mademoiselle
Marie Claire
Marriage Partnership
Media Bypass
Men's Fitness
Men's Health
Middle America News
Midwest Living
Model Railroader
Model Retailer
Money
More
Motor Boating
Motor Boating & Sailing
Motor Magazine
Mountain Bike
Ms.
Muscle & Fitness
National Geographic
National Review
Nationalist Times
New York Magazine
Newsweek
Open Wheel
Organic Gardening
Parenting
Penthouse
People
Playboy
Popular Mechanics
Popular Science
Popular Woodworking
Prevention
Prime Health & Fitness
Printing Impressions
Progressive Populist
Psychology Today
Reader's Digest
Redbook
Rodale's Fitness Swimmer

Rodale's Scuba Diving
Rolling Stone
Runner's World
Salt Water Sportsman
Savage
Savannah
Scale Auto Enthusiast
Self
Seventeen
Shape
Shape Cooks
She
Ski
Skiing
Smart Money
Snap
Snowboard Life
Soap Opera Digest
Soccer Digest
Southern Accents
Southern Living
Spin
Sports Afield
Sports Illustrated
Spur
Stitches
Stock Car Racing
Story
Street & Smith
Successful Farming
Teaching
The Artist's Magazine
The Family Handyman
The Fun Zone
The New American
The New Yorker Magazine
The Saturday Evening Post
The Sporting News
Time
Today's Christian Woman
Town & Country
Traditional Home
Trains
Travel Holiday

TV Guide		Warp	
U.S. News & World Report		Women's Circle	
U.S. News Washington Business		Wood	
Vanity Fair		Working Mother	
Variations		Wrestling Digest	
Victoria		Writer's Digest	
Vogue		Yachting	
VQ		Yankee	
Walking		Your Church	

Foreign owned

4-Wheel & Off Road	UK	Fore!	UK
AAT	ISR	Golden Girl	UKN
Aftersales Manager	UK	Golf Digest	G
AJN Guide	N	Golf World	UK
Allegra	G	Guitar Player	UK
Amateur Gardening	UK	Guns & Ammo	UK
Amateur Photographer	UK	Hair	UK
American Artist	N	Handguns	UK
American Journal of Nursing	N	Home & Décor	SNG
Architects Journal	UK	Home PC	UK
Athletics Weekly	UK	Hot Rod	UK
Audio	UK	Hunting	UK
Automotive Digest	UK	Impressions	UK
Bass Player	UK	Inc.	G
Bike	UK	Information Week	UK
Billboard	N	Interior Design	UK
Boat Angler	UK	Interiors	N
Byte	UK	Keyboard	UK
Car & Driver	FR	McCall's	G
Car Craft	UK	Menswear	UK
Choice	UK	Minx	UK
Circle Track	UK	Model Rail	UK
Construction News	UK	Money Management	UK
Country Walking	UK	Motor Cycle News	UK
Cycle Sport	UK	Motor Trend	UK
DBS	UK	Motorcyclist	UK
Digital Video	UK	Mountain Bike Rider	UK
Dirt Rider	UK	Network Computing	UK
Drag Racing	UK	Our Baby	UK
Elle	G	Parents	G
Family Circle	G	Performance Bikes	UK
Femme Plus	C	Performance Computing	UK
FHM	UK	Photographic	UK
Fishing News	UK	Plant Engineering	UK

Premiere	FR	Sunday Express	UK
Printed Circuit Design	UK	Surfer	UK
Publishers Weekly	UK	'Teen	UK
Pulp & Paper	UK	Today's Runner	UK
Research & Development	UK	Trout & Salmon	UK
Restaurant Business	N	Trout Fisherman	UK
Restaurants & Institutions	UK	Variety	UK
Rodina	SWI	Woman	UK
Rugby World	UK	Woman & Home	UK
Security	UK	Woman's Day	FR
Shoot	N	Woman's Journal	UK
Skateboarder	UK	Woman's Own	UK
Skin Diver	UK	Woman's Realm	UK
Slam	UK	Woman's Weekly	UK
Soccerstars	UK	Women & Golf	UK
Software Development	UK	World Soccer	UK
Sport	UK	Yachting Monthly	UK
Sport Auto	UK	Yachting World	UK
Sport Bild	G	Young Parents	SNG
Sport Truck	UK	Your Cat	UK
Sporting Goods Dealer	N	Your Dog	UK
Steam Railway	UK	Your Garden	UK
Stereophile	UK	Your Horse	UK
Studio	UK	Yours	UK

MATTRESSES

American owned

Aireloom	Imperial Comfort
Beautyrest	Interlude
Beautysleep	King-O-Pedic
Body Perfect	Kingsdown
Cameo	Luxury Comfort
Correct Comfort	Medi-Coil
Craftmatic	New Experience IV
Day Matt	Orthotonic
Dr. Fuller	Perfect Night
Ecstasy	Perfect Sleeper
Energizer	Perma Grip
Fraenkel Bedding Company	Posture Center
Gold Bond	Posture Control
Health Comfort	Posture Cushion
Highland House	Posturepedic
Hydro-Posture	Queensdown

Rest Assured
Rip Van Winkle
Royal Kingsdown
Sealy
Serta
Simmons
Sleep Cushion
Sleeping Beauty
Sleepy's
Slumber
Slumber Comfort
Slumber King
Sof T-Vision

Spinal Aid
Spring Air
Spring-O-Pedic
Stearns & Foster
Sterns & Foster
Super Fetherbed
The American Dream
The Sterling Edition
Tradition
Triple Edge
Unipedic
Vitagenic

Foreign owned

Layezee	UK	Sleepmaker	AUS
Silentnight	UK		

NAPKINS

American owned

Angel Soft
Bella
Big 'N Pretty
Chiffon
Conserv
Coronet
Econofold
Elegance
Guest Ranch
Handi Wipes
Hi Line
Hudson
Iris
Kleenex
Linen Soft
Linenserve
Low Boy
LYS
Mardi-Gras
Mr. Big
Multisoft

Northern
Page
Popee
Scott
Servaides
Sherbets
Slei
Snow-Soft
Softex
Soft-Ply
Sopalin
Sparkle
Splendaides
Sujay
Sunny
Tiss
Unicel
Vanity Fair
Viva
Warwick
Zee

Foreign owned

Duni	SWE

NEWSPAPERS

American owned

Advertiser
Advertising Age
Albany Times Union
Anderson Independent-Mail
Arkansas City Traveler
Athens Daily News
Augusta Chronicle
Beaumont Enterprise
Bremerton Sun
California Plus
Chicago Tribune
Country Weekly
Daily Herald
Daily Press
Daily-Journal
Detroit Free Press
Florida Times Union
Gazette Telegraph
Hannibal Courier Post
Hillsdale Daily News
Houston Chronicle
Kansas City Star
Knoxville New-Sentinel
Las Vegas Sun
Naples Daily News
National Enquirer
News Herald
Northwest Florida Daily News
Orange County Register
Pennysaver
Pittsburgh Morning Sun
Pittsburgh Post-Gazette
Plainview Daily Herald
Reader
San Angelo Standard Times
San Francisco Chronicle
San Francisco Examiner
San Jose Mercury
Savannah Morning News
Seattle Post-Intelligencer

St. Louis Post-Dispatch
St. Petersburg Times
Star Telegram
Sunday Examiner & Chronicle
Sunday Oklahoman
Sun-Sentinel
The Abilene Reporter-News
The Advocate
The Albuquerque Tribune
The Ann Arbor News
The Bakersfield Californian
The Bay City Times
The Blade
The Boston Globe
The Cincinnati Inquirer
The Cincinnati Post
The Courier-Journal
The Flint Journal
The Gazette
The Grand Rapids Press
The Herald
The Herald News
The Jackson Citizen Patriot
The Monitor
The New York Times
The Orange County Register
The Orlando Sentinel
The San Diego Union-Tribune
The Stuart News
The Sun
The Sunday Sun
The Wall Street Journal
The Washington Post
The Wichita Eagle
USA Today
Ventura County Star
Vero Beach Press Journal
Wall Street Journal
Wisconsin State Journal
York News Times

Foreign owned

Chicago Sun Times	C	The Boston Herald	AUS
Financial Times	UK	The New Paper	SNG
Friday Weekly	SNG	The Straits Times	SNG
New York Post	AUS	The Sunday Times	SNG
Sun-Times	C		

OFFICE SUPPLIES

American owned

Acco
American Business Products
American Eagle
Apex
Arrow
Arrow Staplers
Boxelope
Cambridge
Carnival Kraft Envelopes
Damark
Day Runner
Details
Docu-Lok Envelopes
Docu-Lope Envelopes
Eastlight
Elements
Elmers Glue

Execu-Line
Fac-Finders
Fashion Write Envelopes
Fuller's Glue
Galaxy Paper & Envelopes
Gilbert Stationary
Gilcrest
Glare Care
Grip Seal Envelopes
Grip Strip
Hon
Imagemark Envelopes
Mead
Post-It Notes
Rexel Staplers
Swingline Staplers

Foreign owned

Amberg	SWE	Boorum & Pease	SWE
Bensons	SWE	Fiskars Scissors	FIN

PAINT

American owned

Ace
Acme
Aqua Gloss
Behr
Benjamin Moore
Blatz
BPS
California
Crayola
Davis

Decorator
Dezignrite
Dunn-Edwards
Duracolor
Duron
Dutch Boy
Easy Care
Easy Way
Effecto
Elegante

Elite
Empirelac
Enterprise
Envirobase
Fabulon
Fastlac
Fleck Stone Plasti-Kote
Flowkote
Formby's
Four Seasons
Glamor
Graham
Home Decorator
House Saver
Illinois Bronze
Iowa Paint
Kelly Moore
Krylon
Kurfees
LYT-All
M.A.B.
Maestro Colors
Magicolor
Martha Stewart
Masterpiece
Mastertone
Masury
Mautz
Maximum
McCloskey
Metaleaf
Metalhide
Microflo Process
Model Master
Moorgard
Moorglo
Mr. Spray
Muresco
Old Quaker
Olympic Weatherscreen
Overcoat
Pactra
Pasti-Kote
Perfection

Permalize
Perry & Derrick
Pianoramick
Pitt-Cryl
Pittsburgh
Polycron
Polyflex
Pop-Free
Porch Enamel
PPG
Pratt & Lambert
Progress Industrial
Pro-Hide Plus
Proline
Pro-Line
Pro's Choice
Red Devil
Reward
Rich-Lux
Royal Gard
Rust Not
Rustop
Sani-Flat
Satinhide
Satintone
Satin-X
Screamers
Sears
Sherwin Williams
Sparvar
Studio
Sundial
Sun-Proof
Sunset
Super Speed
Super-Kote
Suprime
Surekote
Svenska
Tech-Guard
Touchcoat
True Value
Tuff-Kote
Tweed

Valspar
Vapex
Vitagard Rust-No-More
Vitralite
Wallhide

Weatherbeater
Williamsburg
Withstand
Yenkin-Majestic

Foreign owned

All-Weather	UK	Speed-Wall	UK
Ameritone	UK	Spray-Day-Lite	UK
Blockaid	UK	Spred	UK
Color Key	UK	Spred 2000	UK
Cover Perfect	UK	Spred Enamel	UK
Devoe	UK	Spred Flat	UK
Durocrete	HK	Spred Gloss	UK
Endurance	UK	Spred House	UK
Flexa	N	Spred Kitchen and Bath	UK
Glid	UK	Spred Lo-Lustre	UK
Hancock	C	Spred Lustre	UK
Harris	UK	Spred Satin	UK
ICI	UK	Spred Silk	UK
Imperial Gold	UK	Spred Solo	UK
Lifemaster	UK	Spred Supreme	UK
Modex	HK	Spred-Dura	UK
Mr. Color	J	Triple Cover	UK
Niteline	FR	Vitrakote	HK
Opal	HK	Wonder Shield	UK
Regency	UK	Wonder Tones	UK
Royale	UK	Wonder-Guard	UK
Rustmaster	UK	Wonder-Speed	UK
Sinclair	FR	Xpert	UK
Speedcote	UK		

PAPER TOWELS

American owned

All It Leaves Is Clean
Angel Soft
Big 'N Thirsty
Blue Cross
Bounty
Brawny
Chiffon
Coronet
Delta
Epicure

Gala
Georgia-Pacific
Guest Ranch
Hi-Count
Hi-Dri
Hiway-Wipe
Hudson
Kleenex
Kowtowls
Limpiogar

Marathon

Mardi Gras

Mekan-I-Kloth

Mr. Big

Northern

Page

Papagayo

Pioneer Quadramatic

Popee

Prep-Towls

Rainbow

Scott

So-Dri

Soft Bloom

Soft-Ply

Sparkle

Splendaides

Sujay

Sunrise

Thick & Thirsty

Top-Towls

Trim-Towls

Turn-Towls

Ultima

Viva

Warwick

Wondersoft

Yellow Birch

Zee

Zip-Towls

Foreign owned

Duni   SWE

PENS, PENCILS & MARKERS

In 1991, only 16% of the pencils bought by Americans came from overseas. Today that figure is nearly 50%.

American owned

Ad Mate

Anadel

Astronaut

Avante

Berol

Big Red

Brite-Tone

Calligraphic

Cedar King

Cedar Natural

Charley

Coloron

Crayola

Cross

Custom Color

Dixon Ticonderoga

Eberhard Faber

El Marko

Empire

Eraser Mate

Eversharp

Fast Dry Marker

Fine-Riter

Flair

Furys

Gillette

Honor Roll

Hot Liner

Hunt

Jet Line

Jotter

Kodak

Laddie

Laser-Twist

Lumber

Malibu

Maxxum

Mead

Microroller

Milemaster

Mirado		Selectip Rolling Ball	
My First		Sharpie	
Noah's Ark		Sky Tint	
Oriole		Skyline	
Paper Mate		Slinger	
Paper Mate Flair		Stylist	
Parker		Swiss Army	
Parker Pen		Ticonderoga	
Penit		Trimline	
Powerpoint		Uni-Ball	
Profile		Unipeco	
Quicksilver		Velvet	
Rally		Vision	
Readi-Pencils		Waterman	
Rollerstick		Wearever	
Roll-On		Whale	
Rub-A-Dub		Write Bros.	
Sanford		Y & C	
Scripto-Tokai		Yikes!	

Foreign owned

Crest	FR	Pro Am	J
Dr. Grip	J	Quicker Clicker	J
Encore	J	Razor Point	J
Excalibur	J	Rolling Writer	J
Graphlet	J	Sharp	J
Hybrid-2	J	Sharplet-2	J
Lancelot	J	Sheaffer	FR
Pentel	J	Sign Pens	J
Pilot	J	Superball	J

PLASTIC CUTLERY/DINNERWARE

There are plenty of American brands made in the USA in this category to keep your American picnic or outing all-American.

American owned

Americana	Forster
BasicWare	Guildware
Diamond	Jazz
Diva	Lustra
Dixie	Solo
ElegantWare	Ziploc

Foreign owned

Chinet	FIN	Party Time	UK

SHOE POLISH

American owned

Cavalier	Propert's
Kiwi	Tana
Meltonian	

Foreign owned

Abeille	UK

STAPLERS

American owned

Acco	Boston
Arrow	Swingline

Foreign owned

Stanley Bostitch	BMD

TOOLS

Stanley Tools has shown their true colors recently, and they aren't red, white and blue. Based in Connecticut for over 150 years, Stanley's board of directors unanimously approved a paper scheme to re-incorporate the company in Bermuda to avoid paying U.S. taxes.

Fortunately, there are plenty of other American-based tool makers forging their tools in the USA.

American owned

Allen	Grip-O-Matic
Alligator Power Saw	Hammer Head
AMCO	Hammergun
Ampco	Hanson
AMT	Harig
Arrow Staple Guns	Holgun
Asco	J.H. Williams
Black & Decker	Jack-Hand Saws
Blockbuster	Jensen
Bowen Tools	Klein
Bulldawg	Kodiak
Craftsman	Macho
DeWalt	Matco
DIY	Mr. Ratchet
Doall	Permatrak
Doler	Ridgid/Kollman
Dremel	Snap-On
ELU	Yankee Handyman

Foreign owned

Aeg	SWE	Hole Shooters	SWE
Dymorig	SWE	Makita	J
Facon	FR	Milwaukee	SWE
Hitachi	J	Stanley	BMD
Hole Hawg	SWE		

Chapter 6

Health & Beauty Aids

AFTER SHAVE

American owned

Aqua Velva

Hawk

Saxon

Skin Bracer

Static

Foreign owned

Pitralon   UK

BATH SOAP

American owned

Aquaress

Aveeno

Avon

Boraxo Hand Soap

Camay

Caressa

Cashmere Bouquet

Cleopatra

Coast

Coleo

Dial

Elite

Federal

Fels Naptha

Georgia-Pacific

Grandma's Love-My-Loofah Soap

Grandma's Oatmeal Soap

Grandpa

Handi-Scrubb

Health

Heiress

Irish Spring

Ivory

Kirkman

Kirk's

Lan-O-Soft

Lava

Mahler Oil Soap

Monchel

Moniler

Nature's Accents

Neutrogena

Nube

Oil of Olay

Olay Bath Bar

Old Spice

Palmolive

Protection Plus

Protex

Pure & Natural

Rejoice

Safeguard

Sanitiva

SBS Natural Lotion Soap

Septi-Soft

Septisol Solution

Softsoap

Sulpho-Lac

Tone

Tri-Clean

Ultima

Vel

Vesta

Vetrolin Body Wash

Zest

Foreign owned

Amaze	UKN	Conti	UK
Calgon	UK	Curel	J
Caress	UKN	Dove	UKN

Fenjal	UK	Meadow Blend	J
Gentle Touch	J	Mire	UKN
Imperial Leather	UK	Naturals	J
Jergens	J	Shield	UKN
Jergens Body Wash	J	Spanish Leder	G
Lever 2000	UKN	Suave	UKN
Lifebuoy	UKN	Yardley Lily of the Valley	J
Loanda	UK	Yardley of London	J
Lux	UKN		

CONDITIONER

American owned

Agree (S.C. Johnson)	Right-On Curl
Alberto Balsam	Royal
Australian 3 Minute Miracle	Silkience
Australian Hair Salad	St. Ives Swiss Formula
Clairol	T/Gel
Cortexx	Ultraswim
Icon	Vavoom

Foreign owned

Agree (Schwarzkopf & DEP)	G	Salon Selectives	UKN
Condess	UK	Suave	UKN
Salon Formula Dep	G		

COMBS & BRUSHES

American owned

Ace	Wooster
Goody	

Foreign owned
No foreign brands could be located for this category.

CONTACT LENSES

American owned

Acuvue	Quantum
Boston Envision	Quantum II
Butterfly Lens	Seequence
Permaflex	Sofspin
Permalens	Vistamarc

Foreign owned

Airlens	SWI	Complements	SWI
Aquaflex	SWI	Durasoft	SWI

COSMETICS

American owned

Adrien Arpel
Alberto
Alberto VO5
Alexandra De Markoff
Almay
Alo
Aloe Formula
Apple
Ardell
Avon
Bath Formula Gelee
BeautiControl
Benjamin Ansehl
Betrix
Black Radiance
Blair
Borghese
Bright Girl
Charles of the Ritz
Clarion
Clean Lash
Clear Complexion
Clinique
Contour 35
Corn Silk
Countess Isserlyn
Country Natural
Cover Girl
Creations
Dixie Peach
Ebone
Estee Lauder
Euro Collections
Fashion Fair
Fashion Tan
Flame Glow
Flawless Finish
Georgette Klinger
Germaine Monteil
Gina

Hard As Nails
Irma Shorell's
Lander
Liz Claiborne
Longfella
Lord & Berry
Lush Lips
Marathon Mascara
Mary Kay
Max Factor
Merle Norman
Moisturewear
Nailslicks Nail Polish
Naturade
Neutrogena
Nines
Nouriche
Perfect Blend
Professional
Protectives
Quencher
Quick Tan
Radiant Glo
Revlon
Rich Lash
Roberts
Royal Selections
Sally Hansen
Secrets of Aloe
Semplice
Shape 'N Blush
Sheer Moisture
Skin Saver
Sun Valley
Sweet Georgia Brown
Thick Lash 2
Thick 'N Thin
Ultima II
Ultima II
Ultra Sheen

Visage		Wet 'N' Wild	
Well Of Youth		YA YA	
Foreign owned			
2nd Debut	UK	Margaret Astor	UK
Accentous	FR	Maybelline	FR
Adidas	UK	Miami Chill	FR
AOK	G	Moisture Whip	FR
Ayura	J	No Problem	FR
Biotherm	FR	Now How	THAI
Christian Dior	FR	Nowa	G
Clarins	FR	Orlane	FR
Cosmic	THAI	Phas	FR
Cutex Nail Polish Remover	UKN	Pias	THAI
Cutexcolor Quick	UKN	Pierre Fabre	FR
Cutexcolor Splash	UKN	Pure Care	THAI
Cutexstrong Nail	UKN	Rene Furtherer	FR
Diploma	G	Rene Garraud	G
Dulcia	FR	Revitalizing	FR
Elizabeth Arden	UKN	Scorpio	G
Fresh Lash	FR	Selfit	J
Great Lash	FR	Shades of You	FR
Guerlain	FR	Sheene	THAI
Helene Curtis	FR	Sheer Essentials	FR
Illegal Lengths Mascara	FR	Shine Free	FR
Invite	UK	Shiseido	J
Jil Sander	UK	Sofina	J
Laforre	THAI	Stendhal	N
Lancaster	UK	Stila	J
Lancome	FR	Summer Sensations	FR
Le Chat	G	Theater	UK
Le Crayon Glace	FR	Uno	J
Les Meteorites	FR	Vademecum	G
Long Wearing Lipstick	FR	Vichy	FR
Long Wearing Makeup	FR	Williams	UK
Long Wearing Nail Polish	FR	Yves Saint Laurent	THAI
L'Oreal	FR		

COTTON SWABS

American owned

Handi-Swabs	Senti-Swabs
Johnson's Swabs	

Foreign owned

Q-Tips	UKN

DENTAL FLOSS

American owned
Dentotape   Oral-B
Foreign owned
Butler   J

DEODORANT

American owned

Almay	Mum
Arm & Hammer	No Sweat
Arrid	Old Spice
Ban	Right Guard
British Sterling	Secret
Dial	Shave Stick
Drive	Shower to Shower
Dry Idea	Soft & Dri
Dune	Speed Spray
English Leather	Speed Stick
Feel Free	Sure
Foot Guard	Teen Spirit
Irish Spring	Tickle
Lady Speed Dry	Tom's of Maine
Lady Speed Smooth-On	Top Care
Lady Speed Stick	Trinity
Lady's Choice	Tussy
Mennen	X-Hydra
Mitchum	

Foreign owned

Axe	UKN	Lady Power Roll-On	UKN
Body Mist	UK	Lady Power Stick	UKN
Brut	UKN	Mistral	UK
Chantal	UK	Pierre Cardin	J
Cool Charm	UK	Power Stick	UKN
Degree	UKN	Revive	UK
Dove	UKN	Stetson	UK
Impulse Body Spray	UKN	Suave	UKN
Jovan Musk	UK	Tally-Ho	UK

FEMININE HYGIENE PRODUCTS

American owned

Always	Poise
Amiga	Profile
Camelia	Replens
Fems	Safe & Sfot
Futura	Security
Gards	Serenity Guards
Kotex	Simplicity
Lily	Soft & Thin
Maxithins	Softina
Mimex	Stayfree
Modess	Summer's Eve
Monistat	Sure & Natural
New Freedom	Tampax
Novaera	Tampona
O.B.	Ten & Always
Playtex	Vagisil

Foreign owned

Massengill	UK

FIRST AID

American owned

2nd Skin	Inzo
3M Active Strip	Just-In-Case
9-1-1	Medipore
A & D Ointment	Muellerkold
Ace Bandages	Ouch Kit
Aero Therm Burn Spray	Peroxyl
Band-Aid	Sheer-Gard
Derma-Gel	Skintegrity
Foille	Solarcaine

Foreign owned

Aerugipen	UK	Elastoplast	UK
Coverlet Dressings	G	Medi Quik	J
Cover-Roll Gauze	G	Silvadene Burn Crème	FR
Curad	G	Unguentine	J

FRAGRANCES

American owned

5th Avenue
A Little Sexy
Adolpho
Afta After Shave
Alexandra De Markoff
Ambush
Ann Taylor
Apple
Aramis
Aromatics
Aviance
Aziza
Bandit
Barishnikov
Beautiful
Benjamin Ansehl
Beverly
Blue Grass
Body Fantasies
Body Flowers
Burberry
Cachet (Parfums De Couer)
California
California For Men
California For Women
Canoe
Canoe Sport
Catalyst
Chantilly
Charles of the Ritz
Charlie
Chloe
Clairborne
Confess
Country Breeze
Decollete
Deep Woods
Designer Imposters
Destiny
Devotee
Diamond Fleur

Diffusion
Eddie Bauer
English Leather
Enjoli
Euro Collections
Ever After
Fairchild
Fashion Mood
Fetish
Fifth Avenue
Fire
Fire & Ice
Flora Danica
Fracas
Fred Hayman Beverly Hills
Fresh & Pretty
Fresh Musk
Giorgio Beverly Hills
Golf Club
Haberdasher
Halston
Hawk
Heaven Sent
Helmut Lang
Herbissimo
Herve Leger
Hugo Boss
Incognito
Infinity
Jacques Esterel
Jean Philippe
Jeanne Gatineau
JMF
Jordache Looks
Laura Bigiotti
Liz Claiborne
Love's Baby Soft
Lucien Lelong Parfums
Magic
Malibu Musk
Mesmerize for Men

Midnight
My Islands
Mystic
Navy
Ninja
Paul Sebastian
Perry Ellis
Pheromone
Prestige
Primo!
R & R
Radio Girl
Regine's
Royal Selections
Santa Fe
SCAASI
Sensai
Sensation
Snow Silk

Stanley For Her
Stanley For Him
Sunflowers
Tabu
That's My Girl
Tiffany
Tiffany for Men
Toujours Moi
True Love
Truests
Unforgettable
Unmistakable
Unruly
U-Two
U-You
Wild Rain
Wind Song
Wings

Foreign owned

Adidas	UK	Creations Aromatiques	G
Amando	UK	Crossmen	UK
Anais Anais	FR	Daniel Dafasson	THAI
Aspen	UK	Diamonds & Emeralds	UKN
Azzaro	FR	Diamonds & Rubies	UKN
Azzura	FR	Diamonds & Sapphires	UKN
Bogner	UK	Dioressence	FR
Bridges	J	Diorissimo	FR
Brut	UKN	Drakkar Noir	FR
Byzance	G	Eau Sauvage	FR
Cacharel	FR	Emeraud	UK
Cachet (Chesebrough-Ponds)	UKN	Escape	UKN
Calandre	SP	Eternity	UKN
Calvin	UKN	Exclamation	UK
Capricci	SP	Fahrenheit	FR
Charmers	UK	Farouche	SP
Chipie	UK	Femme	G
Christian Dior	FR	Ferrari	THAI
cK One	UKN	Fille D'Eve	SP
Claire Burke	J	Firmenich	SWI
Clarins	FR	First	N
Cobalt	UK	Fleur De Fleurs	SP
Coeur-Joie	SP	Francesco Smalto	THAI
Coty	UK	Frescolat	G

Gio De Giorgio Armani	FR	Orlane	FR
Giorgio Armani	FR	Paco Rabanne	THAI
Gloria Vanderbilt	FR	Paco-Rabanne	THAI
Gravity	UK	Paloma Picasso	FR
Gridio Terla	THAI	Passion	UKN
Guerlain	FR	Pierre Cardin	J
Guy Laroche	FR	Poison	FR
Heritage	FR	Polo	FR
Hernes	FR	Pparis	ITL
ICI	UK	Preferred Stock	UK
Impulse ''Devotion''	UKN	Qiora	J
Infinitif	UK	Ralph Lauren	FR
Insatiable	J	Ricci-Club	SP
Jean Paul Gaultier	J	Roger & Gallet	THAI
Jil Sander	UK	Route 66	UK
Joop!	UK	Royal Copenhagen	J
Jovan Musk	UK	Samsara	FR
Just Me	FR	Sand & Sable	UK
La Perla	THAI	Sensacion	UK
Lady Stetson	UK	Sergio Tacchini	THAI
L'Aimant	UK	Shalimar	FR
L'Air Du Temps	SP	Signoricci	SP
Lancaster	UK	Sissi	THAI
Lancome	FR	St. Andrews	THAI
L'Heure Bleu	FR	Stetson	UK
Longing	UK	Tommy Girl	HK
Lou Lou	FR	Tresor	FR
Maserati	THAI	Truly Lace	UK
Metal	SP	Tupic	FR
Miss Dior	FR	Universo	UK
Mistral	UK	Vanilla Fields	UK
Molto Smalto	THAI	Vanilla Musk	UK
Monsoon	UK	Verino	UK
Montana	FR	Vol De Nuit	FR
Nahema	FR	Volupte	N
Nikos	UK	White Diamond	UKN
Nina	SP	Windsong	UKN
Obsession	UKN	Yardley Lily of the Valley	J
Obsession For Men	UKN	Yardley London	J
Olivia	G	Zen	J

GENERAL HEALTH & BEAUTY AIDS

French-owned L'Oreal acquired Maybelline in 1997.

American owned

Act
Always
Baby Orajel
Bausch & Lomb
BB Defend
Bikini Bare
Body Fantasies Shower Gel
Complex 15-Skin Care
Derma Klenz
Desquam-E
Desquam-X
Epic
FDS Feminine Deodorant
Fila Fitness
Forest Pure
Fostex-Acne Treatment

Freeman Professional
Georgette Klinger
Good Sense
Grandpa
Herbal Source
Impress Shower Gel
Lip-Ex Lip Balm
Marquee
Nature's Glo
Nudit
Orajel
Secrets of Aloe
Sentinel
Swan
Top Care

Foreign owned

Actibath	J
Desert Wind	J
Gallia	SAF

Jergens	J
Labrosan Lip Care	ITL
Natural Impressions	J

HAIR CARE PRODUCTS

American owned

A.C.T.
Ace Combs
Adorn
Alberto
Alberto VO5
Aloevera 80
Alogen
Alpha
Arista
Aromesentials
Attitudes
Aussie Mega
Balsam Color
Bantu
Beau Kreme

Behave
Black & Beautiful
Bobbi
Body Essence
Bold Hold
Born Blond
Botanical
Breck Conditioner
Breck Hairspray
Brights
Caprice
Casa Di Colore
Clairesse Hair Coloring
Clairmist Hair Spray
Clarion Hair Coloring

Classy Curl
Color Choice
Comb-Thru
Cossack
Crème Relaxer
Curlax
Designer Touch
Dippity Do
Fabulaxer Hair Straightener
Final Net
Finale Hair Spray
Forest Pure
Frames!
Freeman Professional
Frost 'N Tip
Gard Hair Color
Gel Set
Gentle Treatment
Georgette Klinger
Goody
Great Day
Grecian Formula
Guys and Dolls
Hall Tress
Hask Placenta
Henna N' Placenta
Hennalucent
Herbal Essence
Hold & Clean
Hold Tight
Hydrience Hair Color
Icon
Infusium 23
It's Organic Naturally
Jheri Redding
Jhirmack
Just 5
Just For Me
Just For Men
Kaleidocolors
La Coupe
Lectrify
Light Efects
Liminize

Lively Set
Logics Hair Color
Loving Care
Lucky Kentucky
Lustra Colors
Matrix
Men's Choice Hair Spray
Meta 1 Step
Milk N Honey
Moistex
Moxie
New Zealand Hair Paradise Golden
Seal
Nice 'N Easy
Nice 'N Thick
Nutra Care
Option
Palmer's Hair Success
Pantene
PCJ
Perm Life
Perm-Aid
Permathene
Placenta Plus
POR Equal
Prevent
Pro Oxygen
Pro Perm
Prom
Propecia
Protein 21 Hair Spray
Radiant Glo
Ready Set
Revitalique Hair Coloring
Revlon
Revlon Hair Coloring
Right-On
Roffler
Rogaine/Regaine
Roux Hair Coloring
Sanex
Score
S-Curl
Sea Mist

Second Nature
Shapings
Silk & Silver
Snappy Set
Sof N' Free
Soft & Beautiful
Sonatural
Sta-Sof-Fro
Sun-In
System E Biolage
TCB
The Dry Look

Tone Up
Ultra Sheen
Ultress
Vavoom
Vidal Sassoon
Vita Fusion
Vitalis
Vitality
Wash N' Curl
Young Curl
Young Hair

Foreign owned

Agreer Hair Gelling Water	J	Mountain Herbery	UK
Aqua Net	UKN	Optimum	FR
Arrange Hair Spray	J	Parade	G
Blaune	J	Peach Bellini	J
Blondor	G	Pento	UK
Bolty	J	Perfect Control	G
Bristow's	UK	Perform	UK
Brylcreem	UK	Perl Glass	G
Casting	FR	Permavive Technicare	FR
Color Charm	G	Preference	FR
Crisan	G	Proficare	G
Cutrin	FIN	Quantum	UKN
Dep	G	Rave	UKN
Design	G	Rave Microspray	UKN
Excellence	FR	Rolling Hills	G
Falcon Men's Hairspray	UK	Salon Selectives	UKN
Fantastic Silver	UK	Sanara	G
Finesse	UKN	Shaklee	J
Garnier	FR	Shock Wave	G
High Hair	G	So Fine	G
Jojoba Farms	UK	Studio Line	FR
Kerastase	FR	Suave	UKN
Koleston	G	Sunsilk	UKN
Liquid Hair	G	Theorie	G
Living Colors	J	Thermasilk	UKN
L'Oreal	FR	Vibrance	UKN
Lustair Hair Spray	J	Water Hair Pack	J
Luticin	G	Wella Balsam	G
Mill Creek	UK		

HAIR DRYERS

American owned

Apollo	Revlon
Behold	Rocket 2000
Clairol	Select Airstyler
Conair	Selectaire
Crazy Duck	Son of a Gun
Fashion Aire	Sport Mate 1200
Fold N'Go	Style-Aire
Gillette Super Volume	Sunbeam
Jet Set	Sunbeam-Oster
Jheri Redding	Vidal Sassoon
Promotor	VIP Pro
Remington	Windmere

Foreign owned
No foreign brands could be located for this category.

HAIR STYLING AIDS

American owned

Braun	Gold Medal
Crazy Curl	Spin Curlers
Fantas-Stick	

Foreign owned
No foreign brands could be located for this category.

MOUTHWASH

American owned

Act	Oral-B
Arm & Hammer	Plax
Chloraseptic	Rembrandt
Clear Choice	Scope
Colgate	Tom's of Maine
Listerine	Viadent
Listermint	Vince

Foreign owned

Butler	J	Mentadent	UKN
Gly-Oxide	UK	Signal	UKN
Lavoris	G	Targan	UK

OVER-THE-COUNTER MEDICATIONS

American owned

Advil
Advil Cold and Sinus
Afrin
Aftate
Agoral Laxative
Aleve
Amitone
Anacin
APR
Arthricare
Arthriten
Arthritis Foundation
Arthritis Hot
Arthritis Pain Formula
Aspercreme
Asperheart
Aspi Cor Aspirin
Astelin Nasal Spray
Atenolol
Auro Ear Drops
Axid AR
Azelex
Backaid
Backaid PM
Bausch & Lomb Moisture Drops
Benadryl
Ben-Gay
Benylin
Benzodent
Biseptol
Blistex
Blistik
BodyMate
BQ
Bufferin
Caladryl
Carter's Little Pills
Cefepime
Chap-Et
Chapstick
Chericol Cough Syrup

Children's Advil
Children's Tylenol
Chloraseptic
Clear Eyes Eye Drops
Clearasil
Cold-Eeze
Compoz
Comtrex
Cool-A-Ped
Correctol
Cortizone
Creo-Terpin
Datril
Daycare Daytime
Dayquil
Delsym
Dent's Ear Wax Drops
Dexatrim
Di-Gel
Dimetane
Dimetapp
Diurex
Dolobid
Dovonex
Dr. Baker's Aspirin
Dristan
Drixoral
Dry Eye Therapy
Duadacin
Duoplant Wart Remover
Duration Nasal Spray
Efferdent
Encaprin
Excedrin
Feen-A-Mint
FiberCon
Fixodent
Flex-All 454
Formula 44 Cough Syrup
Four Way Nasal Spray
Gelusil

Hall's Cough Drops
Head & Chest
Helps Cough Suppressant
Hudson
Ibutab
Icy Hot
Imodium
Imodium A-D
Kanka
Lanacane
Lanacort
Lockets Cough Drops
Lotrimin AF
Luden's Throat Drops
Maltsupex
Metamucil
Monistat
Motrin
Muellergesic
Multigesic
Murine Eye Drops
Mylanta II
Nix Lice Treatment
Norwich Aspirin
Nose Better
NP-27
Nuprin
Nyquil
OCU Clear Eye Drops
Off-Ezy
Orabase
Oracin
Orajel
Painaid
Pamprin
Pazo Ointment
Pediacare
Pedialyte
Pediatric Formula 44
Pepcid AC
Pepto-Bismol
Percogesic
Peri-Colace
Phazyme

Phenergan
Preparation H
Propa Ph
Regulact
Remegel
Riopan
Robitussin
Rolaids
Rondec
Ryna C
Ryna CX
Rynatan
Scalp Itch
Scalpicin
Scholl
Sexy Lips Lip Balm
Sine-Aid
Sinex
Sinutab
Sloan's
Slumbron
Smith Brothers Cough Drops
Smoke-X
Sonata
St. Joseph Aspirin
Stadol
Stay Moist Lip Balm
Sting-Eze
Sudafed
Sulpho-Lac
Sun Ban Lip Balm
Swiss-Kriss
Syllact
Tam
Tanac
Tempo
Theragran-M
Therapeutic Mineral Ice
Throat Discs
Thylox
Topex
Trans-Ver-Sal
Trinalin
Tronolane

Tylenol
Tyzine
Unisom
Vagisil
Va-Tro-Nol
Vicks
Vicks Blue
Vicks Formula 44

Vicks Formula 44D
Vicks Nyquil
Vicks Vaporub
Victors
Viractin
Visine Eye Drps
Zantac

Foreign owned

Actifed	UK	Junior Lemsip	UK
Acutrim	SWI	Lemsip	UK
Aktren	G	Lookel	J
Alka-Mints	G	Maalox	SWI
Alka-Seltzer	G	MAC Throat Lozenges	UK
Allegra Antihistamine	FR	Mentholatum	J
Ascritpin A/D	SWI	Motofen	IRE
Bactine	G	Nature's Remedy Laxative	UK
Bayer Aspirin	G	N'Ice	UK
Baytril Antibacterial	G	Nicoderm	FR
BC Tablets	UK	Nicorette	UK
Beecham's Pills	UK	Night Nurse	UK
Beecham's Powders	UK	Niquitin CQ	UK
Benzac	FR	Nolahist	IRE
Benzagel	FR	Novahistine	FR
Benzamycin	FR	Novalgin	FR
Betabactyl	UK	Nytol	UK
Caroid Laxatives	J	Oxy	UK
CIBA Vision Eye Drops	SWI	Paramed	UK
Contac	UK	Paynocil	UK
Cope	J	Perdiem	SWI
Daniprol	DEN	Pertussin	UK
Day Nurse	UK	Phensic	UK
Debrox Ear Drops	UK	Philips Milk of Magnesia	UK
Diapid	SWI	Phrenilin	IRE
Disprin	UK	Pollinex	UK
Disprol	UK	Prontalgine	G
Doan's Pills	SWI	Red Cross Toothache Drops	J
Dulcolax	G	Ricola	SWI
Ecotrin	UK	Riopan Plus	SP
Efidac	SWI	Sine Off	UK
Ex Lax	SWI	Singlet	UK
Fiberall Laxative	SWI	Sinulin	IRE
Fletchers Castoria Laxative	J	Softlips	J
Junior Disprol	UK	Sominex	UK

Spagulax	UK	Tenuate	FR
Stimate	FR	Theraflu	SWI
Stop Tou	UK	Toradol	SWI
Sucrets	UK	Triaminic	SWI
Tagamet	UK	Triaminicin	SWI
Talcid	G	Triaminicol	SWI
Tamarine	UK	Tums	UK
Tavist	SWI	Vaseline	UKN
Tavist-D	SWI	Veno's	UK
Tavist-I	SWI	V-Med	SAF
Teldrin	UK		

RAZORS/SHAVERS

American owned

Atra	Microtrac
Bathing Beauty	Oster
Bikini Baby	Outliner II
Braun	Pal
Bump Fighter	Personal Touch
Daisy	Personna
Daisy Plus	Remington
Face-Guard	Schick
Flex Control	Sensor
Flicker	Sensor Excel
Full N Soft	Shower Shaver
Gem	Stubble Device
Gillette	Tech-Razor
Good News	The Knack
Groomsman	Trac II
Jheri Redding	Treet
Just Whistle	Ultrex
Lady Braun	Wahl
Lady Remington	Whisper
Lady Wahl	Wilkinson
Micro Screen	

Foreign owned

Bic	FR	Prepare	J
Norelco	N	Titan	J
Panasonic	J	Twin Pastel	FR

SHAMPOO

American owned

Adorn
Agree (S.C. Johnson)
Alberto VO5
Alpha
Aussie Mega
Aussie Moist
Australian Citrifier
Avon
Baby Magic
Bare Elegance
Biolage
Body On Tap
Breck
Clairol
Condition
Cortexx
Denorex
Earth Born
Elizabeth Arden
Enhance
Equate
Flex
Foho For Oily Hair Only
Formula ZP II
Free 'N Easy
Freeman
Freeman Botanical
Grandpa's Pine Tar Shampoo
Halsa
Head & Shoulders
Heart
Herbal Deep Clean
Herbal Essence
Icon
Infusium 23
Ionil Plus
Ivory
Jheri Redding
Jhirmack
Johnson's Baby
Klorane

Koogalaba
Lemon Up
Matrix
Milk Plus 6
Monterey Naturals
Neutrogena
New Zealand Hair Paradise Dragon Tree
Nizoral
Palmolive Optims
Pantene
Papaya
Pernox
Pert
Pert for Kids
Pert Plus
Prell
Progaine
Prom
Protein 21
Psoriasin S/A
PSSSSSST
Pure Shine
Royal
Scalpicin
Sea Mist
Sebulex
Selsun Blue
Selsun Gold
Shantu
Shimmerlights
Silkience
St. Ives Swiss Formula
Sulfoam
Sulfodene
T/Gel
T/Sal
Tom's of Maine
Top Care
Tresemme'
U.E.S.
Ultima II

Ultraswim

Vavoom

Vidal Sassoon

White Rain

Zincon

Foreign owned

Acclaim Hair Shiners	J	Mineral Water	J
Agree (Schwarzkopf & DEP)	G	Naturelle	J
Aussie	FR	Olapon	G
Bain De Terre	J	Peach Bellini	J
Body & Bounce	G	Rave	UKN
Celsene	FR	Redken	FR
Condess	UK	Salon Formula Dep	G
Conti	UK	Salon Selectives	UKN
Countess	UK	Selecao	G
Cuticura	G	Silvikrin	UK
Design Freedom	J	Studio Line Daily Express	FR
Duett	G	Suave	UKN
Finesse	UKN	Tegrin	UK
Goldwell	J	Tessera	J
Halso	G	Vibrance	UKN
Helene Curtis	UKN	Vosene	UK
Kolestral	G	Wella Balsam	G
Lancome	FR	Wella Flex	G
L'Oreal	FR	Wella So Fine	G

SHAVING CREAM

American owned

Afta

Aveeno

Barbasol

Bikini Bare

Burma Shave

Colgate

Edge

Gillette

Gillette Foamy

Gyro

Hers

Noxema

Old Spice

Palmolive

Pre/Aft

Prep

Rise

Satin Care

Schick

Skintimate

Sof' Stroke

The Hot One

Tom's of Maine

Foreign owned

Brut	UKN	Lectric Shave	UK

SKIN CARE PRODUCTS

American owned

Adrien Arpel
Age Zone Controller
Aloe Vesta
Aloette
Aloevera 80
Alogen
Alpha
Alpha Hydrox
Ambi-Pur
Aveeno
Baby Magic
Badedas
Beauticontrol
Big Wheel
Body Fantasies
Borghese
Bright Girl
Country Natural
Crème of Nature
Gly-Miracle
Hawaiian Tropic
Hydracare
Lanacane
Lournay
Lubriderm
Luxiva
Mariner's Lotion
Millenium
Moisturel
Monterey Naturals
Mycolog II
Nair Dipilitory
Neoteric

Neutrogena Body Lotion
Noxema
Oil Of Olay
Olay
Origins
Palmers Cocoa Butter
Palmer's Skin Success
Pavana
Prom
Pure Care
Rain Bath
Rejuvia
Rose Milk
Royal Jelly Cream
Savane
SBS
SBS-71
Sea Breeze
Sea Mist
Semplice
Sempray-Jovenay
Shower to Shower
Skin So Soft
Sooth & Cool
St. Ives Swiss Formula
Sundance
Topifram
Tritle's
Udder-Wize
Ultraswim
Villa De Jerome
Visible Difference

Foreign owned

Aquaphor	G	Germolene	UK
Aupres	J	Germoloids	UK
Bio Performance	J	Hydra Dior	FR
Biore	J	Integrite	UK
Clarins	FR	Kiehl's	FR
Curel	J	Lancaster	UK
Cuticura	G	Margaret Astor	UK

Mill Creek	UK	Relax Water	J
Minon	J	Rolling Hills	G
Nature's Family	G	Secret D' Angel	FR
Neet Hair Removing Crème	UK	Shaklee	J
Nivea	G	Shiseido	J
Orlane	FR	Somatoline	UK
Plenitude	FR	Stendhal	N
Pond's	UKN	Tiss	J
Porcelana	G	Vaseline	UKN
Pure & Simple	UK	Vital-Perfection	J
Quickargile	UK	Yardley London	J
Rainsilk	J	Za Skin	J
Ralgex	UK		

SUN CARE PRODUCTS

American owned

Almay	Neutrogena
American Fare	Olay
Bain de Soleil	Orange Gelee
Banana Boat	Piz Buin
Beach-Aid	Presun
Biosun	Pre-Sun
Bullfrog	Rite Aid
Coppertone	Shade
Escalol 507	Sundown
Escalol 557	Tropical Blend
Hawaiian Tropic	Walgreen
Herba-Tan	Water Babies

Foreign owned

Anessa Trans Wear	J	Neoheliopan	G
Jil Sander	UK	Programme Solaire	ITL

TOOTHBRUSHES

American owned

Breath of Spring	Oral-B
Colgate	Prevent
Crest Complete	Reach
Crest Deep Sweep	Sensodyne
Dentist Preferred	Sensodyne Search
Gillette Advantage	Tek
Jordan	

Foreign owned

Aquafresh Flex Deluxe	UK	Dental C.	THAI
Butler	J	Pepsodent	UKN
Cleardent	J	Pycopay	UK

TOOTHPASTE

American owned

Arm & Hammer	Oral-B
Colgate	Pearl Drops
Complete	Prodent
Crest	Rembrandt
Darlie	Sensodyne
Denquel	Tom's of Maine
Dentagard	Top Care
Gleem	Ultra Brite
Interplak	Viadent
Listerine	

Foreign owned

Aim	UKN	Mentadent	UKN
Aquafresh	UK	Parodontax	UK
Butler	J	Pepsodent	UKN
Cleardent	J	Popsy	UK
Close-Up	UKN	Protect	J
Dentu-Crème	UK	Signal	UKN
Dentu-Gel	UK	Thermodent	J
Macleans	UK	Topol	G

VITAMINS

American owned

Bedoyecta	Healthbee
Centrum	Hudson Vitamins
Criticare	Imutabs
Dextrevit	Isocal
Family Pharmacy	Jones
Femiron	Kindermins
Fempotane	Malpotane
Funny Chew Chews	Mega Stress
Gerahealth Tabs	Mega-Health 75
Good N' Natural	Nature's Bountry
Grapefruit Diet Tabs	NatureSmart
Health Hair	Nu Skin
Health-A-Day	Nutri Mega

Nutri-Hair
Origin
Poly-Vi-Sol
Puritan's Pride
Radiance
S.F.6
Sesame Street
TGF
The Boxer

Theragran-M
Therahealth-M
Total Formula
Total Nutrition
Tri-Vi-Sol
Vi-Daylin
Vi-Flor
Vi-Sol

Foreign owned

ABCD	DEN	Multi-Tabs	DEN
Avimin	DEN	Nature Made	J
Becoplex	DEN	Nutra	UK
Bugs-Bunny	G	One-A-Day	G
Capsudar	ISR	Rexall	N
Chocks	G	Scott's Emulsion	UK
Covitol	G	Shaklee	J
Elacatonin	UK	Stressgard	G
Extravite	UK	Sundown	N
Flintstones	G	Sunny Maid	J
Geritol	UK	Thompson	N
Healthcrafts	DEN	Vitavel	UK
Ladycare	DEN	Within	G
Lamberts	DEN	Yeast Vite	UK

Chapter 7

Clothing & Accessories

FOOTWEAR

New Balance, with two plants in Maine and two in Massachusetts, still makes about 30% of their shoes in America. There is little or no price difference between American-made New Balance shoes and the Chinese imports of Adidas, Reebok or Nike despite the claim of free traders that imports are beneficial since they supposedly allow consumers to buy similar goods at cheaper prices.

American owned

Aarau
Acme
Air Step
Alden USA
All Star Collection
Allen-Edmonds
Alpen
Altama
American Eagle
American Legend
Angel Treads
Ann Taylor
Anne Klein
Aris
Aristocraft
Arosa
Ascoza
Asics
Astro
ATV's by Knapp
Auditions
Avia
B.A. Mason
Baby Capezio
Baby Deer
Baby Jacks
Bakers
Bandolino
Banister
Barclay
Bare Bottoms
Bass
Bates Floataways
Beverly Hills
Boat-Suns

Boks
Bongo
Born
Bouquets
Brass Boot
Brazilo's
Bria
Bristen
British Knights
Browsabouts
Bumpers
Buster Brown
Calico
Cara Leigh
Carla Cristaldi
Carolina
Caterpillar
Cherokee
Child Life
Chippewa
Chuck Taylor
Cirkids
City Steps
Cole-Haan
Coleman
Comfy Slippers
Compass
Converse
Dan Post Western Boots
Daytimers
Deckers Outdoor
Dee Gee
Deliso
Dexter
Diadora

Dingo Boots
Disney
Dockers Footwear
Domani
Double-H Boots
Dr. Scholl's
Dry Dock
Dry Joys
Dryjoys
Dunes
Durango Boots
E.T. Wright
Easy Spirit
EJ
Endicott Johnson
Enrico Sergio
Enzo Angiolini
Etonic
Evan Picone
Extra Depth
Fanfares
Farm Master
Fashion 10
Fashion Flex
Fashion-Treads
Father & Son
Field & Stream
Flak
Florsheim
Foot Joy
Foot-Joy Classics
Frye Boot Co.
Genesco
Georgia Boot
Georgia Farm & Ranch
Grasshoppers
Gum Drops
H.H. Brown
H.H. West
Hanes Soft Steps
Happy Go Lightly
Herman
Herman Surviviors
Hush Puppies

Hyde
Insbruck
Intrigue
J & M
Jacks
Jarman
Joan & David
Joan Helpern Signature
John Deere
John Eben
Johnsonian
Johnston & Murphy
Journeys
Justin
Justin Boots
Justin Lace R's
Keds
Keepsake
Key Notes
King of the Bench
Knapp
K-Swiss
L.L. Bean
L.A. Gear
Larry Stuart
Lasco
Lehigh
Levi's
Life Stride
Lightwades
Li'l Trolls
Little Capezio
Locarno
Lolly Pops
Lucchese Boots
Lugz
Madye's
Magneforce Golf Shoes
Mark Jeffrey
Mason Shoe
Masseys
Maxwell Shoe
Merit
Merrell

Miralug
Miss Capezio
Moxees
Mushrooms
Nancy Lopez
Naturalizer
NaturalSport
Nautica
New Balance
New Terrain
Night Life
Nike
Nine & Co.
Nine West
Nocona Boots
Northlake Outdoor Footwear
Nubbies
Nunn-Bush
Oomphies Slippers
Outdorable
Pappagallo
Paracord
Pedi-Foam
Penaljo
Perma Bond
Permasole
Pillowbacks
Ponderosa
Pro-Keds
R.J. Colt
Ray Floyd
Realities
Red Wing
Reebok
Rego
Reuna
Revelations
Rigi
Rockport
Rocky
Rodeo Drive
Royal Shield
Ruffhides
Rufi

Ryon's Boots
Saasen
Sabel
Safe-T-Treads
Safety Skids
Saucony
Scuffie Footlights
Scuffies
Selby
Select A Size
Shades of the Old West
Shuperstar
Side Out
Siero-DH
Signature
Simple Shoes
Siricca
Skateboards
Skechers
Ski-Moc
Sneaux
Snow Stalker
Soft Notes
Solar Magic
Solis
Sperry Top-Siders
Splugen
Sport Master
Sport Set
Sportocasins
Spot-Bilt
Stacy Adams
Street Hot
Street Skees
Stride Rite
Stuart McGuire
Sundaes
Sunjuns
Terra
Terry-Threads
Teva
Thermolds
Thorogard
Timberland

Tingley Rubber
Titleist-Foot-Joy
Tony Lama
Topazio
Trail Kings
Trail Queens
Trailbreakers
Trailbuxe
Trak Tred
Treadeasy
Treo
Trimfoot
Trimkids
Trimsteps
Trotters
Tru-Stitch
Tuff Tred
Tura
Two Shot Soles
Ugg Boots
Vancour
Vasque

Versatan
Vicente Collection
Walkchwil
Walker Hill
Wee Kids
Wee Walker
Weebok
Weejuns
Wellco
Westies
Wilbur Coon
Wild Rice
Wildcats
Wilderness
Wimzeez
Windsor Walkers
Wolverine
Wood N' Stream
Woodbuxe
Worx
Yves St. Laurent
Zodiac USA

Foreign owned

Adidas	G	Gucci	N
America Today	N	Hanover	UK
Andiamo	FIN	Hernes	FR
Argyll	UK	John Lobb	FR
Bally	SWI	Kamik	C
Bostonian	UK	Kingtread Workboots	C
Bostonian Windsor	UK	Kodomo	THAI
Campeonato	J	Lotto Athletic Shoes	ITL
Candy	AUS	Mitre	UK
Careca	J	Mizuno	BZL
Cica	UK	Noche	SNG
Clarks	UK	Pony	UK
Cosmic	SNG	Puma	G
Defrosters Boots	C	Racing Star	J
Desert Boot	UK	Radial	AUS
Dunlop	AUS	Radial 500	AUS
Elements	UK	Rainha	BZL
Esprit	HK	Red River	UK
Fila	ITL	Regal	THAI
Foamtread Slippers	C	Runbird	J
Gorshed	J	Salomon	G

Samoa Sandals	BZL	Strada	UK
Scapino	N	Topper	BZL
Shiftlex	J	Tretorn	SWE
Skydragon	J	Tuff Kiks	C
Snowmaster	C	Wallabee	UK
St. Michael	UK	Wave	J
Starfighter	J		

GENERAL APPAREL

America imports almost two-thirds of its apparel, but still makes about 90% of its socks in the USA.

American owned

@Ease
417
A. Byer
Accentuette
Adams Row
Adobe Rose
Aerials
AFRC
AKNY
Alacrity
Alexander Julian
Ali Miles
All That Jazz
Allegheny
Allyn St. George
Alpha
Ambra Sweaters
American Legend
Amy Byer
Amy Too
Andover Togs
Andrew Blues
Angelica-Priest
Anne Leslie
Anything Else Is A Substitute
Appel
Appleseed's
Arcade America
Areo
Areo Sport
Aris
Arnold Palmer

Arrow
Artex
At Ease
AtDenim
Austad's
Austin Reed of Regent Street
Avia
B.A. Mason
B.D. Baggies
Baby 'N' Me
Bali
Barbizon
Barry Ashley
Bassett-Walker
Bath & Body Therapies
Bauer & Black
Bay to Bay
BBW
Beaux Reves
Becky
Beefy-T
Belcor
Beldoch Popper
Berkshire Intimates
Bert Pulitzer
Bestform
B'Gosh
Bibo
Bice
Big Big Dogs
Big Dog Sportswear
Big Dogs

Bike
Bill Blass
Bill Blass Sleepwear
Bill Burns
Bill Robinson
Blair Boutique
Blake & Manley
Blue Mesa
Blue Stone
Boatworks
Bobbie Brooks
Bobby Jones
Body Drama
Bodyflex
Bodysilk
Boltons
Bon Jour
Bongo
Bonkers
Boss Sportswear
Boston Traders
Branders Jeans
Breezin
Bretton Place
Briar
Bristol Lane
Broomsticks
Buckle
Buddy Lee
Bugle Boy
Bunny & Me
Burberrys
C.C. Sox
California Influence
Calvin Klein
Cambridge
Cambridge Bay
Campus
Candie's
Canidae
Cape Cod
Cape Cod Match Mates
Carina
Carter's

Carter's Classics
Carwood
Cascade Sport
Casey & Max
Catalina Swimwear
Cathy Lee
CB
Ceiling Zero Rainwear
Cezani
Chalk Line
Champion
Chams
Chan-Tel Sleepwear
Chantilly Place
Chantilly Place Dresses
Chaparral Ridge
Chaps
Chaps By Ralph Lauren
Chaps Ralph Lauren Formal Wear
Charles Bastion
Chaya
Cherokee
Cheryl Tiegs Hosiery
Christian Aujard
Christian Dior Formalwear
Christian Dior Slacks
Cinema Etoile
Clairborne
Coaster Gear
Code Blue
Colesta
Coliseum Boys
Collarwear (Neckwear)
Columbia Sportswear
Components Sportswear
Cotton Supply
Country By Jax
Country Clothes
Country Cottons
Country Sophisticates
Country Suburban
Country Touch
Country Traditionals
Courchevel Neckwear

Cricket Lane
Cross Creek
Crowntuft
CSK
Curfew
Cushion Roll Knitwear
Cushion Top Knitwear
Custom Club International
Custom Collection Hoisery
Custom Shop
Cutter & Buck
Dana Buchman
Dare To Dress
David Dart
David Harrison
Deb
Debra Lubell
Deckers Outdoor
Defender Outerwear
Delta
Demetre
Designers Originals
Deweese
Dickies
Diplomat Sleepwear
Disney
Dockers Brand
Don Alleson
Doncaster
Donnkenny
Dotti
Dreamwear Lingerie
Dry Foot Socks
Dry Wear Rainwear
Duck Head
Due Date
Dunne & Cole
E. Jovan
Ease Sport
Eddie Bauer
Editions
Elderado
Electric Beach by Jantzen
Elisabeth

Embassy Square
Emily Rose
Enchante
Enro
Enticements
Enticements Sleepwear
Escadrille
Especially You
Esprit
Evan Picone
Eve Byer
Eve Too
Excalibur
Exquisite Form (VF Corp.)
Eyecatchers
Farah
Fashion Galaxy
Fashion Nautigue
Fashion Scoops
Fern Bratten
Field & Stream
Finals
Finery by Freeman
Flags
Flapdoodles
Flight Deck U.S.A.
Flight Tested
Flirts
Flyer's
FM Elements
Foxcroft
Francesca Caretti
Fred Bear
Fred Meyer
Frederick's Of Hollywood
Frostings Lingerie
Fumagalli's
Fun Gear
G-11
Gantner
Garan
Garan by Marita
Gemma
Generra

Genuine Article
Genuine Blues
Genuine Girl
Genuine Kids
Geoffrey Beene
Gieves & Hawkes
Gina Peters
Girbaud
Girls Club
Gitano
Golden Fleece
Graham & Gunn Ltd
Grandoe Dress Gloves
Great Northwest
Grove Avenue
H Orisky
H. Freeman
Haband
Haggar
Hampshire
Handmacher
Hanes
Harbor One
Hardwick Clothes
Harley-Davidson
Harper
Hart Schaffner & Marx
Hathaway
Healthknit
Heavy Survival Gear
Heet
Helen of Troy
Hennessy
Henry Grethel
Herbcraft
Heritage U.S.A.
Hicky-Freeman
Hilton Active
Hilton USA
Horace Small (occupational)
Hot Coles Swimwear
Hot Music
Howard Wolf
Hunt Club

Huntley of York
Hyde Park
I.C. Isaacs
I.C. Winters
I.V.Y.
Identity
Imperial
Imperial Hats
Inside Edge
International Male
Intima Cherry
Irvine Park
Ivy
Izod
Izod Lacoste
J. Chuckles
J. Crew
J.G. Hook
J.J. Cochran Boys
Jack Nicklaus
Jack Wolfskin
Jaclyn B.
Jacques Moret
Jag
James B. Fairchild
Jansport
Jax
Jaymar
Jazz Kids
Jazzertogs
Jeri-Jo
Jerzees
JH Collectibles
Joan Helpern Signature
Joan Leslie Sportswear
Joan Vass, U.S.A.
Jockey
John Alexander
John Blair
John Henry
John Peel Ltd
John Weitz
Johnny Carson
Jones New York

Jones Wear
Jordache
JW's by John Weitz
Karl Lagerfeld
Katherine Bishop
Kathy White
Katin Surf
Kenneth Cole
Kenny Classics
Key
Kicks
Kids "R" Us
Kilgour French & Stanbury
King Louie
King of the Bench
Knockabouts
Kombi
Koret
K-Swiss
Kuppenheimer
LA Gear
Lady Blair
Lady Hardwick
Lady Sansabelt
Lamonts For Kids
Land-N-Lakes
Lands' End
Lanvin
Lanz Of Salzburg
Le Coq
Le Coq Sportif
Lee
Lee Hats
Lee Sport
Les Jeunes
Leslie Fay
Levi's
Lily of France
Lindsy Scott
Linksport
Little Me
Liz
Liz & Co.
Liz And Me

Liz Claiborne
Lizsport
Lizwear
Lobo
Loco Blue
London Fog
Long Gone Banlon
Lord Isaacs
Lord West
Lost River Outerwear
Lou
Lucky Brand Dungarees
M M by Krizia
M.H.M. Dresses
Maggie Barnes
Maggie Lawrence
Major League Baseball
Mallory Men's Hats
Manhattan
Marauder
Marisa Christina
Maryland Square
McGregor
McKid's
Me N You
Me-2
Megaplay
Melissa
Melissa Petites
Melrose
Melrose Studio
Members Only
Men America
Michael Morgan
Mickey Mouse
Miss Elaine
Miss Erika
Miss Pendleton
Miss Sophisticates
M'Lady Bruhn
Monte
Monterey Club
More Intimate
More Jazz

Mountain Lion
Movie Star
Mr. Rags
Mufflings
My Michelle
N.P.W.
N.Y. Lug Co.
Napa Studio
Napa Valley
Natural Baby
Nautica
New Balance
New Dimension
New Generation
Newport News
Nicole Miller
Nicole Summers
Nigel's
Night & Day Intimates
Nightlace Sleepwear
Nightwear By Van Heusen
Nike
Nines By Southwick
Nino Cerruti
Norge Socks
North Bay Outfitters
North Face
Northern Elements
Northern Gataway
Northern Traditions
Northwest Outfitters
Norton McNaughton
Nunus
Nutmeg
Nutmeg Mills
OK Khaki
Olga
Onesies
Oscar de La Renta
OshKosh
OshKosh B'Gosh
Our Gang
Our Girl
Outdoorsman

Outer Banks
Outlander
Oxford Shirtings
P.J. Lane Sleepwear
PAC Knitted Headwear
Pacific Express
Pacific Trading Co.
Page & Tuttle
Pam Undies
Paquette
Pardners
Pasta
Patagonia
Payhalf
Payne Stewart
PBM
Peek A Toe
Penny From Heaven
Perry Ellis
Perry Ellis Sleepwear
Personal Choice
Peter England
Petite August Max Woman
Pheasant Knitted Headware
Philips-Van Heusen
Pierre Cardin
Pierre Cardin Formal Wear
Pine Crest
Pizzazz
Players
Playtex Intimate Apparel
Plaza South
Plums Sweaters
Polar Jac/Vest
Polar King
Polo By Ralph Lauren
Polo for Boys
Polo University Club
Polo/Ralph Lauren
Poppy
Portraits by Northern Isles
PremiumWear
Racquet Club
Radcliffe

Ralph Lauren
Randy River
Raven
Real McCoy
Reebok
Reed St. James
Rena Rowan For Saville
Resistol Hats
Re-Union
Revelation
Richman Brothers
Riders
Risque Undergarments
Rob Roy
Robby Len
Robert Scott
Robert Stock
Robert Terry
Ross & Cromarty
Roust-A-Bout Knitted Headwear
Royal Palm
Runaway Jacket
Russell Athletic
Rustler
Saber
Salem Sportswear
San Francisco Knitworks
Sandcastle Swimwear
Sansabelt
Sarong
Sasson
Satin Francies
Saturday Sun Compnay
Savane
Saville
SCAASI
Schwabe
Screamers
Scroll Embroideries
Seminole
SH Plus
Shimmers
Showtoons
Side Out

Sierra Designs
Signal
Signature II
Signature II by Stan Herman
Siltex
Silver Creek
Silverado Hats
Simply Petites
SJ
Skate N'Ski
Slates
Smart Shirts
Smart Time
Sno-Cat
Sno-Stripe
Society Brand Ltd.
Solaris
Southwest Canyon
Southwick
Spencer
Spencer's
Spiewak
Spoiled Girls
Sportsbra
St. John's Bay
Stafford
Stan Herman
Stanley Blacker
Star Cody
Starter
Stefano
Stephanie K
Stephanie Thomas
Sterling & Hunt
Stetson Hats
Stratamesh
Stratasheen
Stratastretch
Strathmore
Strawberry
Studio 36
Studio Ease
Studio Jax
Style Auto

Style Chief
Suburban Petites
Sudden Impact
Suddenly Slim
Sugar'N Spice
Sunset Blue's
Sweet Tops
Swing West
Swingster
Swirl Directions
Sycamore Hills
Sync
T.L.C.
Tahiti
Tanner
Tanner Sport
Tee-Time
Tepee
Terry Togs
Tex Tan
The American Collection
The Avenue
The End Briefs
The Garan Man
The Right Support For You
Tickets
Timber Topper
Timberland
Titan
Tog
Tom Sawyer
Tony Lama Western Wear
Tony Lambert
Town & Country
Trappings
Trend Club
Trenton Stone
Tropical Sportswear
TSV

Tuff Gear
Tultex
Undergear
Ungaro
Unionbay
Urollit Hats
Van Heusen
Vanity Fair
Vassarette
Veloce 500
VF
Via Max
Victoria Jones
Vintage Blue
Vintage Studio
Violets & Roses
Waist-Watcher
Walter-Morton
Warner's
Weather-Tech
Weathervane
Webdri
Weekend Edition
White Stag
Wigwam
Windmills
WMI
Wolf Mountain
Wonder-Wick
Woolrich
Wrangler
Yankee Rainwear
Yapre
You Babes
Young Stuff
YS Sport
YS Studio
Yves Saint Laurent

Foreign owned

5 Up	THAI	Adidas	G
A/E Sport & Co.	C	America Today	N
Absorba	THAI	American Pie	UK
Addition-Elle	C	Ashworth	J

Baldessarini	ITL	Kangaroo Underwear	CI
Benetton	ITL	Kreymborg	N
Berluti	FR	Kullastri	THAI
Bonfire	G	La Femme	THAI
Borgofiori	ITL	La Seine	THAI
BVD	CI	Laura Ashley	UK
Cannon Socks	MEX	Lebole	ITL
Carrington Viyella	UK	Little Wacoal	THAI
Christian Lacroix	FR	Lofteez	CI
Daks London	THAI	Louis Feraud	THAI
Donna Karan	FR	Louis Joone	THAI
Dusol	J	Louis Vuitton Malletier	FR
East West Clothing Co.	C	Lyle & Scott	UK
Elegance Socks	MEX	M Missioni	ITL
Elle	THAI	Mariner	THAI
Enfant	THAI	Maris	J
Esquire Socks	ITL	Melody	THAI
Excellency	THAI	Michel Klein	THAI
Exquisite Form (AGP Industrial)	PHI	Minna	THAI
Family	CI	Mix Self	THAI
Fine-Flex	THAI	Mizuno	J
Flanie	J	Montagut	THAI
Fred Joaillier	FR	Munsingwear	CI
Freeway	THAI	New Man	THAI
Fruit Of The Loom	CI	Nona	J
Fungals	CI	Nudie	THAI
Funpals	CI	Nurse 'N Easy	PHI
Gant	SWE	O12	ITL
Getaway	THAI	Pan	THAI
Gianfranco Ferre Forma	ITL	Perry Sport	N
Gildan Activewear	C	Pony	UK
Givency	FR	Principe	ITL
Grand Monarch	J	Raysil	UK
Gunze	THAI	Robbie	IRE
Guy Laroche	THAI	Sandella	IRE
Halston	J	Scapino	N
Harmony	THAI	Seascamp Swimwear	IRE
Hilfiger	HK	Southern Comfort	UK
Holeproof	AUS	Speedo	THAI
Hue Legwear	ITL	Spirit of Family	CI
Hugo	ITL	St. Andrews	THAI
Hugo Boss	ITL	St. Michael	UK
Inner	THAI	Sugar	THAI
Jean Arnou	IRE	Sunflair	IRE

Tara	IRE	Wacoal	J
Tee Bazar	THAI	Wacoal Swim Wear	THAI
The One	MEX	Weekenders	THAI
Thiebry Mugler	FR	Wild Bunch	UK
Thyme Maternity	C	Wilson	CI
Tootal	UK	Wisp	IRE
Trombone	THAI	Young Kent	THAI
Underoos	CI	Zazch	THAI
Union Underwear	CI	Zerotondo	ITL

HOSIERY

American owned

747	J.G. Hook
7-Footer	Jockey
Alive	Just For You
BBW	Just My Size
Berkshire	Kicks
Better Than Bare	Lady Supreme
Bonds	L'eggs
Brite Legs	Lineone Socks
Calvin Klein	Liz Claiborne
Cameo (Sara Lee)	Mayer Pantyhose
Cheryl Tiegs	Mr. Lokut Socks
Danskin Legwear	Nur Die
Diams	Olga-Brights
Dim	PAC-Socks
Ebony Rich	Performance
Ebony Supreme	Perry Ellis
Eyecatchers	Pheasant Socks
Field & Stream Socks	Philippe Matignon
Filodoro	Pim
Fitting Pretty	Pretty Polly
Flash Legs	Ralph Lauren
Footnotes	Razzamatazz
Givency	Resilience
Gold Toe	Round The Clock
Hampshire	Roust-A-Bout Socks
Hanes	Seal
Hanes Alive	Sheer Caress
Hue Socks	Sheer Elegance
In Control	Shimmers

Silk Impressions
Silk Reflections
Sirocco
Skate N' Ski
Ski N' Skate
Smooth Illusions
Smooth Silhouetes
Sno-Fire
Sno-Ho
Snugglesox
Sof-T Athletic Socks
Solaris
Spanel
Sport Sox

Summer Legg's
Summer Sheer
Super 60 Socks
Super Tube Socks
Tee-Time
Tepee
Ultimax
Ultra Silk
Valcort
Whisper
Wigwam
Winter Legg's
WMI
Wonder-Wick

Foreign owned

Adler Socks	ITL
Arwa	ITL
Beyond Support	G
Brittania Socks	ITL
Burlington Sheer Hosiery	ITL
Burlington Socks	MEX
Cameo (Grupo Synkro)	MEX
Carla Conti	MEX
Dorian Gray	MEX
Esprit	HK
Foreva	MEX
Fruit Of The Loom Socks	CI

Gabrielle	MEX
Gold Cup Socks	ITL
Interwoven Socks	ITL
Leg Looks by Burlington	ITL
Legart	SWI
No Nonsense Pantyhose	ITL
No Nonsense Socks	ITL
OMSA	ITL
Panti Thermic	MEX
Primanatural Socks	ITL
Saltallegro	ITL
Shalimar	MEX

INTIMATE APPAREL

American owned

Alba Ladies Panties
All Day Long Bra
Appel
Appel Bra
Berkshire Intimates
Bestform
Blanche
Blanche Lingerie
Body Drama
Body Tease
Bodysatin Stretch
Bodysilk
Bolero

Bra Slette
Bra Toppers
Charter Club
Comfort Casuals
Cross Your Heart
Frederick's Of Hollywood
Freedom Back Bra
Full Comfort Bra
Glamorise Bra
Goddess Bra
It's Really Something Bra
Jockey
Just Your Fit Bra

La Difference Bra
Lacy Luxuries Bra
Lacy Textures Bra
Lilyette Bra
Lorraine
Lou
Maidenform Bra
Mara Intimates
Miracle Bra
No Exaggeration Bra
Olga-Brights Bra
Olgalace Bra
Sans Souci
Satin Francies Bras
Scroll Embroideries
Secret Hug
Self Expressions
Shimmerlilies

Shine-On
Sizzles Bras
Suddenly Smooth
Suddenly Smooth Bra
Super Cross Bra
Tailored Sheers
Tailored Sheers Bra
The Right Support For You Bra
The Wrap Bra
Touch of Gloss
Touch of Gloss Bra
Truly Fitting Bra
Variance
Vassarette
Vassarette Bra
Warner's
Wonderbra

Foreign owned

Berlei Bra	UK	Teenform	J
Fruit of the Loom	CI	Teenform Bra	J
Teencharm	J	Young Debs	J
Teencharm Bra	J	Young Wacoal	THAI

LEATHER GOODS

American owned

American Belting Leather
Amity
Bosca
Brighton Bay
Bugle Boy
Buxton
California Saddle Leather
Canterbury
Cinch Belts
Coach
Colours By Alexander Julian
Crossroads
Eagle Ottawa
Enger Kress
Geoffrey Beene
Guess?

Heritage Leathers
Jaclyn
Lyntone
Pierre Cardin
Prince Gardner
Princess Gardner
Rockies
Rolfs
Saddler
Signature
Silkee
Stitchless Billfolds
Swank
Tandy
Wolverine
Yves Saint Laurent

Foreign owned

Bentley	C	Guy Laroche	THAI
Berluti	FR	Hernes	FR
Clarino	J	Louis Fontaine	THAI
Fred Joaillier	FR	Louis Vuitton Malletier	FR
Givency	FR		

JEANS

Some Lee and Wrangler jeans are still made in USA.

American owned

Andrew	Liz Claiborne
Arizona	Lost River
Bon Jour	Manhandler
Brittania	Maverick
Bugle Boy	McGregor
Calvin Klein	New Generation
Chams	Riders
Chic	Rugged Wear
Denver	Rustler
Guess?	Saddle King
H.I.S.	Sasson
Harley-Davidson	Square Rigger
Jones Jeans	Talisman
Jordache	Thin Ice
Kidproof	Two Pepper
Land's End	Wrangler
Lee	Zena
Levi's	

Foreign owned

East West	C	Tommy Hilfiger	HK

LUGGAGE

American owned

Ambassador	Holiday
American Tourister	JanSport
Andiamo	Journeyman
Anvil	Knocabouts
Arnold Palmer	Land's End
Bravado	Lark
Deluxe Square Rigger	Lighthouse
Hartmann	L.L. Bean

Lucas		Slide-O-Matic	
Luggage Gallery		Square Rigger	
Monarch		Summit	
Pierre Cardin		Taylor*Made	
Rimowa		The Ghurka Collection	
Samsonite		Touch-O-Matic	
Sasson		Tuxedo	
Scirocco		U.S. Luggage	
Seward		Valoros	
Skyway		Wings	

Foreign owned

Canvas Classics	K	Quest	K

SUNGLASSES

All Oakley sunglasses are made in California.

American owned

Bausch & Lomb	Eddie Bauer
Blublocker	Gargoyles
Bolle	Guess
Calobar	Oakley
Cosmetan	Polaroid
Delta	Serengeti

Foreign owned

Arnette	ITL	Ray Ban	ITL
Clairborne	ITL	Ray-Ban	ITL
Killer Loop	ITL	Revo	ITL
Liz Claiborne	ITL	Suncloud	ITL
Persol	ITL		

WATCHES

American owned

Accutron	Carriage
Andre Giroud	Citizen
Atlantis	Colours By Alexander Julian
Atlas	Concord
Avante Garde	Corum
Baume & Mercier	Croton
Bulova	Diamond Reflections
Caravelle	Elgin

ESQ
Esquire
Essentials
Faraone
Hampton
Indiglo
Intaglio
Malibu
Movado
Nastrix
Pierre Cardin
Reliance

Riviera
Sculptura
Sports Time
Swiss Army
Tesoro
Tiffany & Co.
Tiffany Classics
Timberland
Timex
Tourneau
Wittnaur

Foreign owned

Bulgari	ITL	Longines	SWI
Casio	J	Omega	SWI
Cellini	SWI	Piaget	SWI
Certina	SWI	Pierre Balmair	SWI
CK Watch	SWI	Pulsar	J
Flik Flak	SWI	Rado	SWI
Gevril	SWI	Reverso	SWI
Hamilton	SWI	Rolex	SWI
Hernes	FR	Seiko	J
Jaeger-Le Coultre	SWI	Swatch	SWI
Lassale	J	Tissot	SWI
Limelight	SWI	Tudor	SWI

Chapter 8

Electronics

ANSWERING MACHINES

American owned

AT&T		Conair	
Bell South		General Electric	
Cobra		Radio Shack	
Code-A-Phone		Southwestern Bell	

Foreign owned

Panasonic	J	Sony	J
PhoneMate	J	Toshiba	J
Sanyo	J		

AUDIO/CASSETTE RECORDERS & PLAYERS

American owned

Optimus	Pocket Secretary

Foreign owned

Aiwa	J	Philips	N
Fisher	J	Pioneer	J
Hitachi	J	Sony	J
JVC	J	Teac	J
Kenwood	J	Technics	J
Marantz	J	Toshiba	J
Onkyo	J	Yamaha	J
Otari	J		

AUDIO TAPES

American owned

3M	Scotch
Memorex	

Foreign owned

Fuji	J	Sony	J
Maxell	J	TDK	J

BATTERIES

American owned

AC Delco	Exide
DieHard	Fulmen
Duracell	Kodak
Energizer	Mallory
Eveready	Master Start
EverStart	Mazda

Motorcraft

NAPA

Photolife

Power Shot

Prestolite

Procell

Pro-Start

Radio Shack

Rayovac

Right Start

Tudor

Willard

Xtralife

Foreign owned

Maxell	J	Sanyo	J
Motor King	J	Sony	J
Omnipack	J	Toshiba	J
Panasonic	J	Varta	G
Renata	SWI		

BOOMBOXES

American owned

Koss

Radio Shack

Foreign owned

Aiwa	J	Philco	N
Casio	J	RCA	FR
Fisher	J	Samsung	J
JVC	J	Sanyo	J
Magnavox	N	Sharp	J
Panasonic	J	Sony	J

CALCULATORS

American owned

Hewlett-Packard

Texas Instruments

Foreign owned

Canon	J	Sharp	J
Casio	J		

CAMCORDERS

American owned

Ambico

General Electric

Kodak

Memorex

Sears

Foreign owned

Canon	J	Hitachi	J
Fuji	J	JVC	J

Konica	J	Quasar	J
Kyocera	J	RCA	FR
Leica	G	Ricoh	J
Magnavox	N	Samsung	K
Minolta	J	Sharp	J
Nikon	J	Small Wonder	FR
Olympus	J	Sony	J
Panasonic	J	Vivitar	J
Pentax	J	Yashica	J
Pro Wonder	FR	Zenith	K

CAMERA FILM

90% of the film Kodak sells to the U.S. market is American made.

American owned
Kodak		Scotch	
Polaroid			

Foreign owned
AGFA	BG	Ilford	SWI
Fuji	J	Konica	J

CAMERAS—DIGITAL

American owned
Hewlett-Packard	Polaroid
Kodak	

Foreign owned
Agfa	G	Olympus	J
Canon	J	RCA	FR
Casio	J	Ricoh	J
Epson	J	Sony	J
FujiFilm	J	Toshiba	J
JVC	J		

CAMERAS—FILM

Kodak's one-time-use cameras are still made in the USA.

American owned
Alphacam	Concord
Bantam	Kodak
Cambo	Linhof

Mega View		Princeton Instruments	
Photometrics		Quickcam	
Polaroid			

Foreign owned

Ansco	HK	Olympus	J
Canon	J	Panasonic	J
Chinon	J	Pentax	J
Fuji	J	Ricoh	J
Hasselblad	SWE	Samsung	K
Konica	J	Sharp	J
Kyocera	J	Sony	J
Leica	G	Vivitar	J
Minolta	J	Yashica	J
Nikon	J		

CAR STEREOS

American owned

Altec Lansing		Jensen	
Audiovox		Kraco	

Foreign owned

Aiwa	J	Kenwood	J
Alpine	J	Panasonic	J
Blaupunkt	G	Pioneer	J
Clarion	J	Premier	J
JVC	J	Sony	J

CELLULAR PHONES

American owned

AT&T		Motorola	
Audiovox		Prestige	
Bellsouth Mobility		Qualcomm	

Foreign owned

Clarion	J	Nokia	FIN
Ericsson	SWE	Samsung	K
Kenwood	J	Uniden	J
NEC	J		

COMPACT DiSC PLAYERS

American owned

Harman Kardon	Optimus
Kodak	

Foreign owned

Aiwa	J	Panasonic	J
Discman	J	Philips	N
Fisher	J	Pioneer	J
Goldstar	K	RCA	FR
JVC	J	Sharp	J
Kenwood	J	Sony	J
Magnavox	N	Teac	J
Marantz	J	Technics	J
Nakamichi	J	Yamaha	J
Onkyo	J		

COMPUTER PRINTERS

American owned

Apple	Laser Writer
Compaq	Lexmark
Hewlett-Packard	

Foreign owned

Brother	J	Minolta	J
Canon	J	Oki	J
Epson	J	Panasonic	J
Konica	J	Samsung	K
Microline	J		

COMPUTERS

American owned

Apple	Hewlett-Packard
Aptiva	IBM
Compaq	Macintosh
Dell	Micron
Gateway	

Foreign owned

Acer	TWN	Tempo	TWN
Sony	J	Toshiba	J
Tatung	TWN		

COPIERS

American owned

Lanier		Xerox	

Foreign owned

Canon	J	Rex Rotary	J
Konica	J	Savin	J
Minolta	J	Sharp	J

CORDLESS PHONES

American owned

AT&T	Lucent
Bell South	Motorola
Cobra	Nomad
Code-A-Phone	Radio Shack
Conair	Southwestern Bell
General Electric	

Foreign owned

Panasonic	J	Toshiba	J
PhoneMate	J	Uniden	J
Sanyo	J	VTech	HK
Sony	J		

DVD PLAYERS

American owned

General Electric

Foreign owned

Hitachi	J	RCA	FR
JVC	J	Samsung	J
Konka	CH	Sony	J
Panasonic	J	Toshiba	J
Philips	N	Yamaha	J
Pioneer	J	Zenith	K

FAX MACHINES

American owned

AT&T	Radio Shack
Hewlett-Packard	Smith Corona
IBM	Tandy
Lexmark	Xerox

Foreign owned

Brother	J	Okidata	J
Canon	J	Olivetti	ITL
Casio	J	Panasonic	J
Epson	J	Quasar	J
Kenwood	J	Samsung	K
Minolta	J	Savinfax	J
NEC	J	Sharp	J

HEADPHONES

American owned

Koss	Recoton
Radio Shack	

Foreign owned

Casio	J	Sony	J
Panasonic	J	Technics	J
Sennheiser	G		

MP3 PLAYERS

American owned

Compaq	Nike
Iomega Hip Zip	

Foreign owned

Creative	SNG	Samsung	K
Panasonic	J	Sony	J

PDAs

American owned

Compaq	Hewlett-Packard
Diamond	Palm
Handspring	Xircom

Foreign owned

Casio	J	Psion	UK
Kyocera	J	Sony	J

PERSONAL STEREOS

American owned

Alaron	Soundesign
Koss	

Foreign owned

Aiwa	J	Philco	N
Casio	J	Philips	N
JVC	J	RCA	FR
Kenwood	J	Sanyo	J
Magnavox	N	Sharp	J
Onkyo	J	Sony	J
Panasonic	J	Walkman	J

RECEIVERS

American owned

Bose Wave Radio	Optimus
Harman Kardon	

Foreign owned

Aiwa	J	Philips	N
Fisher	N	Pioneer	J
JVC	J	Sony	J
Kenwood	J	Teac	J
Marantz	J	Technics	J
Onkyo	J	Yamaha	J

RECORDABLE COMPACT DISCS

American owned

Memorex

Foreign owned

FujiFilm	J	Maxell	J
JVC	J	TDK	J

SCANNERS

American owned

Hewlett-Packard

Foreign owned

Acer	TWN	Epson	J
Agfa	G	Umax	TWN
Canon	J		

SPEAKERS

American owned

Advent	Infinity
Altec Lansing	JBL
AR (Acoustic Research)	Jensen
Audax	Klipsch
Belle Klipsch	La Scala
Bose	NHT
Boston Acoustics	Now Hear This
Cerwin-Vega	Phase Linear
Eosone	Polk
Harman Kardon	Polk Audio
Heresy II	Realistic

Foreign owned

Aiwa	J	Pioneer	J
Cambridge Soundworks	SNG	Sony	J
Fisher	J	Technics	J
JVC	J	Yamaha	J
Kenwood	J		

STEREO SYSTEMS

American owned

Bose Wave Radio	Jensen
Emerson	Koss
GE	Soundesign
General Electric	

Foreign owned

Aiwa	J	Samsung	K
Cambridge Soundworks	SNG	Sanyo	J
Hitachi	J	Sharp	J
JVC	J	Sony	J
Kenwood	J	Technics	J
Panasonic	J	Yamaha	J
Philips	N	Zenith	K
Pioneer	J		

TURNTABLES

American owned
No American brands could be located for this category.
Foreign owned

Aiwa	J	Sony	J
Fisher	N	Teac	J
Pioneer	J	Technics	J

TELEVISIONS

The United States imports almost all of its televisions, but if you visit your local Kmart store, you will find Curtis Mathes still makes their 27'' to 36'' models in the United States.

American owned

Alaron	RCA
Curtis Mathes	Radio Shack
Emerson	Realistic
GE	Sears
General Electric	Soundesign

Foreign owned

Aiwa	J	Pioneer	J
Audiocolor	TWN	Proscan	FR
Casio	J	Quasar	J
Daewoo	K	Samsung	K
Goldstar	K	Sansui	C
Hitachi	J	Sanyo	J
JVC	J	Sharp	J
Konka	CH	Sony	J
Magnavox	N	Sylvania	N
Marantz	J	Thomson	FR
Mitsubishi	J	Toshiba	J
Panasonic	J	Zenith	K
Philips	N		

VCRs

American owned

Admiral	JC Penney
Emerson	Radio Shack
General Electric	Sears
Go-Video	Soundesign

Foreign owned

Fisher	J	Quasar	J
Goldstar	K	RCA	FR
Hitachi	J	Samsung	K
JVC	J	Sanyo	J
Magnavox	N	Sharp	J
Marantz	J	Sony	J
Mitsubishi	J	Sylvania	N
Panasonic	J	Toshiba	J
Philips	N	Zenith	K

VIDEO GAMES

American owned

X-Box

Foreign owned

Nintendo	J	Sony	J
Sega	J		

VIDEO TAPES

American owned

Bell & Howell		Royale	
Kodak		Scotch	
Polaroid			

Foreign owned

BASF	G	RCA	FR
Fuji	J	Sony	J
Maxell	J	TDK	J

Chapter 9

Recreation

BARBECUE GRILLS

American owned

Barbecue King	Jenn-Air
Broilmaster	Kenmore
Char-Broil	Phoenix Grill
Coleman	Sentry
Ducane	Sunbeam
Fiesta	Weber
Grillmaster	

Foreign owned
No foreign brands could be located for this category.

BICYCLES

American owned

Cannondale	ProFlex
GT	Roadmaster
Huffy	Schwinn
K2 Roflex	Trek
Merlin	

Foreign owned

BMW	G	Murray	UK
Bridgestone	J	Peugot	FR
Featherweight	J	Shimano	J
Flame	J	Warrior	J
GTO	J		

BINOCULARS

American owned

Aerolite	Explorer
Audubon	Hawk
Bausch & Lomb	Insta Focus
Bell & Howell	Instafocus
Bobcat	Jaguar
Bushnell	Jason
Condor	Kestrel
Custom	Legacy
Eaglet	Marlin
Eddie Bauer	Micron
Egret	Nightstar
Elite	Plover
Ensign	Powerview

Satellite

Sea King

Sea Wolf

Simmons

Spectatros Series

Sportview

Swift

Tasco

Triple Zoom

Vanguard

Foreign owned

Canon	J
Leica	G
Minolta	J

Nikon	J
Olympus	J

BOATS

American owned

Arriva

Bayliner

Blue Fin

Boston Whaler

Four Winns

Hydra-Sports

Javelin

Lund

Maxum

Mercury Marine

Quantum

Robalo

Sea Ray

Sport Cruiser

Sport Fishing

Trophy

Wellcraft

Foreign owned

No foreign brands could be located for this category.

GAMES

American owned

5 Alive Card Game

Advanced Dungeons and Dragons

Aeon

Babble-On

Baha

Battle Box

Battleship

Bed Bugs

Bee Playing Cards

Bicycle Playing Cards

Big Ben

Bongo Kongo

Booloon Busters

Brass Eagle

Candy Land

Casino Cash

Chutes & Ladders

Clue

Colossus

Connect Four

Cootie

Crossfire

Croxley Puzzles

Deluxe Skip-Bo

Deluxe Uno

Don't Break the Ice

Dungeons & Dragons

First Games

Flip-It

Flipsiders

Frog Feast

Funglasses Card Game

Game of Life
Games Arcade
Girl Talk
Go To The Head Of The Class
Grabbin Grasshoppers
Guess Who?
Hacky Sack
Hands Down
Hearsay
Heroes In A Half Shell
Hoyle Playing Cards
Hungry Hippos
Hydrostrike
Jenga
Jumpin' Monkeys
Jurassic Park
Kem Playing Cards
Kerplunk
Let's Go Fishing
Liar's Maze
Lickin' Lizards
Life
Lite Brite
Luck Plus
Magic 8 Ball
Magna Doodle
Mastermind
Memory Match
Midway
Milton Bradley
Monopoly
Mouse Blaster
Mousetrap
My First Uno
Notebook Games
Odyssey
Operation
Optical Conclusions
Original Memory
Othello
Oxford Puzzels
Parcheesi
Parker Brothers
Password

Pictionary
Pocket Simon
Pokeno
Pressman
Professor Wiley
Rage
Risk
Rock'em Sock'em Crash Dummies
Rock'em Sock'em Robots
Rummikub
Rummy Rumble
Rummy-Up
Scattergories
Scrabble
Simon
Skip-Bo
Slam-A-Rama
Soap Opera Challenge
Sorry
Sounds Great
Springbok Puzzles
Sproing
Sting Card Game
Stratego
Streamer Tag
Stun Card Game
Tally-Ho
Thin Ice
Think Games
Top That
Topple
Toss Across
Tower of Doom
Trax
Tri Ominos
Trivial Pursuit
TSR
Twister
Uno
Uno Dice
Uno Dominos
Uno Rummy
Uno Stacuo
Uno Travel Game

Uno Wild Tiles		Wiggle N' Giggle	
Upwords		Williams Pinball	
Vegas Nite		Word Yahtzee	
Weapons & Warriors		World Of Darkness	
Whitman		Yahtzee	

Foreign owned

Game Boy	J	Sega	J
Madlibs	UK	Sega Genesis	J
Nintendo	J	Top Corner	C
Par Pool	C		

GENERAL RECREATION

American owned

Arctic Cat	Sterling Scooters
Jacuzzi	Sundance Hot Tubs

Foreign owned

Jet Ski	J

MUSICAL INSTRUMENTS

American owned

Baldwin	Leblanc
Bosendorfer Pianos	Sabian Cymbals
Boston Pianos	Steinway Pianos
Hamilton Pianos	Yanagisawa
Holton	Zildjian
Howard Pianos	

Foreign owned

Eterna Pianos	J	Yamaha	J
Silent Series	J		

SPORTS EQUIPMENT

American owned

A-2	Air Cel
AbuGarcia	Air Lite
Accutech	All Star
Acushnet	Ambassador Golf Clubs
Adams Golf	American Angler
Adirondack	AMF
Aerofloat	Arnold Palmer
Aerro Technology	Asics

Astro 2
Astro Star
Astrolane & Design
Austad's
Avanti
Axiom
Banzai
Barrecrafters
Bauer Sports
Bean's
Bell Helmets
Big Bertha
Bikextras
Black Beauty
Black Cat Irons
Black Diamond
Black Jacks
Black Pearl
Blackburn
Blue Chip
Blue Streak Fly Bait
Callaway Golf
Camaro
Cannondale
CB
CG 1800 Golf Clubs
Concept Fishing
Constellation
Coral
Coronet
Cotton Cordell Fishing Lures
Count Imperial
Creek Club Fishing Line
Crown II Fly Reel
D&D Golf Ball
DCI Golf Clubs
De Neve Skiwear
Dry-Ur-Fly
Duck-Pak
Duke
Edge Bowling Ball
Elite Fitness Products (York Barbell)
Elkhorn Camper
Executive Limited

Executive Putters
Fair Play Fishing Line
Finalist
Fireball
Fling
Fly Wate
Garuda
Giro
Gold Crown
Golden Dot Fishing Line
Golden Grip
Golden Ram Golf Clubs/Balls
Golden Scot Golf Clubs
Golden Tour
Golf Pride
Grand Slam
Greenriver
GRF-1000 Fly Rod
Groovies
GTO
Hannay Reels
Harvard
Heddon Fishing Lures
Hercules Fitness Products
Hotfingers Ski Gloves
Hot-z Golf Bags
Huffy Sports
Imperial
Indian
Invincible Fly Line
Jack Nicklaus
Jack Wolfskin
JanSport Backpacks
Jantzen Swimsuits
Jet Black
Jet Blaster
Jet Flow
Johnson
K2
K2 Skis and Snowboards
Katin Surf Apparel
King
King Cobra II Golf Clubs
Kombi

L/E Golf Clubs
Lady Cobra
Lake Placid Ice Skates
Lazy Ike Fishing Lines
Light Gear
Linear
Lolli-Pop
Louisville Slugger
Lustre King
Lynx Golf Clubs
MacGregor
Magna Top-Flite Golf Ball
Magneforce
Malone Skateboards
Marauder
Marigold
Mariner
Mark of a Pro
MCX Golf Clubs
Meteor
Mineralite
Mirage Kayak
Mister Twister
Mitchell Rods & Reels
Monarch
Morrow Snowboards
MT Tourney Golf Clubs
Muirfield Golf Clubs
Nancy Lopez
Nassau
New England Camp and Supply
NFL Guardian
Nicklaus
Nitro Golf Balls
No Balls No Glory
Nova
Olin Skis
One Up Golf Gloves
Orbital
Orvis
Pacer Roller Skates
Pacesetter
Pangaea Camping Gear
Panther Spotting Scopes

Peerless
Pennray
Penthouse Ski Wear
Performance Line
Perma-Tube Golf Bags
Pin Finder
Pin Life
Ping Golf
Pinnacle Distance
Pinnacle Equalizer
Planet Earth Skateboards
Playmaster Billiards
Portex
Powerbilt
Precision I Fly Rods
Premiere
Pro Custom
Pro Maker
Promark
Quantum
Queen
Raider
Rainmaker Paintball Guns
Rally Checkmate
Rally Pinto
Ram Golf
Range-Finder
Rascal
Rawlings
Red Wolf
Regal
Renaissance Billiards
Rhode Gear
Riddell
Ridgeway
Rimfly Fly Reel
Rogue
Roller Derby
Scamp
Scientific Anglers
Scooter
Score King
Scotty Cameron by Titleist
Scout Spotting Scope

Scubapro
Sea Strike
Senator
Shakespear Fishing Tackel
Sierra Designs
Silver Scot
Skate Attack
Smartee
Sof-T Athletic Socks
Soft Scot
Spiderline
Sportcraft
Sportsman
Sportsman Dream
Star Shield
Starfire
Stearns
Stiga
Striker
Subway
Super "G" Fishing Line
Super-Brite
Sweet Spot

Swift
Tear Drop Golf
The Working Ball
Tiger
Titleist
T-Line Golf Clubs
Tommy Armour Golf
Top Flite
Torino
Tour
Tour Hockey Skates
Triangle
Tri-Force
Triple Crown
Tuffy Fishing Rods
Voit
XI Archery
York Fitness Products
York USA
Zebco Fishing Equipment
Zebra Golf Clubs
Zeus Fishing Reels

Foreign owned

Altawand	J	
Altawand Golf Clubs	J	
Blade Runner Rollerblades	ITL	
Campeonato Shoes	J	
Canvas Classics	K	
Careca	J	
Cleveland Golf	FR	
Cooper	C	
Davis Cup	J	
Dynastar Alpine Skis	FR	
Elektra Racquetball & Racquet	AUS	
Elite Racquetball and Racquet (Head)	AUS	
Emeral Bay	K	
Grand Monarch	J	
Harry Day	AUS	
Head	AUS	
Hot Shot Tennis Raquet	AUS	
Lange Ski Boots	FR	
Los Andes Skis	J	
Macroblades In-Line Skates	ITL	
Maxfli	AUS	
Maximizer Golf Club	J	
Mitre Sports	UK	
Mizuno	THAI	
Mizuno Pro Golf Clubs	J	
Oxygen	FIN	
Penn Racquetballs	AUS	
Penn Tennis Balls	AUS	
President XD Golf Clubs	J	
Prince	ITL	
Pro Penn	AUS	
Pro-Guide Hunting Knives	FIN	
Pro-Max	J	
Proto Forged Ti Clubs	J	
Quest	AUS	
R-5 Skis	J	
R-7 Skis	J	
Raichle	AST	
Redline Racquet Strings	AUS	

Rollerblade	ITL	Taylor Made	G
Salomon	G	Tournament Racquetball	AUS
Seaquest	FR	Tretorn	SWE
Ski-Doo	C	Vanguard Golf Clubs	J
Slazenger	AUS	Wilson	FIN
St. Andrews	THAI	Yamaha	J
Swix	NOR	Zetra In-Line Skates	ITL

THEME PARKS

American owned

Adventure Island
Adventure Lands of America
American Adventures
America's Rollercoast
Canada's Wonderland
Cedar Point
Discovery Cove
Disneyland
Disneyworld
Dorney Park & Wildwater Kingdom
Knott's Berry Farm
Ocean's of Fun
Paramount's Great America
Paramount's Kings Dominion
Paramount's Kings Island
Real Thrills
Seaworld
Silver Dollar City
Six Flags Astroworld

Six Flags California
Six Flags Fiesta Texas
Six Flags Great Adventure
Six Flags Houston
Six Flags Hurricane Harbor
Six Flags Magic Mountain
Six Flags Over Georgia
Six Flags Over Texas
Six Flags St. Louis
Six Flags Water World
Six Flags Wild Safari Animal Park
Soak City
The Amazement Park
Valleyfair
Walt Disney World
Water Country U.S.A.
White Water
Worlds Of Fun

Foreign owned

Wet N' Wild	FR

TOYS

American owned

Aliens
Amanda Star
American Girls Collection
American West
Annette Himstedt
Aqua Blaster
Baby Check-Up
Baby Face

Baby Get Well
Baby Shivers
Baby Tenderlove
Babygund
Barbie
Batman
Betty Spagetty
Big Bruisers

Bitty Baby Collection
Bitty Bear
Bob The Builder
Bongo Kongo
Brass Eagle
Bubble Machine
Bubble Thing
Buddy L
Busy Beads
Cabbage Patch Kids
California Roller Baby
Caterpillar
Century
Chatty Cathy Doll
Chemtoy
Color 'N Recolor
Creator
Creepy Crawlers
Disney Classics
Duncan
Easybake Oven
Esquire–ichols
Etch-A-Sketch
Fashion Magic
Feather Touch
Fisher Price
Flair Dolls and Accessories
Flexible Flyer Snow Sleds
Floam
Frisbee
Fruit Snack Maker
G.I. Joe
Galoob
Great Adventures Playsets
Guild Jigsaw Puzzles
Gund Stuffed Animals
Hacky Sack
Hard Body
Heros
Hot Cycle
Hot Keys
Hot Wheels
Hula Hoop
Ideal Nursery Dolls

Imperial Yo-Yo
Jakks Pacific
Joe From Below
Johnny Quest
Joy Toy
Junkbots
Jurassic Park
Just Toys
Kenya Doll
Koosh Ball
Laser Challenge
Leapfrog
Let's Play Dolls
Lil Brutes
Li'l Miss Dress Up
Li'l Miss Make Up
Lionel Trains
Little People
Little Pretty Doll
Little Tikes
Little Women Journals Doll
Madame Alexander Collectible Dolls
Magic Bottle Baby
Magic Copier
Magic Maker
Magic Nursery Dolls
Magic Rocks
Magic Slate
Magna Doodle
Matchbox
Mattel
Mega Bump Foam
Merry Rider
Metal Molder
Mighty Mo's
Monsters, Inc.
Motorcity
Mr. Boggs
Mr. Bubbles
Mr. Potato Head
My First Buddys
Nerf
Newborn Baby Bubbles
Newborn Baby Checkup

Nickelodean

Oopsie Daisy Doll

P.J. Sparkles Doll

Penny From Heaven

Play By Play

Play-Doh

Playskool

Pocketools

Polly Pocket

Pound Puppies

Power Changers

Power Drivers

Power Mites

Power Wheels

Precious Metals

Pressman

Pride

Qunits Dolls

R/C Revolver

R/C TMH Psycho

Real Cookin' Food

Remco

Rescue Heroes

Roadmaster

Rub-A-Dub Doggie

Rubbermaid

Ruggie Bear

Sabrina

Sandberg

Sandi Dolls

See 'N Say

Sesame Street

Shop & Cook

Silly Putty

Sky Dancer Flying Doll

Slinky

Slip and Slide

Slip 'N Splash

SLM Snow Goods Sleds

Smud

Softina

Spear's Games

Speckled Smud

Spy Tech

Starting Lineup

Starwars

Steven

Sticker Fun

Stuffins

Super Blocks

Super Brutes

Talking Tina

Tangle Twist

The Little Mermaid

Tim Mee

Today's Kids

Tonka

Tootsietoy

Toybars

Trac-Ball

Twinkles

Tyco

Wham-O-Ring

Willy Water Bug

Wonder

Foreign owned

Amazing Amy	HK	Nano	HK
Belville	DEN	Playstation	J
Duplo	DEN	Primo	DEN
Fabuland	DEN	Slinky Pets	C
Franklin	C	Star Trek	HK
Hogwart's Castle	DEN	Teenage Mutant Ninja Turtle	HK
Kissy Kissy Baby	C	Toolo	DEN
Lego	DEN	VTech	HK
Lil Oopsie Daisy	C	Waterbabies	HK
Meccano	C		

TRADING CARDS

American owned

Donruss	Topps
Fleer	Upper Deck
Stadium Club	

Foreign owned

No foreign brands could be located for this category.

Chapter 10

Services

AUTO REPAIR CENTERS

American owned

Big O Tires
Discount Tire
Earl Scheib
Goodyear
Maaco
Midas

Monro Muffler/Brake
Precision Tune
Quick 10
Sears Auto Centers
Tuffy

Foreign owned

Car-X	C	Speedy	C
Firestone	J	Speedy Brake & Muffler	C
Meineke	UK	Speedy Muffler King	C

BANKS

American owned

American National Bank & Trust
American Savings Bank
AmSouth
Atlantic Savings
Banc One
Banc One Wisconsin
Banco Popular
BancWest
Bank of America
Bank of Boston
Bank of Canton (Ga.)
Bank of Commerce
Bank of Hawaii
Bank of Lake County
Bank of New York
Bank of North Dakota
Bank of Smithtown
Bank of The Hudson
Bank of The West
Bank of Tidewater
Bank Plus
BankAmerica
Brookline Savings
California Federal
Capital Banks
Carolina First
Century South

Chase Manhattan
Citibank
Citizens Commercial
Citrus Bank
Civitas
Colonial
Comerica
Crestar
Dime Savings
Eastern Heights
Eastland National
Farmer's Bank & Trust
Farmers State Bank
Fidelity Federal
Fifth Third
First American
First Arizona Savings
First Chicago NBD Bancorp
First Citizens
First Consumers National Bank
First Federal Savings
First Hawaiian
First Interstate
First Interstate Bank of California
First Interstate Bank of Oregon
First Interstate Bank of Washington
First Mariner Bank

First Midwest
First National Bank of St. Louis
First Northern Savings
First Security
First Tennessee
First Union
First Virginia
Firstar
Frost National Bank
Grossmont
Haywood
Hereford State
Hibernia National
Horizon
Household Bank
Hudson City Savings
Huntington
J.P. Morgan
Jefferson Savings
Lafayette American
Lakeview Savings
Landmark Bank
Langham Creek National
Lone Star
M&T
Marquette Bank
Mellon Bank
Merchants National
Metrobank
Mid-America
Morgan Guaranty Trust
Napa Valley
Nashville Bank of Commerce
National Bank of Alaska
National Bank of Arizona
National Bank of South Carolina
Nations Bank/Bank South
Nazareth National
Northern Trust
Northfield Savings
Old Kent
Pacific Century Bank

Park National
People's Bank & Trust
Peoples Heritage Savings
Pittsburgh National
PNC Bank
Prime Bancorp
Progress Bank
Provident
Providian
Reliance Federal Savings
Republic Bancorp
Republic Banking
Riggs
Roslyn Bancorp
Seafirst
Seattle-First
Security Bank & Trust
SierraWest
Society First Federal
Sothwest Bancorp
SouthTrust
Strongsville Savings
Suburban Savings
Summit
Sun Bank
SunTrust
Superior Federal
Swiss Avenue
Texas Bank
U.S. Bancorp
Union Planters
United Bankshares
United Southern
United States National
Valley National
Wachovia
Washington Federal Savings
Washington Mutual
Webster
Wells Fargo
WestAmerica

Foreign owned

Allfirst Bank & Trust	IRE	Citizens Bank	
ANR	AUS	of New Hampshire	UK
Asahi	J	Citizens Bank of Rhode Island	UK
Bancomer	MEX	Citizens Trust	UK
Bank Brussels Lambert	N	Commerzbank	G
Bank Hapoalim	ISR	Dauphin Deposit Bank and	
Bank of Bermuda	BMD	Trust Co.	IRE
Bank of China	CH	Dundee Bancorp	C
Bank of Montreal	C	First Maryland Bancorp	IRE
Bank of Pennsylvania	IRE	First Omni Bank	IRE
Bank of Pennsylvania	IRE	Harris Bank	C
Bank of Yokohama	J	LaSalle National	N
Barclays	UK	Manufacturers Bank	J
Canadian Western Bank	C	Sakura Bank	J
Centura Banks	C	Sumitomo	J
Century Bank	C	Tokai	J
Citizens Bank of Massachusetts	UK	Union Bank of California	J

INSURANCE

American owned

AAA	Avemco
Acceptance	Boston Mutual Life
Aetna	Central Mutual
Aflac	Central United Life
Alexander & Alexander	CIGNA
Alico	Citzens
All Nation	Connecticut General
Allied Group	Consolidated American
Allstate	Country Companies
American Centennial	Deerbrook
American Family	Empire
American Foundation Life	F & T Life
American General	Farm Bureau
American Hardware Mutual	Farmers & Traders Life
American Republic	Farmers Mutual
American Standard	First Allmerica
American United Life	First Colony Life
Americare	Franklin Life Insurance
Amerisure	Frontier
Ameritas	Glenbrook Life
Amica Mutual	Golden State Mutual
Auto-Owners	Graward General

Guardian Life
Hanover
Hanover Lloyds
Hartford
Homebiz
Horace Mann Educators
Horizon
Integrity Mutual
Kemper
Kentucky Home Life
Keyport
Keyport Life
Liberty Life
Lutheran Brotherhood
Massachusetts Bay
Massachusetts Mutual Life
Metropolitan Life
Midland Life
Modern Woodman of America
Mutual of Omaha
National Deposit Life
National Life
Nationwide
New England
New England Financial
New York Life
Norlen Life
Northbrook Life
Northwestern Mutual
Northwestern Mutual Life
Old American

Pacific Life Insurance
Pan-American Life
Partners in Progress
Peninsula
Pioneer Life
Presidential Life
Protective Life
Provident Mutual Life
Pyramid Life
RLI Corp.
SBLI
Scottsdale
Security Plus Life Insurance
Sentry
Shipmate
South Carolina
Southwestern Life
SunAmerica Life
Target Life
The Guardian
The New Hampshire
Travelers Life
United Insurance (UICI)
Universal
Unum
Utica National
Wausau
West Coast Life
Weyerhauser Co.
White Mountain
Woodmen Accident & Life

Foreign owned

Academy Life	N	National Liberty Life	N
Allfirst Life	IRE	People's Security Life	N
Ark Life	IRE	Royal Life	UK
Commonwealth Life	N	Safeguard	UK
Derbyshire Manx Bond	UK	Unigard	SWI
First Maryland Life Insurance	IRE	Universal Underwriters	SWI
Gerber Life	SWI	Veterans Life	N
Jackson National Life	UK	Zurich Life	SWI

HAIR CARE SALONS

American owned

Fantastic Sams	Mastercuts
Great Clips	Regis
Great Expectations	Supercuts
Haircrafters	Vidal Sassoon

Foreign owned
No foreign brands could be located for this category.

HOTELS

American owned

Adams Mark Hotel	Knights Inn
Amerihost Inn	La Quinta
AmeriSuites	Loews
Atlas	Mainstay Hotels
Aztar	Marriott
Baymount	Microtel
Best Western	Miraval
Clarion	Omni
Comfort Inn	Outrigger Hotels
Country Hearth Inn	Parker House Hotel
Country Inn	Quality Inn
Courtyard by Marriott	Radisson
Days Inn	Ramada Express
Daystops	Ramada Int'l Hotels & Resorts
Doubletree	Red Lion Hotels
Econo Lodge	Renaissance
Embassy Suites	Residence Inn by Marriott
ExecuStay	Rodeway
Fairfield Inn	Royal Orleans
Family Inns Of America	Sands Oceanfront Resorts
Forte Hotels	Sheraton
Four Points	Shoney's Inn
Hampton Inn	Sleep Inn
Harrah's	Spring Hill Suites
Hilton	Super 8
Homestead Village	The Ritz-Carlton Hotel
Homewood Suites	The Shoreham
Howard Johnson's	Tollman/Hundley
Hyatt	Town Place Suites
James K. Polk	Travelodge

Wellesley Inns

Westin

Wilson Inn

Foreign owned

Crowne Plaza	UK	Motel 6	FR
Fairmont Hotels	C	Orient-Express	BMD
Four Seasons	C	Red Roof Inn	FR
Holiday Inn	UK	Stamford Hotel & Restorts	SNG
Inter-Continental	UK	Studio 6	FR
Lansbury	UK	Travel Inns	UK
Meridien	UK		

Woodfield Suites

Wyndham Hotels

MAIL ORDER CLUBS

American owned

Arrow Book Club

Book-Of-The-Month Club

Carnival Book Club

Columbia House

Dolphin Books Club

Firefly Book Club

Fortune Book Club

Lucky Book Club

North Light Book Club

Scholastic Book Club

TAB Book Club

Trumpet Book Club

Foreign owned

Doubleday Book Club	G

MOVING COMPANIES

American owned

Global Van Lines

Interstate Van Lines

United Van Lines

Foreign owned

Allied Van Lines	UK

OIL CHANGE CENTERS

Shortly after Pennzoil and Quaker State merged in 2001, they sold out to Royal Dutch Shell, giving the Netherlands-based company control of most of the brands listed below.

American owned

Mobil

Texaco

Foreign owned

Jiffy Lube	N	Q Lube	N
McQuick's Oilube Inc.	N	Quick 10	N

RESTAURANTS

American owned

76 Auto/Truckstops
A & W
Abdow's Restaurants
Acapulco Mexican
Allies
American Bandstand Grill
American Café
Applebee's Neighborhood
  Grill & Bar
Arby's
Arthur Treachers
Atlas
Au Bon Pain
Aunt Sarah's Pancake House
Back Street Brewery
Bahama Breeze
Bakers Square
Barnie's Coffee & Tea Co.
Bavarian Pretzel Bakery
Benihana Grill
Bennigan's
Bertolini's
Bickford's
Big Apple Bagel
Big Boy
Big T
Bill Knapps
Bishop's Buffets
Bistro 110
Blackhawk Lodge
Blazing Hearth Grill
Blimpie Subs
Bob Evans
Bob's Big Boy
Bojangles
Bonanza
Boston Market
Bridgeman's
Bristol Bar & Grill
Brown's Chicken
Bruegger's Bagel Bakery

Buena Vista
Bugaboo Creek
Cadillac Bar & Grill
Café Braur
Café Chicago
Café Spaggia
California Pizza Kitchen
Canyon Café
Captain D's
Carlos Murphy's
Carl's Jr.
Carraba's
Carrows
Carvel Ice Cream
Casa Bonita
Casa Gallardo
Casa Lupita
Casa Ole
Charley Brown's
Charley Horse
Charley's Place
Charlie Brown's Steakhouse
Checkers
Cheese Cellar
Chef's Express
Chesapeake Bagel Bakery
Chi Chi's
Chick-Fil-A
Chili's Grill & Bar
Chop House
Chuck E. Cheese's
Church's
Cinnabon
Coco's
Colorado Steakhouse
Cooker Bar & Grill
CookieTree Cookies
Corner Bakery Café
Country Buffet
Country Kitchen
Country Market

Country Roadhouse Buffet & Grill
Cousin's Submarines
Cozymel's
Cracker Barrel Old Country Store
D.B. Kaplan's
D'Angelo Sandwich Shops
Darryl's
Dave & Busters
Del Taco
Denny's
Diary Queen/Brazier
Digital Java
Dixie House
Domino's
Don Pablo's Mexican Kitchen
Donatos Pizza
Dos Hermanos
Dunfey's Tavern
Eat N Park
Einstein Bros. Bagels
El Chico
El Pollo Loco
El Torito
Family Inns Of America
Famous Dave's
Fat Boys BBQ
Faxasak
Fazoli's
Fifth Quarter
Fred Gang's
Fred P. Ott
Fresh Choice
Friday's Front Row
Friendly's Restaurants
Frisch's
Fuddruckers
Furr's Cafeterias
Gallery Café
Garcia's Mexican
Garfield's Restaurant & Pub
Gloria Jean's Coffee
Godfather's Pizza
Golden Corral
Grady's American Grill

Grandy's
Granny's Buffets
Green Burrito
Grisanti's
Ground Round
H. Salt Seafood Galley
Hamburger Hamlet
Hardees
Helmsley
Hogate's
Holly's Bistros
Holly's By Golly
Holly's Landings
Hometown Buffet
Hooters
Hops
Hot Sam Pretzels
Houlihan's Old Place
Howard Johnson's
IHOP
Il Fornaio
Iron Skillet
Italianni's
J.B. Winberie
Jack Baker's Lobster Shanty
Jack in the Box
JB's Restaurants
Jerry's
Joe's Crab Shack
Karmelkorn Shoppes
Kenny Rogers Roasters
Kentucky Fried Chicken
Kettle Restaurants
Koo Koo Roo California Kitchen
Krispy Kreme
Krystal
La Salsa
Lamp Post Pizza
Landry's Seafood House
Lawry's
Le Peep
Lee's Famous Recipe Chicken
Lettuce Entertain You
Lily's/Cricket's

Little Caeser's
Little Mexico
Lobster Shanty
Logan's Roadhouse
Long John Silver's
Luby's Restaurants
Lucille's Country Dinner House
Lyons
Maggiano's Little Italy
Mamma Ilardo's
Manhattan Bagel Co.
Maui Tacos
Max & Ermas
McCormick & Schmick's Seafood
McDonalds
McGuffey's
Mesquite Beach
Miami Subs
Mom N Pop's Buffet & Bakery
Monterey's
Morrison's Cafeterias
Morrison's Fresh Cooking
Morton's of Chicago
Mr. Gatti's
Mr. Hero
Mrs. Field's
Mrs. Levy's Deli
Mrs. Winner's
Nathan's Famous
New World Coffee
Noble Roman's
Old Chicago
Old Country Buffet
Olive Garden
On The Border Café
Orange Julius
Original Roadhouse Grill
Outback Steakhouse
Owens Family Restaurants
Pancho's Buffet & Grill
Pancho's Mexican Buffet
Papa Gino's
Papa Vino's
Paragon Steakhouses

Pargo's
Parkers' Lighthouse
Pasta Central
Peet's Cofee & Tea
Pepperoni Grill
Perkins
Petitbon's American Grill & Bar
Phineas & Carnegies
Piccadilly Cafeterias
Pizza Hut
Pizza Inn
Pizza Parlor Sandwich
Pizzeria Uno
Pollo Tropical
Ponderosa Steakhouse
Popeye's
Poppies
Potowmack Landing
Pretzel Time
Pretzelmaker
Prime Sirlion
Pump Room
Quincy's
R.C. Cooper's
Ragazzis
Rainforest Café
Rally's
Ralph & Kacoo's
Rax
Red Lobster
Rehearsals Room
Rib Room
Ribsters
Rising Star Grill
Rock Bottom Restaurant & Brewery
Romano's Macaroni Grill
Rubio's
Ruby Tuesdays
Rusty Scupper
Ryan's Family Steakhouse
Sadie Buffets
Saint Louis Bread Co.
Sbarro
Seaport Café & Bar

Seattle Coffee Co.
Shells Seafood Restaurants
Shoney's
Sirloin Stockade
Sizzler
Skyline Chili
Smoothie Island
Sonic Drive-In
Sonny's Real Pit Bar-B-Q
Spageddies
Spageddies Italian Kitchen
Spires
Starbucks
Steak & Ale
Steak 'N Shake
Stuart Anderson's
Subway
Sushi Doraku
T.J. Cinnamon's
Taco Bell
Taco Bueno
Taco Cabana
Taco John's
Tahoe Joe's Famous Steakhouse
Tastee Freez
TCBY

Terry's Old Fashioned Donuts
TGI Friday's
The Aquarium
The Black-Eyed Pea
The Capital Grille
The Fireworks Factory
The Original Cookie Co.
Tia's Tex Mex
Tim Horton's Donuts
Timber Lodge Steakhouse
Tony Roma's
Tortuga's
Tropigrill
Victoria Station
Vie De France
Village Inn
Waffle House
Wendy's
Western Steer
Whataburger
White Castle
Willie G's
Willoughby's Coffe & Tea
Woody's
Wyatt Cafeterias
Zoo-Kini's Buffet

Foreign owned

Autogrill	ITL		Mister Donut	UK
B&Burger	FR		Mrs. Baird's	MEX
Baskin-Robbins	UK		Pasqual's	BG
Beefeater	UK		Peter Piper Pizza	J
Burger King	UK		Pizza Mart	C
Dunkin' Donuts	UK		Sky Chef	C
East Side Mario's	C		Skylark Gardens	J
Four-S	MEX		Steak & Burger	C
Haagen-Dazs	SWI		Swensen's	C
Hard Rock Café	UK		Swiss Chalet	C
Harvey's	C		Togo Sandwich Shops	UK
Java Coast	C		Upper Crust	UK
Kirin City	J		Winchell's Donut House	C
Manchu Wok	C			

Chapter 11

Appliances

AIR CONDITIONERS

American owned

Amana		Kenmore	
American Standard		Lennox	
Bryant		Mammoth	
Carrier		Nordyne	
Coleman Evcon		Nortek	
Comfortmaker		Payne	
Fedders		Philco	
Fraser-Johnston		Powermiser	
General Electric		Slant/Fin	
Gibson		Tappan	
Governair		Tempstar	
Heil		Temtrol	
Intertherm		Trane	
Johnson		Whirlpool	
Kelvinator		York	

Foreign owned

DeLonghi	ITL	Quasar	J
Frigidaire	SWE	Rheem	J
Goldstar	K	Ruud	J
LG	K	Sharp	J
Panasonic	J	White-Westinghouse	SWE

DEHUMIDIFIERS

American owned

Emerson		Kenmore
General Electric		Magic Chef
Kathabar		Whirlpool

Foreign owned

DeLonghi	ITL	Gibson	SWE
Frigidaire	SWE	White-Westinghouse	SWE

DISHWASHERS

American owned

Amana	Magic Chef
Estate	Maytag
General Electric	Talisman
In-Sink-Erator	Versatronic
Jenn-Air	Viking
Kenmore	Whirlpool
KitchenAid	

Foreign owned

Bosch	BRZ	Tappan	SWE
Fisher & Paykel	NZ	White-Westinghouse	SWE
Frigidaire	SWE		

HUMIDIFIERS

American owned

April-Aire	Lennox
Emerson	Sunbeam
Kaz	Toastmaster
Kenmore	

Foreign owned

No foreign brands could be located for this category.

MICROWAVE OVENS

Amana still makes microwave ovens in America.

American owned

Amana	Magic Chef
Emerson	Maytag
GE	Meal-In-One
General Electric	Menumaster
Hotpoint	Roper
JC Penney	Sandwich-Master
Jenn-Air	Spacemaker
Kenmore	Tupperwave
KitchenAid	Whirlpool
Litton	

Foreign owned

Brother	J	Samsung	K
DeLonghi	ITL	Sanyo	J
Goldstar	K	Sharp	J
LG	K	Tappan	SWE
Matsushita	J	Toshiba	J
Panasonic	J	White-Westinghouse	SWE
Quasar	J		

RANGE HOODS

American owned

Brogan	Nortek
Eclipse	Rangemaster
Nautilus	Silhouette

Foreign owned
No foreign brands could be located for this category.

RANGES/OVENS

American owned

Amana	Magic Chef
General Electric	Maytag
Hardwick	Recon
Hotpoint	Versatronic
Jenn-Air	Viking Range
Jetzone	Whirlpool
Kenmore	Wolf Range
KitchenAid	

Foreign owned

Frigidaire	SWE	RCA	FR
Garland	UK	Tappan	SWE
Gibson	SWE	U.S. Range	UK
Kelvinator	SWE	White-Westinghouse	SWE

REFRIGERATORS & FREEZERS

American owned

Admiral	Maytag
Amana	McCall
Estate	Norge
Foster	Revco
General Electric	Roper
Hotpoint	Talisman
Jenn-Air	Versatronic
Kenmore	Viking
KitchenAid	Whirlpool
Magic Chef	

Foreign owned

Frigidaire	SWE	Sanyo	J
Gibson	SWE	Tappan	SWE
Haier	CH	Welbilt	UK
Kelvinator	SWE	White-Westinghouse	SWE
RCA	FR	Zipel	K

SEWING MACHINES

American owned

Husqvarna Viking		Viking	

Foreign owned

Bernette	SWI	New Home	J
Durkopp	G	Singer	C

SMALL APPLIANCES

American owned

Acme Juicerator	Fry Baby
Admiral	Fry King
Aerohot	Frydaddy
Affordable Portable	Grindmaster
Aqua Sentinel	Hamilton Beach
Astro Popcorn Machine	Hot Spa
Bagel Perfect Toaster	In-Sink-Erator
Betty Crocker	Ironmaster
Black & Decker	Kaz
Black Angus	KitchenAid
Blendor	Kitcheneer
Braun	La Machine
Breadman	Little Pro
Bunn-O-Matic	Magic Hostess
Clairol	Mardi Gras
Conair	Mini Chill
Corner Bakery	Mirro
Crock-ette	Mixmaster
Crock-Grill	Monitor
Crock-Pot	Mr. Coffee
Cuisinart	Mr. Mustache
Deluxe Whiz Bang Popcorn Machine	National Presto
Dogeroo	Nesco
Econo-Pop Popcorn Machine	Oster
Evenmist Humidifier	Osterizer
Family Bakery Coffee Maker	Perfect Hair Care
Farberware	Perfection
Fiesta	Pinto Pop
Flavorcell Food Processor	Pitco Frialator
Flavor-Lock Coffee Makers	Pop-A-Lot
Flavormax Coffee Maker	Popcornnow
Flint	Popeil

Power Pierce
Presto
Proctor-Silex
Regal
Regal Ware
Republic
Rival
Saladshooter
Salton Hotray
Salton Maxim
Salvajor II
Scrap Master
Select Cut
Select Steam
Selectemp Curling Iron
Selectric Typewriter
Servalot
Shredmaster
Shred-O-Mat
Simer Pump
Simmer-Safe
Sinkmaster

Smith Corona Typewriters
Society & Design
Speed-Compounder
Spray Mist Irons
Stir Crazy
Sunbeam
Super Dogeroo
Thurmaduke
Toastmaster
Travl-Mates
Trough-Veyor
Vidal Sassoon
Viking
Vista
Wafflemaster
Waring
Waste King
Welch's Juicemakes
West Bend
Whirlaway
Whiz Bang

Foreign owned

Brother Typewriters	J	Pop-Down	UK
DeLonghi	ITL	Rowenta	FR
Frymasters	UK	Sanyo	J
Hitachi	J	Savory	UK
Krups	FR	Tefal	FR
Melitta	G	T-Fal	FR
Morphy Richards	IRE	The Boss Cordless Hand Vac	SWE
Nespresso	SWI	Vulcan	AUS
Olivetti Typewriters	ITL	Welbilt	UK
Panasonic	J		

STEAM IRONS

American owned

Black & Decker
Braun
General Electric
Kenmore
Oster

Proctor-Silex
Remington
Salton
Sunbeam
Toastmaster

Foreign owned

Krups	G	Singer	C
Norelco	N	Tefal	FR
Panasonic	J	T-Fal	FR
Philips	N	White Westinghouse	SWE
Rowenta	FR		

TOASTER OVENS

American owned

Black & Decker	KitchenAid
Hamilton Beach	Proctor-Silex
Kenmore	Toastmaster

Foreign owned

DeLonghi	ITL	Panasonic	J

TOASTERS

American owned

Betty Crocker	KitchenAid
Black & Decker	Oster
Cuisinart	Proctor-Silex
Farberware	Rival
General Electric	Salton
Hamilton Beach	Sunbeam
Kenmore	Toastmaster

Foreign owned

DeLonghi	ITL	Savory	UK
Krups	G	T-Fal	FR
Philips	N	Welbilt	UK
Rowenta	FR		

VACUUM CLEANERS

American owned

Bissell	Kirby
Dirt Devil	Majestic
Douglas	Oreck
Dustbuster	Princess
Empress	Rainbow
Filter Queen	Readivac
Futura	Royal
Generation 3	Steamvac
Hoover	Tempo
Kenmore	Vista

Foreign owned

Adspray	DEN	Mighty Mite	SWE
Advac	DEN	Nilfisk	DEN
Aquaclean	DEN	Panasonic	J
Arid Foam	DEN	Regina	N
Electrolux	SWE	Samsung	K
Eureka	SWE	Sanyo	J
Fantom	C	Sharp	J
Goblin	IRE	Singer	C
Jetvac	N	Tiger	G
Kobold	G	White-Westinghouse	SWE
Matador	DEN		

WASHERS & DRYERS

American owned

Admiral	Maytag
Amana	Norge
Estate	Roper
GE	Sears
General Electric	Speed Queen
Hotpoint	Talisman
Kenmore	Versatronic
KitchenAid	Whirlpool
Magic Chef	

Foreign owned

Bosch	G	Frigidaire	SWE
Fisher & Paykel	NZ	White-Westinghouse	SWE

WATER HEATERS

American owned

Bradford White	Maytag
Burkay	Micro Mix
Constantemp	Permaglas
General Electric	Whirlpool
Glascote	

Foreign owned

Andrews	UK	Range	UK
Craftmaster	AUS	Redring	UK
Marathon	J	Rheem	J
Mor-Floamerican	AUS	Richmond	J
Polaris	AUS	Ruud	J
Powermax	UK	Santon	UK

WET/DRY VACS

American owned

Ridgid

Sears Craftsman

Foreign owned

Genie   J

Shop Vac

Stinger

Chapter 12

Beverages

BOTTLED WATER

Since U.S.-owned AquaPenn Spring Water Co. agreed to be acquired by French-owned Dannon in 1998, bottled water brands Great American and Pure American are now owned by the French.

American owned

Alaskan Falls	Mountain Valley Water
Aquafina	Natural Springs
Dasani	Naya
Deer Park	Purely Pacific
Diamond Water	Saratoga Springs
Glacier Springs Water	Silver Glacier
Krank2O	Silver Rock
La Croix	Vermont Pure Natural Spring
Manhattan	

Foreign owned

Adelbonder	UK	Labrador	FR
Alhambra	FR	Lanjaron	FR
Apollinaris	G	Lindoya	SWI
AquaPenn	FR	Minere	SWI
Arrowhead	SWI	Mont Dore	FR
Ashborne	SWI	Montclair	SWI
Baraka	SWI	Neptune	J
Blaue Quellen	SWI	Oasis	SWI
Calistoga	SWI	Ozarka	SWI
Canada Dry	UK	Penafiel	UK
Cascade	J	Perrier	SWI
Castle Rock	FR	Petropolis	SWI
Clearly Canadian	C	Poland Spring	SWI
Crystal Spring	FR	Pure American	FR
Dannon	FR	Rainbow Water	J
Eads	J	Rock Spring	BG
Evian	FR	San Bernardo	SWI
Five Springs	J	Sao Lourenco	SWI
Font Vella	FR	Schweppes	UK
Great American	FR	Sierra	J
Great Bear	SWI	Silver Springs	J
Hayat	TUR	Sparkletts	FR
Hickory Springs	J	Suntory	J
Hinckley & Schmitt	J	Vera	SWI
Ice Mountain	SWI	Volvic	SWI
Kerryspring	IRE	Zephyrhills	SWI

COCOA

American owned

Chipits	Swiss Miss
Hershey's	Taste of the Alps
Kayo	

Foreign owned

Carnation	SWI	Royal Dutch	BG
Rowntree's	SWI		

COFFEE

American owned

Bonus Blend	Marcilla
Brim	Mauna Kea
Cain's	Maxim
CDM	Maxwell
Chase & Sanborn	Maxwell House
Chock Full O' Nuts	McCarvey
Diedrich	Mellow Roast
Douwe Egberts	Meridian
Finley	Merrild
Flavorsum	Metropolitan
Folgers	Millstone
Friele	Nabob
General Foods International	Onco
Georgia Coffee	Park Avenue
Gevalia	Park Regency
Grand Mere	Postum
Greenwich Mills	Red Label
Hag	Royal Kona
Harris	RT
High Point	Saimaza
Hillside	Sanka
Ireland	Starbucks
Jacobs	Superior Benchmark
Jacques Vabre	Superior Cafe Royal
JFG	Superior Sucaf
Kanis & Gunnick	Superior World's Finest
Keystone	Vendor's Select
Laurentis	Wechsler
Luzianne	Winslow's Gourmet
Maison Du Café	Yuban

Foreign owned

Alta Rica	SWI	Melitta	G
Birdy	J	MJB	SWI
Bokar	G	Mr. Automatic	UK
Bonjour	SWI	Nescafe	SWI
Brown Gold	UK	Nescore	SWI
Café Do Brasil	J	Nespresso	SWI
Café Oquendo	UK	Perfect Balance	SWI
Café Ristretto	SWI	Red Circle	G
Caro	SWI	Rombouts	UK
Eight O'Clock	G	Sark's Supreme	SWI
Hills Bros.	SWI	Savarin	UK
Jack	J	Sunrise	SWI
Martinson	UK	Taster's Choice	SWI
Master Choice	G		

GENERAL BEVERAGES

The Dr. Pepper/7-Up Co. was acquired by Britain's Cadbury Schweppes in 1995. Since then, the acquisitive company has bought RC Cola and the Snapple Iced Tea brand.

American owned

All Sport	Country Time
American Dry	Crystal Bay
Americola	Crystal Light
Apple Slice	Dad's Root Beer
Arctic Blast	Del Monte
Aunt Wick's Root Beer	Diet Citra
Awake	Double-Cola
Aylmer	Double-Dry
Barq's Root Beer	Dr. McGillicuddy's
Brights	Dr. Wells
Bubble-Up	Everfresh
Buffalo Rock	Farleys Hard Cider
Capri Sun	Faygo
Carrotonic	Frappuccino
Choco-Cream	Frappuccino Coffee Drink
Choco-Riffic	Fresca
Coca-Cola	Frost Drink Mix
Cool & Fruity	Frostie Root Beer
Cool N Fresh	Fruitopia
Copperhead Cider	Gatorade

Gatorlode
Gaymers Old English Cider
Grape King Grape Juice
Grapette
Grapico
Green Spot
Hansen's Natural Sodas
Hansen's Super Smoothie
Hawaii's Own
Herbal Aloe
Herbalife Weight Control Drink
   Mixes
Hershey's Chocolate Drink Box
Hi-C
Hires Root Beer (Proctor & Gamble)
Jake's Diet Cola
Jolly Good
Jolt Cola
Jumbo
Kayo Hot Chocolate
Kickapoo Soft Drink
Kool-Aid
Lady Carolyn
Lion Brewery Root Beer
Mason's
Mello Yello
Minute Maid
Mountain Dew
Mountain Dew Sport
Moxie Soft Drink
Mr. Pibb
Mug Crème
Mug Root Beer
Nesbitt's
Nugrape
Ocean Spray
Old New England Egg Nog
Orange Driver
Orchard Park
Overbrook Egg Nog
Party Club

Pepsi
Pepsi Max
Pepsi One
Pepsi-Cola
Pepsi-Free
Planet Java
Polar
Postum
Powerade
Powerized Louisville Slugger
Punch-N-Fruity
Quench
Robert Corr
Rooty Fruity
Royal Crown Cola
Saranac Root Beer
Sharon Corr
Shasta
Sioux City
Sioux-Mox
Ski
Slice
SoBe
Sprite
Sun Crest
Sun-Drop
Surge
Sweet Celebration
Tab
Tang
Teem
Thirst Quench'r
Toddynho
Upper 10
Vitamite
Welchade
Welch's
West Soy
White House
White Rock
XTC Energy Drink

Foreign owned

10-K Sports Drink	J	Nescao	SWI
7 Up	UK	Nescau	SWI
A & W	UK	Nesquick	SWI
ACM	SWI	Nestea	SWI
Ades	UKN	Nestle Quick	SWI
Agruma	FR	One A Night	J
Alpro	G	One-Cal	UK
Aperio Sports Drink	J	Orange Crush	UK
Athlon	FR	Orangina	UK
Banania	UKN	Orchard	SWI
Berry Springs	ITL	Oronamin-C Drink	J
Blendy Coffee Drink	J	Ovaltine	SWI
Canada Dry	UK	Ovoline	SWI
Carnation	SWI	Pilkil	J
Chocolate Cow	UK	Poky	MEX
Crush	UK	RC Cola	UK
Daily's Fruit Juices	N	RC Edge	UK
Diet Rite	UK	Radical Blast	UK
Dr. Koch	G	Rose's	UK
Dr. Pepper	UK	Rush	ITL
Eckes	G	Sandhurst Farms	ITL
Florida Citrus Orange Juice	BG	Schweppes	UK
Fruco	UKN	Seagram's	FR
Frutsi	MEX	Shandy Bass	UK
Gala	ARG	Slim-Fast	UK
Gini	UK	Slurpee	J
Hawaiian Punch	UK	Snapple	UK
Hires Root Beer (Schweppes)	UK	So Fruity	ITL
I.B.C. Crème Soda	UK	So Juicy	ITL
I.B.C. Root Beer	UK	Solo	UK
Ice Break	ITL	Sportplus	UK
Icebreaker Canned Ice Coffee	SWI	Squirt	UK
Janeiro Fruit Drink	FR	Star	POR
Jero Drink Mixes	UK	Stewart's	UK
Koko Blanco	UK	Sundrop	UK
Lady's Choice	UKN	Sunkist	UK
Lipton Iced Tea	UKN	Sweet Success	SWI
Mauna La'i	UK	Tahitian Treat	UK
Milo Chocolate Drink	SWI	Tarino	UK
Mistic	UK	Vernor's	UK
Mocha Cooler	SWI	Vitasoy	HK
Nehi	UK	Wink	UK
Nescafe Iced Coffee	SWI	Yoo-Hoo	FR

JUICE

American owned

Adams
After The fall
Apple Dandy
Ardmore Farms
Birds Eye
Bluebird
Campbell's
Capri Sun
Chiquita
Citrus Hill
Coastal Breezes
Dole
Donald Duck
Everfresh
Five Alive
Flav-R-Pac
Florida Gold
Florida's Natural
Fresh Juice
Fresh Samantha
Fruitland
Fruitopia
Gentle Juice
Green Spot
Healthy Start
Hi-C
Home Juice
Hygeia
Jjust Jjuicy
Juice-Ups
Knudsen
Lake Niagra
Lamb-Weston
Lincoln
Martins
Meiers Non-Alcholic Sparkling Grape
Minute Maid
Mr. Juice
Mr. Pure
Nature's Own
Northland
Ocean Spray
Odwalla
Old South
Party Treat
Realemon
Realime
Refreshers
Sabra
Sacramento Tomato Juice
Santa Cruz Organic
Schwan's
Seneca
ShopRite
Simply Fruit
Simply Nutritious
Speas Farm
Squeezit
Squeezit 100
Sunchee
Sun-Flo
Sunkist
Sunny Delight
Sunsweet
Sun-Vi
Tangy
Texsun
Tree Ripe
Tree Sweet
Tree Top
Treefresh
Tropical Squeeze
Tropicana
Twister
V-8
V-8 Splash
Veryfine
Welch's
White House
Winter Hill

Foreign owned

2nd Foods	SWI	Mott's	UK
Agruma	FR	Natura	SWI
Beatrice	ITL	Pam-Pam	FR
Calistoga	SWI	Pampryl	FR
Cepita	ARG	Paw Paw	J
Clamato	UK	Picnic	C
Florida Citrus	BG	Presta Light	G
Frutsi	MEX	Raison Cider	FR
Hawaiian Punch	UK	Real	UK
Indian Summer	J	Rose's	G
Juicy Juice	SWI	Shloer	UK
Junior Juice	C	Squeeze Six	C
Just Juice	UK	Tender Harvest	SWI
Kern's	SWI	Valle	MEX
Kist	UKN	Vita	HK
La Cidraie Cider	FR	Vita Gold	C
McCain	C	Zip	PHI
Merrydown Cider	UK		

MILK

American owned

Alta-Dena	Maplehurst
Barber	Mayfield
Bell	McArthur
Berkeley	Meadow Gold
Borden	Milnot
Bowman	Pevely
Bridgeman	Prairie Farms
Creamland	Price's
Fieldcrest	Purity
Friendship	Reiter's
Gandy's	Sani-Dairy
Goldenrod	Sealtest
H. Meyer	Silk Soy Milk
Hart's	Suncoast
Hillside	T.G. Lee
Hygeia	Verifine
Lite-Line	Wingut's

Foreign owned

Abbotts	BG	Parmalat	ITL
Bay City	ITL	Pauls	ITL
Beatrice	ITL	Pensupreme	N
Big M	ITL	Piknik	J
Curtis Farm	ITL	Quebon	C
Dairy Wise	ITL	Riviera	ITL
Froth Top	ITL	Sandhurst Farms	ITL
Johanna	BG	Shayks	ITL
Lactaid	ITL	SkimPlus	ITL
Lactania	BG	Trim	ITL
Lancashire Dairies	UK	Trim & Terrific	ITL
Lehigh	BG	Unigate	UK
Morinaga	J	Vita Plus	ITL

TEA

American owned

AC	Ireland
Arizona	Laci Lebean
Banquet	Luzianne
Celestial Seasonings	Pickwick
Douwe Egberts	R.C. Bigelow
Fruitopia	Red Rose
Greenwich Mills	Tea House
Harris	Tender Leaf

Foreign owned

Jamy	J	Ryokucha	J
Kirin Lemon	J	Snapple	UK
Lipton	UKN	Tetley	UK
Nestea	SWI	Twinings	UK
Our Own	G	Vita	HK
Royal Estates	UKN		

Chapter 13

Alcohol & Tobacco

ALE

American owned

Balantine
Blue Moon Belgian White
Croft
Dempsey's
Genesee
Henry Weinhard's
Little Kings
McSorley's
Pacific Ridge Pale

Pickwick
Point Pale
Redhook Blond
Redhook Hefe-Weizen
Redhook India Pale Ale
Redhook Nut Brown Ale
Redhook Rye
Samuel Adams

Foreign owned

Allbright	BG	Melbourne Bitter	AUS
Barbican	BG	Newcastle	UK
Bass	BG	North Eastern	BG
Beamish	AUS	Redback Bitter	AUS
Boddington's	BG	Smithwick's Ale	UK
Chiswick Bitter	UK	Stella Artois	BG
Courage	AUS	Tennants	BG
Golden Pride	UK	Theakston	UK
Highgate Old Ale	BG	Toby	BG
John Courage	AUS	Victoria Bitter	AUS
John Smith's	UK	White Shield	BG
Kent Old Brown	AUS	Worthington	BG
Kronenbourg 1664	AUS	Younger's	UK
McEwan's	UK		

BEER

Since Phillip Morris has agreed to sell the Miller Brewing Co. to South African Breweries PLC, and it is unlikely that there will be significant regulatory opposition, I have listed all of the Miller brands as foreign owned.

American owned

Alpine
Amber Bock
American
Anheuser Marzen
Anheuser-Busch
Ausburger
Baderbrau
Balantine
Banks
Bartels

Bavarian Club
Beck's
Berghoff
Bert Grants Ales
Bicentennial
Birell
Blatz
Boh
Braumeister
Buckhorn

Bud Dry
Bud Ice
Bud Light
Budweiser
Burger
Busch
Busch Light
Busch NA
Caramel Porter
Carling
Carlsberg
Christian Moerlein
Colt 45
Coors
Corona
Coronita
Dixie
Dixie Basin Street Ale
Dixie Blackened Voodoo Lager
Dixie Jazz Amber Light
Double Diamond
Esslinger Premium
Falstaff
Foster's
Genesee
Genny Ice
Genny Spring Bock
Gibbons
Goebel
Goetz Pale
Grain Belt
Griesedieck
Haffenreffer
Hamm's
Hanley
Henry Weinhard
Hi-Brau
Holiday
Honey Amber
Huber
Hudepohl
Hudy Bold
Hudy Delight
I.C. Golden Lager

I.C. Light
Iron City
Jacob Best
Jacob's Best
Jax
Jed's Hard Lemondade
JW Dundee's
Keystone
King Cobra
Koch's Golden Anniversary
Krueger
Landmark
Leinenkugel's
Liebotschoner
Lionshead
Lone Star
Lowenbrau
Lucky Draft
Meister Brau
Michelob
Michelob Dry
Michelob Light
Modelo Especial
Molson
Mustang
Natural Light
Natural Light Ice
Northstone
O'Doul's
Old Chicago
Old Dutch
Old German
Old Milwaukee
Old Milwaukee Red
Old Style
Olympia
Olympia Gold
Pabst
Pabst Blue Ribbon
Pabst Genuine Draft
Pacifico
Pale Ale
Pearl
Pearl Light

Pearl Premium
Pickwick
Piels
Pig's Eye
Pocono Lager
Pocono Pilsner
Pocono Raspberry
Point Amber Classic
Point Bock
Point Maple Wheat
Point Special
R.J.'s Ginseng
Rainier
Red Bull
Red Wolf
Regal
Regal Brau
Rhinelander

Samuel Adams
Saranac
Schaeffer
Schlitz
Schlitz Ice
Schmidt's
Southpaw
St. Ides
St. Pauli Girl
Stag
Steg Light
Stegmaier
Stegmaier 1857
Stroh's
Texas Pride
Utica Club
Winterfest
Wisconsin Club

Foreign owned

1664	FR	Dos Equis	BG
Aguila	N	Drafty Black	J
Alcazar	UK	Elders	AUS
Alexander Keith's	BG	Extra Old Stock	C
Amstel	N	Fischer	N
Amstel Light	N	Foster's Lager	AUS
Anchor	N	George Killian's	N
Ancre	N	Grolsch	N
Bitburger	G	Guinness	BG
Black	J	Harp Lager	UK
Black Label	AUS	Heineken	N
Black Stout Draft	J	Highgate Mild	BG
Brau	J	Hoegaarden	BG
Braugold	SWI	Hokkaido	J
Breaker Malt Lager	BG	Icehouse	SAF
Buckler	N	Imperial	POR
Calanda	N	John Courage	AUS
Carling O'Keefe	AUS	John Smith's	AUS
Carlton	AUS	Jubilee	BG
Cascade	AUS	Kaiser	BZL
Cristal	POR	Kanterbrau	FR
Cristal Alken	FR	Kestrel	UK
Crowl Lager	AUS	Kirin	J
Dave's	C	Kokanee	BG
Diebels Alt	G	Kronenbourg	FR

Kylian	N	Nastro Azzurro	FR
L & B DPA	BG	Nautic Light	POR
Labatt	BG	OB-Lager	BG
Labatt 5	BG	O'Keefe	AUS
Labatt's	BG	Olde English 800	SAF
Lamot	BG	Old Vienna	AUS
Larossa	BG	Onix	POR
Leffe	BG	Original Ale 6	J
Lingen's Blong	N	Pelforth Beer	N
Lite	SAF	Pelican	N
London Pride	UK	Puregold	J
Maes	FR	Red Dog	SAF
Mahou	FR	Resch's	AUS
Matilda Bay Bitter	AUS	Rickard's Red	C
Melbourne Bitter	AUS	Rolling Rock	BG
Mickey's Malt Liquor	SAF	Ruddles	AUS
Miller	SAF	Sagres	POR
Miller Genuine Draft	SAF	San Miguel	FR
Miller High Life	SAF	Sapporo	J
Miller Lite	SAF	Sapporo Draft	J
Miller Lite Ice	SAF	Sharp's	SAF
Miller Molson Ice	SAF	Shokunim	J
Miller Reserve	SAF	Sol	BG
Milwaukee's Best	SAF	Spiess	SWI
Molson Canadian	C	Stella Artois	BG
Molson Dry	C	Suntory Draft	J
Molson Export	C	Tennants	BG
Molson Golden	C	Topazio	POR
Molson Ice	C	Toronto's Own	C
Moosehead	BG	Victoria Bitter	AUS
Moretti	N	Worthington Dark Mild	BG
Moussy Non-Alcholic	BG	Yebisu	J
Murphy's Irish Stout	N	Younger's	UK
Mutzig	N		

BOURBON

American owned

Ancient Age	Country Club
Baker's	Eagle Rare 101 Proof
Barclay	Elijah Craig
Blanton's	Evan Williams
Booker's	Fighting Cock
Colonel Lee	Forester 1870

Hancock's Reserve
Heaven Hill
Henry McKenna
Jim Beam
Kentucky Gentleman
Knob Creek
Mohawk
Old Charter
Old Fitzgerald
Old Forester Kentucky
Old Grand-Dad

Old McCall
Old Taylor
Private Stock
Rebel Yell
Rock Hill Farms
Schwegmann's
Ten High
Tom Moore
Very Old Barton
W.L. Weller

Foreign owned
No foreign brands could be located for this category.

BOURBON WHISKEY

American owned

Jim Beam
Kentucky's Tavern
Old Crow

Old Grand-Dad
Woodford Reserve

Foreign owned

Wild Turkey	FR

BRANDY

American owned

Allen's
Blansac
Boston 5 Star Brandy
Captain Applejack
Christian Brothers
Deschaux
E. & J. Brandy
Inca-Pisco
Jacque Bonet

Jean Danflou
Jenkins
Korbell
Laird's
Laird's Applejack
Mohawk
Premium Canadian
St. Cyr
Straight Apple B-I-B

Foreign owned

Asbach Uralt	UK	Louis XIV	UK
Bols	UK	Macieira	FR
Chantre	G	Mariacron	G
Don Pedro	UK	Mercian Brandy X.O.	J
Dorville	FR	Metaxa	UK
Dreher	UK	Mouquin	FR
Eckes	G	Richelieu	UK
Hiram Walker	UK	Viceroy	UK

CANADIAN WHISKEY

American owned

Alberta Canadian	Lord Calvert
Black Velvet	Triple Crown
Corby's	Windsor
G.M. Tiddy's	

Foreign owned

Crown Royal	FR	VO	FR
Rich & Rare	UK	Wiser's	UK

CHAMPAGNE

American owned

Andre	Jacquert
Ballatore	Korbell
Chateau Chardon	Louis Roederer
Chateaulet	Pol Roger
Cook's American	Stanford
Eden Roc	Tott's
Henri Marchant	

Foreign owned

Canard-Duchene	FR	Mercier	FR
Dom Perignon	UK	Moet And Chandon	FR
Dom Ruinart	UK	Piper Heidsieck	FR
Laurent Perrier	UK	Rozes	FR

CHEWING TOBACCO

American owned

Apple Jack	Moore's Red Leaf
Big Kick	Old Taylor
Black Maria	Peach
Cannon Ball	Peachy
Chattanooga	Rail Road Mills
Conwood	Rainbow
Copenhagen	Red Coon
Country Blend	Red Fox
Kentucky King	Red Rose
Kodiak	Red Seal
Lancaster	Rose Bud
Levi Garrett	Rough Country
Lieberman's	Seal
Mail Pouch	Silver Creek

Skoal

Taylor's Pride

Union Workman

Warren County

WB Cut

Wild Cat

Winter's Clippings

Yankee Girl

Foreign owned

No foreign brands could be located for this category.

CIGARETTES

American owned

Alpine

American Spirit

Basic

Bristol

Bucks

Cambridge

Camel

Cartier

Century

Chesterfield

Dave's

Derby

Doral

English Ovals

Eve

Fortune

Galaxy

Harley-Davidson

Heritage

Kent

L&M

Lark

Lider

Magna

Marlboro

Maverick

Max

Merit

Mistura Fina

Newport

Now

Old Gold

Parliament

Peter Jackson

Philip Morris

Players

Price/Value Brand

Pyramid

Raffles

Salem

Saratoga 120's

Satin

Spring

Spring Lemon Lights

Sterling

Style

Superslims

Taste of America

Triumph

True

Vantage

Virginia Slims

Winston

Foreign owned

Amadis	J	Belair	UK
American Lights	UK	Belomor	J
Arsenal	J	Benington	J
Aspen	J	Benson & Hedges	UK
Barclay	UK	Berkeley	UK
Bars	J	Brooklyn	SP

Cabin	J	Misty	UK
Capri	UK	Montclair	UK
Carlton	UK	More	J
Carrolls	UK	Otamah	UK
Caster	J	Pall Mall	UK
Colt	J	Parisienne	UK
Craven "A"	UK	Peace	J
Cresent	J	Peter Stuyvesant	UK
Crown's Of London	UK	Plaza	UK
Davidoff	G	Prime	UK
Dickens & Grant	J	Private Stock	UK
Dorchester	J	Raleigh	UK
Ducados	SP	Richland	UK
Dumaurier	UK	Richmond	UK
Dunhill	UK	Rothmans	UK
Embassy	UK	Royale	SP
Fotuna	SP	Silk Cut	UK
Freeman's No. 1	J	Silva Tall	UK
GPC	UK	Silva Thins	UK
Hollywood	UK	Sobranie	UK
Jan III Sobieski	UK	Sopianae	UK
John Player	UK	Sovereign	UK
Kool	UK	Special 10's	UK
Kozak	UK	St. Michel	J
Krone	UK	State Express 555	UK
Kurmark	UK	Summit	UK
Lucky Strike	UK	Tareyton	UK
MacDonald Select	J	Viceroy	UK
Matinee	UK	Vogue	UK
Mayfair	UK	Winfield	UK
Mild Seven	J	Yves Saint Laurent	J

CIGARS

American owned

Bering	Optimo
Don Thomas	Santa Fe
El Trellis	Swisher
King Edward	Swisher Sweets

Foreign owned

1886	SP	Ben Franklin	SP
Antonio Y Cleopatra	SP	Cabanas	SP
Backwoods Smokes	SP	Canaria D'Oro	SWE
Bances	SWE	Captain Black	UK

Cararia D'oro	SWE	Mexican Bundles	SP
Carl Upmann	UK	Montecristo	SP
Cohiba	SP	Montecruz	UK
Corps Diplomatique	UK	Muriels	SP
Cruzeros	SP	Onyx	UK
Don Diego	SP	Out West	SP
Don Miguel	SP	Panama	UK
Dunhill	UK	Partagas	SWE
Dutch Masters	SP	Playboy By Don Diego	SP
Dutch Treats	SP	Pleiades	SP
El Dorado	SP	Por Larranaga	SP
El Producto	SP	Primo Del Rey	SP
Flamenco	SP	Punch	SWE
Flor De Copan	SP	Ramon Allones	SWE
Garcia Y Vega	SWE	Reinitas	SP
Gauloises	SP	Riata	SP
George Burns Vintage	SP	Robt. Burns	SWE
Gitanis	SP	Romeo and Juliet	SP
H. Upmann	SP	Romeo y Julieta	SP
Hamlet	UK	Royal Jamaica	UK
Harvesters	SP	Rustlers	SP
Havanitos	SP	Santa Damiana	SP
Headlines	SP	Schimmelpenninck	UK
Henri Winterman's	UK	Shakespeare	SWE
Henry Clay	SP	Super Value	SP
Hoyo De Monterrey	SWE	Supre Sweets	SP
La Coronas	SP	Te Amo Cigars	SP
Laflorde Cano	SWE	Temple Hall	SWE
Las Cabrillas	SP	Tijuana Smalls	SWE
Longchamps	SP	Tiparillo	SWE
Macanudo	SWE	Tresado	UK
Masters Collection	SP	White Owl	SWE
Matacan Bundles	SP	Wm. Penn	SWE
Medal of Honor	UK		

COGNAC

American owned

Albert Robin		Gautier	
Ansac		Normandin	
Basilica			

Foreign owned

Hine	FR	Salignac	UK
Martell	FR	XO	UK

GENERAL TOBACCO

American owned

B.G.	Happy Jim
Barking Dog	Mammoth Cave (smokeless)
Bighorn	Mapleton
Bond Street	Old Joe
Borkum Riff	R.T. Junior
Cotton Boll	Revelation
Douwe Egberts	Samson's Big 4
Field & Stream	Yellow Tag
Happy Days	

Foreign owned

Amber Leaf	UK	House of Lords	UK
Black Knight	UK	John Henry	UK
Blend Eleven	UK	John Rolfe	UK
Demarks's	SP	Kite	UK
Don Pablo	UK	Red Juice	UK
Dunhill	UK	Rum & Maple	UK
Edgeworth	UK	Sir Walter Raleigh	UK
Gold Block	UK	Smoker's Pride	UK
Golden Virginia	UK	St. Bruno	UK
Hayward	UK	Three Nuns	UK
Heine's Blend	SP	Three Star	SP

GIN

American owned

Bankers Club Blend	Kimnoff
Barclay	Laird's
Barton	London Tower
Boston	Majorstea
Caldwell's	Mohawk
Carnaby's	Monogram Blend
Chatham	Nikolai
Cossack	Pikeman Gin
Crystal Place	Rainbow
Five O'Clock	Ruble
Fleischmann's	Schwegmann's
Glenmore	Senators Club
Heaven Hill	Skol
Jenkins	Taaka
Kassers '51' Blend	

Foreign owned

Beefeater	UK	Ginebra San Miguel	PHI
Black Jack	FR	Gordon's	UK
Bombay	BMD	Huntly & Gunn	UK
Boodles British Gin	FR	Johnnie Walker	UK
Booth's	UK	Seagram's	FR
Chelsea	UK	Seagram's Extra Dry	FR
Dewar's	BMD	Somers	FR
Gilbey's London Dry	UK	Tanqueray	UK

LIGHTERS

American owned

Casco	Zippo
Contempo	

Foreign owned

Bic	FR

LIQUOR

American owned

A. Hardy	Du Bouchett Cordial
After Shock	Fairview Liquer
After Shock Cordial	Fireball Liquer
Age Preferred	G.M. Tiddy's Liquer
Allen's Liqueur	Gold Crown
Amaretto Crème Di Amoure Liquer	Heather Cream Liquer
Amaretto De Sabrosa Liquer	Heather-Glo Liquer
Amaretto Di Loreto Liquer	Ice 101 Liquer
Amaretto Di Padrino Liquer	Jacquin
Arrow Cordials Mixers	Jenkins Liquer
Ashbourne Irish Cream	Kamora
Barton	Liquore Cordial
Basilica	Mazzetti Cordial
Basilica Amaretto Liquer	Melone Liquer
Basilica Liquer	Montebello
Boston Liquer	Noilly Prat
Casalini	O'Mara's Irish Cream Liquer
Casalini Liqueur	Paramount
Copa De Oro Liqueur	Peychaud's Bitter
Cynar Apertif	Poland Springs Liquer
Dekuyper Cordial	Praline Liqueur
Devonshire Crown	Rosita Liquer

Rosso Antico Aperitif
Sabrosa Liqueur
Sambuca Sarti Liqueur
San Francisco Cookies 'N Cream

Sante Gran Spumante
Tombolini Verdicchio
Tomintoul Liqueur
Tuaca Liquer

Foreign owned

Alaska	FR	Emmets Liquer	UK
Amaro Ramazotti Liquer	FR	Fior Di Vite Apertif	FR
Amarula	UK	Fratelli Oddero	UK
Ambassadeur Aperitif	FR	Galliano Liquer	FR
Americano 505 Aperitif	FR	Godiva Liquer	FR
Aperol Aperitif	ITL	Grand Marnier Liqueur	UK
B&B	BMD	Hiram Walker Liquer	UK
Bailey's	UK	Irish Mist Liqueur	UK
Bailey's Irish Cream	UK	Kahlua Liquer	UK
Baileys Liquer	UK	La Pommeraie Calvados	UK
Bartissol Apertif	FR	Licor 43 Liquer	UK
Benedictine Liquer	BMD	Midori	J
Berentzen Appel	UK	Mount Royal Light	FR
Bols	UK	Nassau Royale Liqueur	BMD
Bols Liquer	UK	Pisang Ambon Liquer	UK
Byrrh Apertif	FR	Romana Sambuca Liqueur	UK
Cederberg	UK	Rumple Minze Liquer	UK
Chiswick Bitter	UK	Sabra Liqueur	FR
Chivas Regal	FR	Sambuca Romana Liqueur	UK
Coloma Liqueur	J	Seagram's V.O.	FR
Courvoisier Liqueur	UK	Springfield Bitter	UK
Crown Royal	FR	Tia Maria Liquer	UK
Di Saronno Amaretto	UK	Zoco Apertif	FR
Eckes Liquer	G		

MALT LIQUOR

American owned

Coqui	Mickey's
Country Club	Red Bull
Elephant	Schlitz
King Cobra	Silver Thunder
Magnum	St. Ides

Foreign owned

Red Horse	PHI

PIPE TOBACCO

American owned

Argosy		Model	

Foreign owned

Captain Black	UK	Mellow Virginia	UK
China Black	SP	Mountain Leaf	UK
Clan	UK	Mountbatten	UK
Condor	UK	Pipe Mate	SP
Cookie Jar	UK	Troost	UK
Crown Achievement	UK	V I P	UK
Holiday	UK	Walnut Flake	UK
Medal of Honor	UK		

RUM

American owned

Barton	Jenkins
Bocador	Kingsport
Boston Rum	Mohawk
Caldwell's	Old Sea Dog
Calypso	Rainbow
Cockspur	Ron Bermudez
Depaz	Ron Pontalba Rum
Gosling's Black Seal	Ron Roberto
Heaven Hill	Ronrico

Foreign owned

Anejo	BMD	Lemon Hart	UK
Bacardi	BMD	Limon	BMD
Black Heart	UK	Malibu	UK
Captain Morgan	FR	Mount Gay	FR
Carta Blanca	BMD	Myer's	FR
Castillo	BMD	Myers's Original	FR
Crown Jewel	UK	Ron Llave	FR
Havana Club	FR	Tondena Manila	PHI
Lamb's Navy	UK		

SCHNAPPS

American owned

Boston	Maui
Dekuyper	Mohawk
Dr. McGillicuddy's	White Birch
Fire Water	Wintergarten

Foreign owned

Echter Nordhauser	G	Hulstkamp	G

SCOTCH

American owned

Bankers Club Blend	John Handy
Barristers Scotch	Kennedy's
Cluny	Kings Crown
Crown Sterling	Lauder's
Dental	M.S. Walker
Duncans	Schwegmann's
Dunheath	Scots Lion
Findlaters	Sir Malcolm
Glayva	Speakers
Glenfarclas	Speyside 21-Year-Old
Highland Mist	The Claymore
Inver House Scotch	W.E. Garrett
Isle of Jura	

Foreign owned

100 Pipers	FR	J&B Select	UK
Ballantine's	UK	Johnnie Walker	UK
Balvenie	UK	Old Smuggler	UK
Black & White	UK	Passport	FR
Black Bottle	UK	Queen Anne	FR
Buchanan's	UK	Royal Lochnagar	UK
Chivas Regal	FR	Royal Paisley	FR
Consulate	UK	Royal Salute	FR
Cutty Sark	UK	Royal Stewart	UK
Dewar's	BMD	Scoresby	UK
Glen Ord	UK	Something Special	FR
Glengoyne	UK	Tamdhu	UK
Glenlivet	FR	The Famous Grouse	UK
Glenturret	UK	The Macallan	UK
Highland Park	UK	Vat 69	UK
J&B Rare	UK		

SCOTCH WHISKEY

American owned

Ardbeg	The Dalmore
Highland Mist	Tomintoul-Glenlivet
Kennedy's	Usher's
McColl's	Whyte & Mackay
The Claymore	

Foreign owned

Aberlour	FR	Old Smuggler	UK
Chivas Regal	FR	Teacher's	UK
Highland Park	UK	White Heather	FR
J&B	UK		

SPIRITS

American owned

B.J. Holladay	Rhum Barbancourt
Caldwell's	S.S. Pierce
Pines Brook Vintners	

Foreign owned

Archer's	UK	Opal Nera	UK
Bersano	J	Passoa Liqueur	FR
Chateau Mercian	J	Peachtree Fizz	J
Cointreau	FR	Phillips Old English	UK
Fundador	UK	Pommery	FR
Karuizawa	J	President	UK
Long John	UK	Red Heart	UK
Maker's Mark	UK	Remy Martin	J
Malibu	UK	Seven Seas Cane	UK
Malliac Armagnac	UK	Sheridan's	UK

TEQUILA

American owned

Captain Tequila	Puerto Nuevo
Don Eduardo	Rosita
El Condor	Tijuana
El Toro	Tina
Heaven Hill	Torada
Montezuma	Twisted Sheila's Lime Tequila
Ole Tequila	Two Fingers
Pepe Lopez	Zapata

Foreign owned

Arandas	UK	Jose Ceurvo	UK
Camino Real	BMD	Tequila Sauza	UK
Coyote	FR	Tequila Yacatan	FR
Herradura	FR		

VODKA

American owned

Alexi	Laird's
Argent	McCalls
Banff Ice	Mims
Bankers Club Blend	Mohawk
Barclay	Nikolai
Barton	Pertsovka
Boston Vodka	Priviet
Caldwell's	Rainbow
Chaska	Romanoff
Cossack	Ruble
Crown Russe	Schenley
Crystal Place	Senators Club
Czarinavodka	Simka Kosher
Don Cossack	Skol
Finlandia	Stolichnaya
Five O'Clock	Stulski
Fleishman's	Taaka
Glenmore	Vladimir
Goldring	Vladivar
Heaven Hill	Vodstok
Kamachatka	Wolfschmidt
Kasser	Zhenka
Kimnoff	

Foreign owned

Absolut	FR	Johnnie Walker	UK
Altai	FR	Popov	UK
Banzai	J	Seagram's	FR
Borzoivodka	UK	Smirnoff	UK
Count Pushkin	UK	Suntory	J
Denaka	UK	Tanqueray	UK
Dimitri	UK	Wyborowa	FR
Gordon's	UK		

WHISKEY

American owned

Bankers Club	Brittania
Barton Reserve	Canadian Gold
Black Bush	Canadian Host
Black Velvet	Canadian Mist
Booker's	Corby's

Corby's Canadian
Corby's Reserve
Early Times
Five Star American
Fleischmann's Preferred
Four Queens Blend
Gentleman Jack
Golden Wedding
House of Stuart
Imperial
Jack Daniels
Jacob's Well
James Foxe
Jenkins
Jim Beam
Kennedy's Canadian
Kentucky Gentleman

Kessler
Lord Calvert
MacNaughton's
Mar Lodge
McCalls Canadian
Northern Light
Press Club Blend
Private Stock
Senators Club
Seven Star
Southern Comfort
Tangle Ridge
The Dalmore
Tom Moore
Triple Crown
William Penn

Foreign owned

7 Crown	FR		Loch Dhu	UK
Ballantine's	UK		Macleans	UK
Bushmills	FR		McNaughton Canadian	UK
Canadian Club	UK		Milton Duff	UK
Cardhu	UK		Rich & Rare	UK
Crystal Decanter	UK		Royal Canadian	FR
Curtis	UK		Royal Reserve	UK
Four Roses	FR		Suntory	J
George Dickel	UK		Suntory Reserve	J
J&B	UK		Suntory Royal	J
Jameson	FR		Suntory Signature	J
Johnnie Walker	UK		Teacher's Wall Street	UK
Knockando	UK		Tullmore Dew	UK
Laphroaig	UK		William Lawson	BMD
Laphroaig Islay	UK		Yamazaki	J

WINE

American owned

Alexis Lichine
Allegrini
Almaden
Alsace Willm
Andre
Andre Gaston & Cie
Antonelli

Antonin Rodet
Armstrong Ridge
Asti Spumante Banfi (Castello Banfi)
Balkan Crest
Banfi Asti
Banfibrut
Barberani

Baron Langwerth Von Simmern
Bartles & Jaymes
Batasiolo
Beau Rivage
Bel Arbor
Belnero-Pinot Noir
Benzinger
Bersano Piedmont
Black Tower
Blesius
Bodegas Palacio
Bolla
Bonterra Vineyards
Boone's
Boutari
Brolio
Browio Tuscan
Burati
C.K. Mondavi
California Cellars of Chase-Limogere
California Fortune
Campo Leonardo
Canandaigua Lake Niagra
Canyon Road
Carlo Rossi
Carobbio
Castellarin
Chappellet
Charles Krug
Charles Le Franc
Chase Limogere
Chateau & Estates
Chateau Chardon
Chateau Clark
Chateau D'Arch
Chateau Grand-Puy Ducasse
Chateau Haut Pagaud
Chateau La Coronne
Chateau La Joya
Chateau Lartigue
Chateau Liversan
Chateau Oliver
Chateau Palmer
Chateau Reysson

Chateau Rothschild
Chateau Roubine
Chateau St. Jean
Chateau Ste. Michelle
Chateaux Senejac
Christian Brothers
Cisco
Cockburn's Port
Colour Volant
Columbia Crest
Cook's Captain Reserve
Cool Breeze
Corte Sant'Alda Amarone
Corvo
Costa do Sol Rose
Cribari
Curlier Freres
Cuvaison
Domaine
Domaine St. Michelle
Douinus
Ducia
Duna
Dunnewood
Elk Ridge Vineyards
Enzo
F. Chauvenet
Fassati
Fazi-Battaglia
Ferrari
Fetzer Vineyards
Folonari
Fourcas Hosten
Francois Labet
Franz Weber
Franzia Winetaps
Frescobaldi
Fu-Ki
Fuki Plum
Gallo
Gancia
Gerhard Schulz
Geyser Peak
Gibson Vineyards

Glen Ellen (Glen Ellen Winery)
Grandin
Graziosi
Hartley
Henkell
Henkell Trocken
Ingelnook
ISC
J. Moreau
J. Roget
Jacque Bonet
Jacques Depagneux
Jean Dorsone
Jekel Vineyards
Joseph Victori
Justino
Karl Von Stetter
Kasser
Keller-Geister
Kettmeir
Kitchens Best (cooking)
Korbell
Krizia
La Chablisienne
Lake Country
Lake Niagra
Le Domaine Champagne
Leonardini
Livingston Cellars
Louis Roederer
Lucien Deschaux
M. Chapoutier
M.G. Vallejo
Mandrielle-Mellot
Manischewitz
Marchesi De Gresy
Marcus James
Marega
Marega Pinot
Marega Tocai
Masi
Mateous
Mazzoni
McPherson

Meiers
Melini
Michel Picard
Mirafiore
Mogen David
Moletto
Mommessin
Monarch
Mondoro
Monsieur Henri
Monterra Promise
Nardi Brunello
Nardi Rosso De Montalcino
Noilly Prat
Noilly Prat Vermouth
Old Brookville Chardonney
Olivier Leflaive (Burgandy)
Partager
Pastene Foods
Paul Jaboulet Aine
Paul Masson
Perrier Jouet
Pio Cesare
Placido
Premiat
Principessa Gavi
Renato Ratti
Ricasoli Tuscan
Rivera
Robert Mondavi
Rocche Castagmagna
Rochioli
Romano
Rougemont Castle
Round Hill
Rozes
Saddle Mountain
San Angelo
San Donato Chianti
San Rocco
San Vincenti
Santa Anita
Santa Carolina
Santa Margherita

Santi

Savory and James (Sherry)

Schwegmann's (Burgandy)

Signature

Silverstone Cellars

Skye's Hollow

Snoqualmie

Sonoma Cutrer

St. Leonard

Stag's Leap

Stival

Stival Chardonnay Le Rive

Stival Le Rive Merlot

Stival Pinot Grigiom Merlot

Stones

Sutter Home

Talentie Brunello

Tavernelle

Taylor California Cellars

Thevenin

Thunderbird

Trakia

Tribuno Vermouth

Viginia Dare

Villa Mt. Eden

Vintner's Choice

Walnut Crest

Wente

Widmer's

Wild Irish Rose

Wincarnis

Woodbrook Vineyards

Yves Roche

Foreign owned

Akadama	J	Cune	SWI
Alto Estate	UK	Dom Perignon	FR
Andean	ARG	Domecq (Sherry)	UK
Andres	C	Dragon Seal	FR
Antinori	FR	Drosty-Hoff	UK
Asti Mondoro	ITL	Dry Sack (Sherry)	UK
Asti Spumante (Gio. Buton)	UK	F.O.V.	FR
Atlas Peak	UK	Feist	FR
B&G	FR	Franciscan	C
Beaulieu Vinyard Wines	UK	Gainey	UK
Beringer	SWI	Glen Ellen (UDV North	UK
Bigi	SWI	America)	
Blanc De Fruit	FR	Goedehoop Estate	UK
Blossom Hill	UK	Gold Coast	C
Blue Nun	UK	Harveys	UK
Bouchard Pere & Fils	UK	Harveys (Sherry)	UK
Café De Paris	FR	Haywood	G
Callaway	UK	Hennessy	FR
Canei	FR	Heublein	UK
Casa Di Pescatore	UK	Hillebrand	C
Chateau De Pez	FR	Hine	FR
Chateau Giscors	FR	Hochtaler	C
Chateau Gloria	FR	Jacob's Creek	FR
Chateau Souverain	SWI	Jacobsdal Estate	UK
Clos Du Bois	UK	Jaffelin	FR
Coolabah	FR	John Harvey (Sherry)	UK

Kaiser Stuhl	AUS	Piper Sonoma	FR
Kijafa	FR	Pommery	FR
Kirsberry	DEN	Queen Adelaide	AUS
Krug	FR	Riccardo Falchini	UK
La Ina (Sherry)	UK	Rietvallei Estate	UK
La Motte Estate	UK	Robert Stemmler	G
Lancers	UK	Rosemount	AUS
Le Bonheur Estate	UK	Rothschild Wines	UK
Leo Buring	AUS	Rouge Homme	AUS
Les Fleus Des Champs	UK	Ruffino	UK
Lindemans	AUS	San Pedro Wines	FR
L'Ormarins Estate	UK	Scarletta	UK
Macon-Lugny Les Charmes	FR	Seaview	AUS
(Burgandy)		Sichel	UK
Maison Deutz	SWI	Stellenryck	UK
Martini & Rossi	BMD	Sterling Vineyards	FR
Meridian	SWI	Sterzi	ITL
Middelvlei Estate	UK	Tollana	AUS
Napa Ridge	SWI	Trapiche	ARG
Ozeki-Sake	J	Travaglini	SWI
Paolo Cordero Barolo	SWI	Tulloch	AUS
Peller Estates	C	Two Oceans	UK
Penfolds	AUS	Vajra Barolo	SWI
Peter's	SWI	Viala	G
Piat D'Or	UK	William Hill	UK
Piat Pere & Fils	UK	Woodley	AUS
Piemontello	UK	Zinn	G
Pionero	G		

WINE COOLERS

American owned
Bartles & Jaymes
Foreign owned

Quenchette	BG	Seagram's Coolers	FR

PART II

Chapter 1

The Joy of Statistics

America doesn't buy free trade—even during what were once called buoyant times prior to the recession of 2001—and it is most likely because of the unique features found in a global, free-trade economy that have never been seen before. To be sure, America has never willingly tread upon such untested waters. The recent New Economy has shot holes into many textbook theories once held as standard economic foundations.

Globalization has resulted in an era characterized by a series of broken records, but most are records that were set during economic crises that America would be wise not to revisit and should motivate America to change its policies. Not all the items listed below are record-setting items, but they are good candidates for explaining why, as our economy spreads out globally, most Americans still think nationally or locally.

- America has a negative savings rate not seen since the Great Depression.
- Consumer debt levels are at their highest point since at least World War II, when recordkeeping for this statistic began.
- 10% of Americans receive at least some portion of their food from a food bank or some other charitable organization.
- Second-hand clothing stores have increased their sales volume 100% in the last decade.
- Requests for food aid rose 23% and requests for emergency shelter rose 13% between 2000 and 2001 alone.
- America leads First World nations in income inequality.
- In 1975, the average American worker could purchase a new car after 18 weeks of wages. By 1995, it took the average American worker 28 weeks of wages to buy a new car.
- In 1975, the average car loan was 36 months. In 1995, the average car loan was 54 months.
- The average American works 140 hours more per year than in 1982, and America has surpassed Japan as the most over-worked nation.

- Corporate profits are now 8% of national income, down from 12% in the 1960's.
- America leads all First World nations in the percentage of married women in the work force. The percentage of working mothers with children under 6 rose to 63% by 1995 from 30% in 1970.
- The income tax, at 3% in 1950, has risen at least 800%.
- What cost $30 during the Kennedy administration cost $144 in 1992, even though free-traders claim that cheap imports hold down consumer prices.
- By 1993, the value of the dollar in 1971 had fallen to under 40 cents.
- U.S. factories produce over 3.5 times more than in 1960, but the American worker in manufacturing makes less than in 1960.
- Productivity increased 20% between 1989 and 1999, and while women saw a 4% gain, real wages for men decreased.
- The average American works 30 hours more per year than in 1995.
- Trade is responsible for 25% of the increase in income inequality for the last 30 years.
- Almost 33% of all American workers were paid $8 an hour or less during the 1990's.
- No large corporation founded during the New Economy of the 1990's provides their employees with the option of a traditional pension plan based on salary history, years with the company, and adjustments for inflation.
- Although medical bills remained flat for many years, annual price hikes for employees who have access to health care are to be expected. Insurers increased premiums 11% in 2000 and corporate America is likely to pass future projected increases on to their workers.
- The health care sector was responsible for 30% of GDP growth and 45% of new jobs in the year 2000. The housing sector, which is credited for temporarily keeping the economy out of recession, was only 18% of GDP and responsible for only 25% to 30% GDP growth.
- Despite an expansion of 21 million new jobs in the 1990's, the rate of increase was the smallest in recent decades.
- Productivity in the 1990's, although it outpaced the 1980's, was no match for the 1960's and 1970's. Productivity in the 1990's was a full percentage point less than the 1960's, the last full decade before the U.S. could declare itself a free-trade, open economy.
- Compared to the 1960's, the 1990's unemployment rate was one percentage point higher and inflation was 20% higher.
- Although it is still claimed by many that a rising tide lifts all boats, a phrase coined by President John F. Kennedy, it did not apply to the 1990's.
- GDP for the wage-gain recovery years of 1995-2000 was 2.5%, much better than when wage rates declined for the American worker 22

straight years between 1973 and 1995 when GDP averaged an anemic 1.3%. But the recent booming economy years were still no match for the post-war, more-protectionist era between 1947 and 1973, which showed a GDP pace of 2.9%.

- Both consumer and corporate debt have increased two-fold in two decades.
- Since real wages for working Americans began their steady decline in 1973, they began to rise in 1996, but halted again in 1999 despite a booming economy.
- Higher wages provided income for only about half of America's families between 1996 and 1999, as the other half increased family income by working longer hours.
- Although over 40% of employees in the private sector had employer-sponsored pension plans in 1980, only 20% do today. The average 401(k) account in 1998 had only $16,000.
- Contrary to the popular economic theory that higher productivity means higher wages, wage rates of the 1960's outpaced those of the 1990's although the American worker produced three times as much as his counterpart did in 1960.
- Alan Greenspan has identified America's low-savings rate as "the key domestic policy problem of this country."
- The savings rate, which has recently turned negative for the first time since the Great Depression, averaged at least 7% throughout the 1960's, the 1970's and the 1980's.
- The wage-growth period in the 1990's, from 1995-1999, did not recover the lost ground of declining wages in the earlier part of that decade.
- Despite a jobless rate that was at a 29-year low in 1999, the growth of real wages stagnated.
- Only one-fifth of employees that are eligible for 401(k) plans actually pay into the system, and 66% of those contribute less than the maximum. Less than 10% of eligible Americans contribute to IRA's. Despite the booming economy, Americans with low-savings rates simply don't have enough disposable income to contribute to their own retirement.
- In 1988, the average corporate executive made 42 times the wage of the average factory worker. By 1998, executive pay had risen to 419 times as much.
- Employee absenteeism was at its highest level in 1998. Stress as a cause of absenteeism increased three-fold since 1995. Workers are now just as likely to skip work because of stress as they are actual physical illness.
- The United States fueled economic expansion with borrowed money equaling almost $1 billion a day.

- The number of uninsured Americans reached 44.3 million in 1998, representing 16.3% of the population. Half of America's poor full-time employees lacked health insurance, as well as 11.1 million children.
- The top two individual states of the most uninsured Americans were George W. Bush's Texas and John McCain's Arizona, followed by California.
- Elderly Americans spend 19% of their annual income on health care that is not covered by Medicare.
- U.S. corporate debt increased 60% between 1995 and 2000, setting a record at 46% of America's GDP.
- An American worker employed full time was just as likely to fall below the poverty line in the 1990's as the 1980's, and was at a greater risk of doing so than a 1970's counterpart.
- Child poverty rates reached a record 22.5% in 1993, and stood at 19% in 1998. The percentage of children in poverty was 16% in 1979.
- The rate of personal bankruptcies has risen 400% since the late 1970's.
- A thirty year-old with a High School diploma earned 20% less in 1998 than in 1974.
- 53 million households in 1980 were supplemented with more than one paycheck. Twenty years later, there were 68 million, with much of the increase supplemented with more than two paychecks.
- 51% of working Americans are currently happy with their jobs, compared to 59% in 1995.
- There is one key difference between the Fed's aggressive rate-cutting that occurred in 1982 and pre-recession February 2001. In 1982, the Fed was trying to pull the economy out of a deep recession. In February 2001, the economy was still able to avoid entering into recession.
- Americans are working more and sleeping less. 38% of those surveyed by the National Sleep Foundation work 60 hours a week, 40% struggle to stay awake at work, and only 37% get at least 8 hours of sleep a night.
- Household net income fell in 2000 for the first time in 55 years.
- 10 million Americans don't have bank accounts.
- Mortgage delinquent rates are at their highest level since 1992.

Chapter 2

The New Economy
Meets the New Reality

All four presidents carved into Mt. Rushmore warned of the folly of free trade and endorsed protectionism for the U.S. market. British Economist John Maynard Keynes in the 1920's, and 2000 presidential candidate Patrick J. Buchanan in the 1990's both turned their back on free trade in favor of protectionism. Thomas Jefferson, who once endorsed free trade, said " . . . experience has now taught me that manufactures are now as necessary to our independence as to our comfort . . . " in 1816. When such well-respected men agree to change their long-held views, it is evidence that once popular theories do not match reality. Today's advocates of free trade advocate what was widely ridiculed by our founding fathers.

Pre-September 11 polls showed that most Americans today don't support free trade either, and believe that too many "old economy" jobs have to be destroyed for the "new economy" jobs that are created. And they are right. One only has to look at the constantly increasing trade deficit as evidence that America's trade policy is not working for America. If our free-trade policy was working, our exports would outpace our imports and we would eventually narrow our massive trade deficit down to a trade balance. But this is not the case. For the first 26 years after WWII, the U.S. reaped the gains of trade surpluses every year, resulting in a total of $98 billion. After our new-found dedication to free trade, we have suffered accumulated trade deficits literally in the trillions of dollars. Everyone seems to benefit from America's love affair with free trade except America and her people. Under a protectionist trade policy, America churned out trade surpluses every year between 1893 and 1971.

The Asian crisis of 1997 has been called the worst financial crisis in 50 years. Free trade President Bill Clinton admitted in 1999 that even though he believed "A failure to expand trade further could choke off innovation and diminish the very possibilities of the *information economy*," (emphasis added) he added "Unfortunately, working people the world over do not believe this." We should not be increasing our trade volume with other nations just for the sake of trade. Our trade volume has never been greater, and our trade deficit has never been worse.

Of course the information economy of which Bill Clinton spoke is also known as the "New Economy," which turned out to be a bubble that brought harsh realities on many investors and stockholders when it finally burst. Bankers, for instance, were not surprised that the Asian crisis of 1997 took place, since they knew many Asian countries were living beyond their means. It is unfortunate that America finds itself in a similar situation today. Still, many bankers are in favor of free trade. This is less surprising when one realizes that banks simply lend money for those who want to consume, and enabling corporations and individuals to consume is their business.

The information economy may not be the savior America is looking for to solve her trade problems. A quick look at the number of workers employed by one of America's leading manufacturing companies—Ford—and America's leading software company—Microsoft—reveals what should be a heavy blow to "New Economy" advocates. Microsoft, even though it has been exalted as an information technology success story, only employs 1/20th the workers that Ford employs and ranked below 400 in the Fortune magazine's ratings of the top 500 American companies. Over 5000 India-born engineers were instrumental in developing Windows 98 software. Despite America's hope that software will be a significant export industry for the United States, Ireland is currently the world's number one exporter of software. Such sobering statistics should point to manufacturing as having the most potential for American employment—not information technology.

This comparison between Ford and Microsoft also does not take into account the American workers missing in the numbers comparison who supply parts for Ford cars and trucks since many are employed by companies other than Ford. This is an especially important factor since the number of workers in the parts sector for the automobile industry is fast approaching the number of workers required to assemble the finished product, and software has no parts content. This makes the argument for manufacturing as the key to American employment even more credible.

According to economist Paul Craig Roberts, the United States has "the export profile of the 19th century third-world colony." We have trade surpluses in hides and skins, scrap and pulp, crude fertilizers, corn, soybeans and cigarettes. We have trade deficits in automobiles, TVs, VCRs, industrial machinery, electrical components, optical goods and power-generating machinery.

Even though we were fortunate enough to escape the Asian crisis of 1997 without too much problem, we have not always been totally immune to crises given our policy of increasing interdependence. When Russia defaulted on its government debt in 1998, it was enough to seize up the U.S. bond market. And even though Mexico's peso crisis wasn't as serious as the Asian crisis of 1997, it caused Latin America's markets to fall 38% in sixty days.

Although there is an appearance of national prosperity, every nation appears to be prospering when they are living beyond their means. The flaw in measuring prosperity today is that it is measured by an accumulation of things, rather than by real wages, and we should be paying less attention to the unemployment rate and more attention to what the workers who are employed are actually earning.

Many laid-off Americans have realized that the majority of new jobs available for them to replace their old jobs pay less money. According to the Bureau of Labor Statistics, the number of workers discouraged because they believe there is a lack of jobs available to them increased 40% between June 1999 and June 2000.

A state agency in Minnesota seeking to diversify its economy in the wake of 4,000 potential steel-related job losses found that as they tried to attract new jobs into the area to soften the blow of the layoffs, most did not pay as well as the old steel jobs. The majority of the 3,000 jobs to be provided by new employers attracted to the area are in the service sector. Former steelworkers simply aren't going to make the same money working in call centers, which make up the majority of jobs coming to the area. And if steel is one of the hand-picked losers in America, former steelworkers won't find call center jobs more stable. Calls placed to call centers from many areas of the country are just as likely to reach an operator in Canada or elsewhere as they are an operator in America.

Another thing to keep in mind is that each manufacturing job lost creates a ripple effect that costs at least 4 other jobs, and the ripple effect in the steel industry in particular is argued to be even higher. University of California at Santa Cruz Economist Lori Kletzer estimates that the average American worker who loses a job because of trade or technology earns 13% less in their new job, and close to one-fourth earns a whopping 30% less. This of course does not take into account the income that was lost while trying to land that new job, and even if a new job is found at the same pay, workers will not be able to replace income that was lost in the transition. Further research showed that laid off manufacturing workers who were forced to take jobs in the retail sector experienced and average wage decrease of 34%.

Other Americans in the manufacturing sector who don't lose their jobs suffer pay cuts instead. Workers employed by Trico Products Company, currently a subsidiary of Britain's Tomkins PLC, started to see their jobs migrate south to Mexico as early as the mid-1980's. By 1995, only 300 jobs remained, and the remaining workers took pay cuts to keep their jobs. Wages at $14.50 an hour were cut to $12.50 an hour and remained frozen for at least 4 years. Americans might wonder how an economy is supposed to grow in an atmosphere of mass layoffs and forced wage reductions.

These examples are all the more reason why the unemployment rate is increasingly an unreliable indicator of national prosperity. Our trade policies force many American workers to take pay cuts or find new jobs that pay less, but the unemployment rate in each of these cases remains unchanged. The result, however, is a nation of less affluent consumers that pay fewer taxes to support the increasing cost of government with their new, lower-wage jobs. Again, we should be less concerned with how many Americans are working and more concerned with what the Americans that are still working are actually making. Still, the inaccuracies of the unemployment rate in America should not go unnoticed. According to the September 11, 2001 issue of the Wall Street Journal, the last issue printed before the tragedy at the World Trade Center, the unemployment rate in August 2001 of 4.9% did not take into account an estimated 70 million potential workers who had stopped looking for work for one reason or another.

Many workers find their only option is to work more than one job. Barbara Ehrenreich, author of ''Nickel and Dimed,'' tried to make ends meet working two jobs in Minnesota with no children, living in a cheap $245-a-week hotel, and driving a Rent-A-Wreck car, but she found the exhausting experience absorbed all her energy and failed to pay the bills as well.

Even President Clinton worried that the U.S. trade deficit could halt national prosperity while at the same time admitting to using the U.S. as a buffer to prevent what he believed could turn into a global recession. Clinton admitted that he purposely allowed the U.S. to ''run quite a large trade deficit to help our friends in Asia and Russia get through this crisis,'' and that ''with a lot of our wealth in the stock market . . . difficult events in one place can have a big reverberating effect in others.'' But what steps were taken to help Americans who worked in industries that were being hit hard by imports get through this crisis? Then Treasury Secretary Robert Rubin said ''I think it will take the world a long time to work through the effects of this financial crisis.'' Recurring crises like the Enron scandal further highlight the dangers of relying too heavily on the stock market for wealth creation.

With all these sobering announcements highlighting the risk of continuing with a free-trade, globalized new economy, why do these leaders continue to push free trade, and why do Americans continue to elect legislators who support it?

"I have heard of patriotism in the United States, and I have found true patriotism among the people, but never among the leaders of the people."

Alexis de Tocqueville

One possible answer, summed up amazingly well by Motorola's Malaysian country manager, Roger Betelson, is that "Americans don't have the foggiest idea what is happening to them and why." Most Americans don't realize they are being led down the gradual path of transferred or stolen prosperity. Alan Greenspan said "What is happening amongst our trading partners has a greater effect on the United States than we can understand directly," and that "leads us to be, obviously, quite sensitive to what we see going on abroad."

The voter who casts his ballot primarily because of a candidate's stance on trade policy is certainly no one-issue voter. American jobs used to pay the highest wages in the world, but now rank ninth among industrialized nations. America's free trade stance also reveals its flaws in comparison to a more protectionist Japan and Germany. Since they were both devastated during WWII, both have eventually surpassed the United States in real wages. In the 1950's, U.S. workers earned 8 times the wages of Japanese and German workers, but both passed the United States in real wages in the 1980's. American workers now put in more hours on the job than Japan, the former primary nation of overwork. Japan also used to trail the United States in life expectancy after WWII, but Japanese citizens now live 4 years longer. Certainly the fast pace of increase in living standards has played a major role.

These examples should clearly show that increased manufacturing does not destroy a country's industry. Germany has the highest wage rates and the shortest workweek compared to other first world nations, and they also have one-third less the U.S. poverty rate to boot. America's fall from once paying the highest wages in the world did not happen overnight. It has been a gradual, and obviously for the most part, an unnoticeable phenomenon starting in 1973 when wages stopped increasing with productivity. In little more than a decade between the late 1970's and 1990, real wages fell in America's manufacturing sector even though productivity increased an impressive 35%. Real wages for the average American worker finally started to rise in 1995, but then stagnated again in 1999—a serious blow to New Economy proponents. In Mexico, productivity has risen 40% since 1980, but wages have fallen by 40%. One might wonder where the incentive is to be more productive if wages do not rise as a result.

Another possible answer is that the policies that have engulfed America into so much risk of their financial well-being are the same reasons Americans aren't marching in the streets protesting these trade policies. If the jobs of working Americans are cut or wages are reduced in order to increase corporate profits, are the workers, who may increasingly have a stake in the stock of their employer, supposed to applaud the wage reductions and layoffs or frown upon them? Such a policy creates opposing factions in our economy, as well as special interests that turn a blind eye to the destruction of certain Americans' livelihoods as long as it doesn't involve "me." The same risk factor we accepted—exchanging increasing wage rates for increasing stock values—has now caught up with us. Now that the majority of Americans' stock portfolios aren't looking as rosy as they were in the boom years of the 1990's, there is no longer the once reliable guarantee of annual wage gains to fall back on. If Americans can't save, the government can't significantly pay down the national debt, wages don't rise with productivity, and an extra-tight labor market fails to show significant wage gains among the majority of American workers during the so-called boom years of the 1990's, when will we ever realize such sought-after gains? Even in the 1970's, during which we experienced the oil crises, the beginning of decreasing real wages for working Americans, and the first ever de-linking of the traditional rising productivity and rising wages, the savings rate was over 10% for eight years in that decade. The guarantee of rising real wages—wages that outpace inflation—was solidified during the policies of trade protection for the U.S. market, but America has since traded-off the guarantee of reliable rising wages in favor of using the much-less stable stock market as their primary tool for increased prosperity. And since 2001 went down in history as the worst year for stocks in the last 23 years, there is considerable credibility for the theory that this was not a good trade off. We traded a protected market that all but guaranteed continued rising wages for an unprotected market, open to predatory foreign nations and their investors who do not have America's best interest at heart.

"There is no longer an automatic connection between a growing economy and rising prospects for ordinary workers."

Robert Reich

Under a protectionist trade policy, what was good for General Motors really was good for America. I doubt anyone would suggest that what is good for Wal-Mart is good for America, as Wal-Mart has replaced GM as America's largest private employer in terms of the most employees. If Toyota were to some day overtake GM in market share, would the day ever come where Americans would feel comfortable saying "What's good for Toyota is also good for America?"

America switched from being generally a closed economy to being generally an open economy in 1973. No economy is, or can be, a completely open or completely closed economy, but for all intents and purposes, the U.S. became an open economy in 1973. As many exalted the benefits of free trade during times of perceived prosperity, the same trade policy is now coming under greater scrutiny. With free trade, only employees in certain sectors benefit, and one's personal prosperity depends heavily upon which sector or industry within the economy you work in. Under the policy of trade protection through the 1960's, workers in every sector of the economy benefited, and wages rose with productivity. But by the summer of 1999, with unemployment just over 4%, most economists agreed that American workers should be seeing more gains from such a tight labor market. While wage gains were prevalent in high-demand industries like computer technology, the wage rates for middle-income workers stagnated.

The 1990's were definitely a time of increased consumerism, but much of the perceived prosperity was because of heavy borrowing, both by individual Americans and American corporations. American consumers continually spent more than they earned, and when the debt ceilings were reached, they borrowed against their homes for yet more consumption. This seemed to make perfect sense since the whole theory of free trade is based on consumption, but it is now evident that we cannot consume our way to greater prosperity. Heavy borrowing only makes us more vulnerable in an economic downturn, which will inevitably occur. We have forgotten that only production truly creates wealth, while consumption dissipates wealth. America must retain and build upon its capacity to manufacture, thereby retaining its power to create wealth.

"The power of producing wealth is . . . infinitely more important than wealth itself."

Friedrich List

When financial crises hit America in the past, the suggested answer was to save. With September 11, the suggested answer was not only to spend, but it also supposedly did not matter what we spent our money on, where we spent it, where the products were made, or whose pockets we were lining, as long as we spent. "Just don't sit there, spend something!" seemed to be the mind set. One reason for this suggestion is that since we have grown into such a mature free-trade economy, retailing has become one-third of our economy. Soon after the first edition of this book was printed in 1996, it was projected that the number one job category for the next five years in terms of growth was cashier. Just over 5 years later, it seems the projections were right.

Another reason is because the United States was supposedly the only obstacle standing in the way of a global recession, and if Americans saved their money instead of spending it, that feared global recession may have begun. Eventually American consumers are going to have to decide to spend less and pay down more of their personal debt, especially since Americans currently spend nearly 14% of their disposable income servicing such debt. Bankruptcy filings in the second quarter of 2001, before September 11, rose 25% compared to the second quarter of 2000.

A sad reinforcement of this disappointing outlook is that Wal-Mart has now replaced General Motors as the company in America having the most employees. The very ability of Americans to consume is almost guaranteed to decrease when America's former largest employer, who paid over $20 an hour with full benefits, was replaced by a new largest employer whose pay averages less than $10 an hour with little or no benefits and whose workers cannot afford company-supplied health insurance. Since the majority of Americans are employed at lower wages, tax collections also decrease, and there is less money for social services such as education, social security, national defense, the military and health care. Our manufacturing capability has been in a state of forced decline over the last 30 years. It seems like we were pretending not to care whether or not we manufactured the products for our own consumption, and that all we cared about was supplying the jobs to ring up the cash register, even if the product was imported from another country.

"I attach great importance on strong and balanced global growth in the context of interdependent U.S., European and Japanese economies. A healthy global economy requires all of us to perform to our full potential."

Treasury Secretary Paul O'Neill, April 27, 2001

"I sympathize, therefore, with those who would minimize, rather than those who would maximize, economic entanglement between nations. Ideas, knowledge, art, hospitality, travel—these are things which should of their nature be international. But let goods be homespun whenever it is reasonable and conventionally possible: and, above all, let finance be primarily national."

John Maynard Keynes, British Economist

The nations of Southeast Asia were performing to their full potential, even to the point of living beyond their means, but it still resulted in what has been called the worst financial crisis in 50 years.

Despite the rhetoric of free traders, history has taught us that there is no such thing as universal prosperity. While the economies of some nations were booming, others were always in recession. While one economy was prospering, another was always in financial crisis. Globalization now guarantees us that, since our economies have become increasingly interdependent, the paychecks of American workers can be shredded by events unfolding on the other side of the world. Even though free traders realize this, they have attempted to soften the blow of interdependence by attempting to spread prosperity around the globe at the expense of the American worker. Former White House Chief of Staff Leon Panetta claimed in January 2000 that we should strive to guarantee prosperity for all citizens of emerging democracies. This statement begs the question that if we cannot ensure prosperity for all American citizens, what qualifies us to be able to assure prosperity for workers in distant, foreign nations who pay no taxes to the U.S. government and do not elect our leaders? The only guarantee that free trade and globalization can make good on is that we cannot sustain our growth independently from other nations, which will ultimately call for world government. When nations are totally dependent on each other, every nation must have an interest in what each nation's trade and economic policy will be, since both crisis and prosperity will ripple throughout the larger world economy.

As we will need to focus more attention on helping with damage control for foreign economies that get into trouble, it will not be possible to retain the same level of attention or focus on our domestic economy. America will be so pre-occupied with preventing economic crises literally all over the globe that it will have to neglect attempting to legislate prosperity for America. Complete interdependence will require this sort of damage control since crises unfolding in any nation with which we are interdependent will expose America to crises as well.

America has already been warned by Japan, China and the European Union to stop meddling in their economic affairs, which hints at the possibility that every nation does not share America's dream of a free trade free-for-all as the answer to the question of how to synchronize prosperity globally.

In early 2000, when Treasury Secretary Lawrence Summers was offering America's advice to Europe, Bundesbank President Ernst Welteke responded that "In Europe, we discuss the problem of disequilibrium in the U.S., but we don't tell the U.S. what to do about it." It is indeed dangerous to expect that since America is still believed to be the world's foremost economic superpower that all other nations will rubber stamp our economic and trade policies and adopt them as their own. Both European and Asian nations would obviously like the positives they see in the New Economy, but they don't want the poverty that comes along with it, and they are not receptive of the mentality of shopping at all hours of the day and night, which has been fueled by the fact that retailing is now one-third of our economy. They also would rather do without the chaos that comes from an increasingly unregulated market with an invisible hand at the wheel. Nor do they want the huge pay inequalities we have created in our nation between ordinary workers and their CEO's. Former French Prime Minister Lionel Jospin summed it up this way: "We want a market economy, not a market society."

"We have to be more flexible and mobile, but we don't take the American hire-and-fire system as our model. We have a different tradition and culture in Germany."

Horst Teltschick, member of the board, BMW

Even Mexico is doubtful about America's direction towards a deeper commitment to free trade and free markets.

"The greatest paradox is that since 1982 we've followed free-market policies that failed and we had to be bailed out twice, not by the Mexican government, but by a foreign government."

Carlos Heredia, Former Mexican Government Economist.

The foreign government Mexico is talking about is the U.S. Government.

"Either democracy has to be tamed for the sake of the market, or the market has to be tamed for the sake of democracy . . . Globally and nationally, we shall sooner or later have to choose between the free market and a free society."

David Marquard, a British political scientist

We should take a hands-off approach to Japan and their economic problems. Had their economy mirrored ours at the onset of that country's banking crisis and had they been exposed to the world economy through interdependence instead of isolated through independence, their troubles could have easily affected the rest of the global economy.

At least currently, when one nation's economy gets sick, we are bound to catch a cold or at least get the sniffles. The only way to avoid this scenario and prevent complete interdependence and a world government that will be more sovereign than our own is to protect the American market from undercutting by foreign competition. We need to secure the American market for the American producer. Commenting on the Asian crisis of 1997, Business Week editor Gary Becker believes that the recommended economic medicine is prone to make the countries involved even sicker, admitting that a profit-based system of global capitalism may cause periodically unavoidable economic crises.

It should be clarified at this point that protectionism does not or should not imply that America should isolate itself from the world, nor does it imply that America should stop trading with all other nations. Abraham Lincoln declared that trade should be used "where it is necessary" and avoided "where it is not." This type of thinking allowed U.S. imports of coffee, which the U.S. did not grow, and disallowed U.S. imports of cotton. Henry Clay's tariff bill of 1832 eliminated duties on goods America did not grow or produce. Tariffs were capped at high levels, however, on imported goods that were also produced in the United States.

The policy of protection merely seeks to protect our economy from unfair or undercutting competition where foreign producers get a better deal in accessing America's market than American producers receive.

Perhaps some quotes from some of the greatest men in our history can more accurately explain or further reinforce why the tariff system is more beneficial than the free trade system.

"By adopting free trade, we give our markets and our money to foreigners; by adhering to protection, we secure both to our own people . . . The fate of the country depends on the result."

Representative Andrew Stewart, 1846

"Thank God I am not a free trader. In this country pernicious indulgence in the doctrine of free trade seems inevitably to produce fatty degeneration of moral fibre. These forty odd years have been the most prosperous years this nation has ever seen; more prosperous years than any other nation has ever seen. Every class of our people is benefited by the protective tariff."

Theodore Roosevelt

"Free trade in the United States [among the states] is founded upon a community of equalities and reciprocities. It is like the . . . obligations of a family."

Representative William McKinley

The foreign producer, McKinley went on to say, had no "right or claim to equality with our own. He is not amenable to our laws. . . . He pays no taxes. He performs no civil duties. . . . He contributes nothing to the support, the progress, and the glory of the nation. Free foreign trade . . . results in giving our money, our manufactures, and our markets to other nations, to the injury of our labor, our tradespeople, and our farmers."

"Free trade gives to the foreign producer equal privileges with us. . . . It invites the product of his cheaper labor to this market to destroy the domestic product representing our higher and better-paid labor. It destroys our factories or reduces our labor to the level of his. It increases foreign production but diminishes home production. . . . it destroys the dignity and independence of American labor, diminishes its pay and employment, decreases its capacity to buy the products of the farm and the commodities of the merchant.''

Gov. William McKinley, 1892

The only thing McKinley would have gotten wrong were he alive to say this today is that free trade doesn't give the foreign producer equal privileges with us. The foreign producer now has greater privileges than we.

Even as the party of Lincoln was traditionally in favor of protection for the U.S. market, some of their platform language did still resemble their long tradition as late as 1972, but the language was removed in 1976.

''We deplore the practice of locating plants in foreign countries solely to take advantage of low wage rates in order to produce goods primarily for sale in the United States. We will take action to discourage such unfair and disruptive practices that result in the loss of American jobs.''

1972 Republican platform

Consider other portions of former GOP platforms that further demonstrate that the Republican party's roots were in the tariff system—not the free-trade system.

''Protection, which guards and develops our industries, is a cardinal policy of the Republican Party. The measure of protection should always at least equal the difference in the cost of production at home and abroad.''

1904 Republican platform

''The Republican party stands now, as always, in the fullest sense for the policy of tariff protection to American industries and American labor.''

1916 Republican platform

Republicans successfully used protectionism to win the White House in 14 out of 18 elections between 1860 and 1928.

''Protection . . . of our own labor against the cheaper, ill-paid, half-fed, and pauper labor of Europe, is, in my opinion, a duty which the country owes to its own citizens.''

Daniel Webster

"Give us a protective tariff, and we will have the greatest country on earth."

Abraham Lincoln

Lincoln's prediction turned out to be right on target. The tariff system did enable the United States to become the greatest nation on earth. Contrary to the belief of free traders today, Lincoln believed the tariff system was the cheaper system.

"The tariff is the cheaper System. . . . By the direct-tax system the land must be literally covered with assessors and collectors going forth like swarms of Egyptian locusts. By the tariff system the whole revenue is paid by the consumer of foreign goods, and those chiefly the luxuries, and not the necessities, of life. By this system the man who contents himself to live upon the product of his own country pays nothing at all."

Abraham Lincoln

In 1892, then-Governor William McKinley believed that free trade would either cause us to abandon American industry or lower American wages. Unfortunately, he was right on both predictions, and both unwise circumstances have been the result.

"This country will not and can not prosper under any system that does not recognize the difference of conditions in Europe and America. Open competition between high-paid American labor and poorly-paid European labor will either drive out of existence American industry or lower American wages, either of which is unwise."

Gov. McKinley, 1892

"Practically every country in the world . . . has some type of restriction, some type of barrier, some type of subsidization for their own people, that gives their own manufacturers and workers an unfair advantage over the American worker . . . . When have we ever retaliated against the unfair barriers put up by these other countries which go back many, many years? And if we are to have a trade war, if that's the only answer, I imagine if we had an all-out trade war we would do quite well for one simple fact: We have the market. We have the greatest market in the world right in this country.

George Meany, first AFL-CIO President

If Mr. Meany was correct that we have the most to win in a trade war, that would mean we have the most to lose in maintaining our current trade policies. No one enters any kind of "war" unless they are fighting for something they feel they don't already have, or something they have is being threatened and is in danger of being lost. In this case, we have the greatest market in the world, and it is being threatened by foreign producers in unfair trade agreements. Our current U.S. Trade Representative, Robert B. Zoellick, has already admitted that our trade policies are crafted so that foreign countries have the most to gain.

When the United States tried to shore up support from India for a new round of global trade talks in August of 2001, Zoellick said the following:

"The developing world has the most to gain from a new round, and the most to lose without one."

Robert B. Zoellick, U.S. Trade Representative.

In 1890, then-Representative William McKinley warned America that low tariffs had been tried before, and the results were not desirable. Our current president and trade representative would do good to read up on U.S. trade history. If we would only learn from history, we wouldn't have to keep repeating the same mistakes.

"[W]hat these other countries want is a free and open market with the United States. . . . wherever we have tried reciprocity or low duties we have always been the loser."

Representative William McKinley, 1890

Britain once lamented the American advantages through a protectionist system while they advocated free trade. Between the years of 1870 and 1913, yearly production growth increased 4.7% in protectionist America and 4.1% in protectionist Germany, but only 2.1% in free-trade Great Britain.

"Where is the American competition to end? The Yankees are threatening to take the leather trade out of our hands now. American locks are superseding those of Staffordshire; American apples are taking the place of those of Somersetshire and Devon in the dye-works. American furniture is to be found in many forms in more houses than the inhabitants themselves are aware of, and many English sideboards next Christmas will probably groan under American barons of beef. You cannot go into an ironmonger's shop without finding his cases full of American notions. . . . Even the English agriculturists themselves are cultivating their fields, reaping and gathering their crops, when they gather them at all, with implements of American invention and American manufacture."

England's "Times and Mirror," 1879

"There is scarcely an operation in every-day life, in which an American device is not required."

B.H. Thwait, British Writer

Today, the United States finds itself on the other side of the coin, yet continues to advocate increasing trade volume as if nothing but positives were happening. We practice free trade with a protectionist Japan, and Japan has a trade surplus with the United States. We practice free trade with a protectionist China, and China has a trade surplus with the United States. This should be ample proof that trade protectionism triumphs over a policy of free trade without having to refer to U.S. trade history, but our elected officials continue to prescribe the same medicine to reduce our burgeoning trade deficit, somehow expecting different results.

Our tariffs on Chinese imports, for instance, are almost negligible, so the U.S. has nothing with which to negotiate a reduction of tariff rates applied to American exports. The only course of action we can take, as President Bush did recently concerning the U.S. steel industry by raising tariffs to nearly 30%, is to increase import duties to make up for the difference in production costs between each country with which we engage in trade in every industry where such differences exist. The United States must show it is willing to defend its own laws instead of making empty threats of retaliation. Such empty threats prompted one business leader in Japan to comment that America's intimidating talk on trade issues was "about as frightening as walking through a zoo of caged lions." Even Ronald Reagan, who slapped tariffs on Japanese motorcycles to save Harley-Davidson, once said that we cannot compete against goods sold at prices below the cost of production.

House Minority Leader Richard Gephardt (D-MO), speaking against approval for MFN (Most Favored Nation) Status for China, once noted that the United States exports more products to Singapore than to China. Singapore has roughly the population of St. Louis, Missouri which resides in Representative Gephardt's district.

History shows protectionism was even likened to higher quality and lower prices, although textbook free-trade theorists would have you believe that protectionism results in lower quality and higher prices. Are we to believe what is documented throughout history or believe free trade theory that contradicts the wisdom of our founding fathers?

The truth is that the success of free trade as the prevailing U.S. policy is a triumph of ideas over facts. Only in theory can free trade be deemed beneficial to the United States. However, facts proven through U.S. trade history clearly document the success of protectionism. It is truly sad to see ideas and theory that don't work to the benefit of America in the real world when implemented to prevail over policies that have proven to work well for America in the past.

Secretary of State John Hay said in 1900 that "The United States is approaching . . . a position of eminence in the world's markets, due to superior quality and greater cheapness of . . . its manufactures."

The former Secretary of State was speaking from experience. From 1870 to 1900, domestic prices for American products made behind protective tariff walls fell substantially. Prices for textiles and household furnishings fell 30% in that 30-year period, while metal products fell 49% and chemicals fell 41%. The increased efficiency of domestic production protected behind tariff walls was well on its way to paying off for both workers who saw their incomes rise and consumers who saw prices drop. The economic connection between high tariffs and low prices was solidified during the golden age of protectionism.

President Theodore Roosevelt once commented that tariffs "must never be reduced below the point that will cover the difference between the labor cost here and abroad. The well-being of the wage-worker is a prime consideration of our entire policy of economic legislation." He advocated a policy that would at minimum put all competitors on the same level playing field. As mentioned previously, foreign producers today are allowed to undercut American producers on price in nearly every industry. Calls to end this special treatment for foreign producers prompt free traders to invoke the Smoot-Hawley Tariff, whose myths are thoroughly exposed in Part II Chapter 4.

"The question of what tariff is best for our people is primarily one of expediency, to be determined not on abstract academic grounds, but in the light of experience."

Theodore Roosevelt

Today's free traders also equate the tariff system with trade isolationism, and free trade with trade engagement. Complete isolationism severing all trade with all countries is an unfair characterization of the tariff system since it is not possible, and no one should advocate such a policy. The question before us is *how* to engage other nations, and not if we will or if we will not. According to Teddy Roosevelt, free traders pursued "a course of folly which threatens more than anything else the maintenance of the protective system which I deem so essential to our economic well-being."

When America's prosperous protectionist history is mentioned as proof to free traders as why the tariff system should become the America system once again, many claim that this is no longer the 1900's and that times are different. I wonder how Teddy Roosevelt would have been accepted if, in 1912, he claimed we should have abandoned the tariff system on the grounds that it wasn't the 1800's anymore. If we do not equalize the difference between production costs at home and abroad, we allow the foreign producers to gain an unfair advantage over our own producers.

"I believe in the protection of American industry and it is our purpose to prosper America first. The privileges of the American market to the foreign producer are offered too cheaply today, and the effect on much of our own productivity is the destruction of our own self-reliance, which is the foundation of the independence and good fortune of our people. . . . imports should pay their fair share of our cost of government."
                    President Warren G. Harding after his inauguration, 1921.

What U.S. president, being elected by the American people, would fail to support a trade policy that puts Americans first? Unfortunately, since President Theodore Roosevelt, most U.S. presidents have failed to do so by unilaterally lowering tariffs on imports for either nothing in return or unrelated foreign policy gains.

In seeking Brazil's support in May 2001 concerning the FTAA (Free Trade Area of the Americas), President Bush promised to "iron out any differences" with the country in the interest of maintaining positive relations. Although the FTAA has steep opposition by the textile, steel and other key manufacturing industries, President Bush maintained that "the important thing is spirit of cooperation."

You would think that if any country would be given an advantage to be able to better access American markets, it would be America, but the reverse has been the case.

When President Harding was challenged by the argument that consumers benefit from cheaper imports, he replied "One who values American prosperity and . . . American standards of wage[s] and living can have no sympathy with the proposal that easy entry and the flood of imports will cheapen our cost of living. It is more likely to destroy our capacity to buy." Surely a system that creates an over-abundance of goods but reduces the ability for the average American to buy them cannot be headed for general prosperity.

"I am *not* prepared to concede that anyone, whether it be a foreign government or a foreign firm, has a vested right in lax enforcement of our international fair trade statutes."
                    President Richard Nixon

Protecting domestic manufacturing was also associated with national security and independence.

"The wealth . . . independence and security of a Country, appear to be materially connected with the prosperity of manufactures."
                    Alexander Hamilton, 1791

The U.S. should not strive to compete in the trade arena with all nations for the sake of competition simply to see who can win that competition. Competition is only honorable if the U.S. is required to compete in the world marketplace based on terms at least as favorable as those afforded to their foreign rivals.

The livelihoods of Americans and their families should not be arbitrarily engaged in competition for mere bragging rights. We should advocate a strategic trade policy that seeks to keep us as independent, as self-sufficient and as self-reliant as possible. We should not intentionally depend on others for things we can provide for ourselves. After all, isn't that what we strive to teach our children as individuals and strive for as adults? A nation of citizens that believes they should advocate such honorable virtues in their personal lives should also advocate them collectively for the nation.

When Nike moved its factories from the U.S. to Asia, their footwear prices did not drop. But Americans see their jobs disappear, see their wages stagnate or drop because of a new direct and cheaper competition, and see their taxes go up to cover social costs brought on by higher unemployment or for sponsoring government programs to retrain workers for the jobs they didn't want in the first place. Americans are less happy today with their jobs today as well. Statistics show that less than 51% of working Americans are currently happy with their jobs, when 59% were happy with their jobs just five years earlier. We would do best to allow Americans to remain in their chosen employment and protect them from undercutting by import competition with a fair-trade policy. It is mind-boggling to know that the government spends $400 million each year for the privilege of laying off Americans from their chosen employment and retraining them for the hand-picked winners in the global economy. We are again going against a proven and prosperous history of protectionism.

Foreign workers pay no taxes for the purposes of retraining dislocated American workers even though they are the primary reason Americans are being retrained. The American taxpayers are burdened with retraining their fellow citizens who have been victimized by unfair foreign competition allowed by our own government's trade policies.

"Our kind of tariff makes a competing foreign article carry the burden, . . . supply the revenue; and in performing this essential office it encourages at the same time our own industries and protects our people in their *chosen* (emphasis added) employments. That is the mission and purpose of a protective tariff."

Congressman William McKinley, 1888

When Nike closed their factories in the U.S. and moved overseas to avoid the high cost of American laws and regulation, we gave them a better deal in accessing the U.S. market than New Balance, who remained here to employ American workers at higher wage rates and to abide by American laws. We have failed to impose the same costs on foreign producers as we have on our own producers, and have allowed our own people to become poorer because we have encouraged our companies to produce in foreign countries under the somewhat honorable goal of raising their living standards. As honorable as this professed goal may seem, although every good American should have sympathy for poor workers in other countries, that sympathy should end when we start making our own people poorer as a result by destroying their jobs, their livelihood, and their belief that government should protect those who operate under the cost burdens of American laws and regulations from those who do not. The U.S. Government's hand-picked winners should not result in damage to the hand-picked losers. A truly healthy economy does not intentionally abandon entire industries, thereby preventing a large portion of its citizens from participating in prosperous times that have been custom designed for a select group of its people.

"Poverty befalls any nation that neglects and abandons the care of its own industry, leaving it exposed to the action of foreign powers—there is a remedy and that consists in—adopting a Genuine American System accomplished by the establishment of a tariff—with the view of promoting American industry—the cause is the cause of the country, and it must and it will prevail."

Henry Clay

Free trade has not caused a noticeable increase in unemployment, since those in the manufacturing industry who got fired from their high wage jobs are often able to find lower wage jobs in the service industry. Remember, the service industry is expanding and the manufacturing industry is shrinking. This also agrees with the statistic that a high percentage of workers who get laid off find replacement jobs at lower pay. Who wants the stress of leaving one job they chose at higher pay for another job the government chose as a "winner " for them that they don't want at lower pay? Our government sure picks some lousy winners!

In embracing free trade and demonizing protectionism as it is currently understood, we have ushered in a new type of protectionism of which many Americans are completely unaware. But this protectionism is not for the benefit of those who would honor American laws. It is a protectionism that is solely for the benefit of those who decide that American laws are too burdensome and costly and are to be evaded. It is a protectionism for those who want to compete for their share of the most lucrative market in the world, without paying the same price for the privilege. It is the same as allowing another poker player to the table that doesn't have to ante up, but can still compete for his share of the pot just like everyone else. It is a protectionism for those who want to exempt themselves from costly U.S. laws, and one that victimizes those companies that do not voluntarily exempt themselves from those same laws. The companies seeking this form of protectionism for themselves know that they cannot be subjected to identical costly U.S. regulations that have been imposed on American producers. They stand to have their imports subsidized since we have given cost privileges to them without granting the same cost privileges to American producers. As the saying goes, if you subsidize anything, you will get more of it, and we have subsidized those who would follow the free trade path of exempting themselves from U.S. laws. Is it any surprise that this form of protectionism has continued to increase imports more than exports with no end in sight? It is a sad fact that in the name of increased competition we have rendered our laws meaningless, since those who operate under them are not protected from those who do not. The free trade global economy has been exalted for forcing American companies to become more efficient to ''compete'' against ever-increasing foreign competition, but no one has stepped forward to explain clearly just what the rules of this supposedly beneficial competition should be.

Competition, we are told, goes hand in hand with the free-market system, but this too is misleading since there is no such thing as a free market. The Congress of the United States, unknowingly to free traders, has solidified this fact by passing literally thousands of laws since the beginning of this country that restrict what we can do, what we can buy, and how we can act. Neither the U.S. Constitution nor the Declaration of Independence says anything about free markets, and a national economic system geared towards free markets is nowhere implied. A free market, as well as free trade, in the purest sense of the term, is not even possible, and the fact that no founding national document mentions them should be proof enough that they were never intended to be a governing philosophy.

To advocates of what today is called fair trade, which is merely a politically correct word for protectionism, the rules of competition should be the same for trade policy as they are for any other competitive activity or event. Baseball games, for instance, require both teams to have the same number of strikes per batter and the same number of outs per side. Baseball requires that both teams should play by the same rules, and should be allowed to win the game based upon the same rules of play. One team doesn't get 4 strikes per batter or 6 outs per side. The agreement is not that if one less productive team gets an unfair advantage for a time, at the expense of the opposing team, that they eventually become better players and raise their skill level, allowing them to better compete in the future.

If this were the case, the fans would cry foul, declare the competition rigged, and would stop supporting either team. In like manner, American workers subject to unfair competition from abroad, where foreign producers are subsidized since they do not bear the same costs that American producers must bear, become much less enthusiastic supporters of what their country supposedly believes in and their political system. American workers would like to believe in a country that holds to its principles of equal protection ensuring justice for all.

But there is a serious lack of equal protection and justice for American companies and workers that are continuously subject to unfair competition from abroad by foreign companies that are granted more preferential access to America's lucrative market.

What's more is that there is more at stake here than just numbers in a win or loss column. The lives and financial and social well being of literally millions of Americans are at stake. The U.S. government has failed in its duty to abide by the Constitutional mandate of equal protection. It has failed to impose the same costs on foreign producers seeking access to the U.S. market that we impose on our own producers.

Fair traders (protectionists) want tariffs raised to sufficient levels so that the terms and cost consequences for all producers, foreign and domestic, are the same. Free traders, were they true to their beliefs, would favor such a policy since all producers would be on equal footing and the winners in the global economy would depend strictly on the basis of efficiency and productivity. It is likely that producers would find that prevailing in an atmosphere where the rules of competition were equal for all competitors was encouraging.

Protectionism has been vilified, even though it would merely protect Americans from less costly foreign production. But free traders fail to realize or admit that free trade is a form of protectionism all its own. Free trade is clearly protectionism for producers who do not want to operate in accordance with U.S. laws in favor of less costly foreign laws. American citizens don't realize they have passively endorsed and are the recipients of many forms of protectionism already. Social Security is a form of protectionism since it protects those who are beyond their working years and keeps them healthy financially. Welfare is a form of protectionism since it protects those who are out of work or are not able to find a job. The same applies to unemployment compensation and workman's compensation—both are forms of protectionism. It is amazing to me that we will endorse these kinds of protectionism that the U.S. taxpayer will ultimately pay for, but we will not endorse the form of protectionism that would keep workers from losing their jobs in the first place!

No matter which trade policy our government chooses, they will inevitably choose one form of protectionism or another. The choice that must be made will depend upon which form of protectionism is the most fair, and who deserves to be protected from the laws that "We, the people" have demanded and the government has enacted.

By adopting free trade, we subsidize foreign producers, since we fail to impose the same costs on foreign producers seeking access to the U.S. market as we have on our own producers.

Free trade economists also claim that America's trade policy since 1973 has served to keep inflation in check. But when one discovers that products costing $30 in the Kennedy administration cost $82 when Reagan took office in 1980, this puts the assertion that free trade keeps inflation and consumer prices low in serious question. Furthermore, by 1992, the same products that cost $30 during the Kennedy years cost $144. So much for free trade keeping costs down.

A 1999 Tax Foundation report found that American taxpayers pay more in total federal, state and local taxes than for food, clothing and shelter combined. We have shifted the burden of paying for the cost of government from the foreign producer to the American producer and consumer. We have raised taxes on American producers while simultaneously lowering taxes (tariffs) on foreign producers to the point that our remaining American producers must transfer more of their production offshore where they can get a better deal accessing the U.S market along with their foreign rivals.

Higher tariffs force foreign producers, rather than the U.S. taxpayer, to finance the costs of American government. The American taxpayers are not only picking up the tab because of reduced import tariffs, they are also paying a higher share of the costs of government than corporations in general. As recently as 1996, corporate income taxes made up 23% of all government revenue, but by 1999, that figure was down by more than half at 10.1%.

The old national economy was more or less under local or national control. That local control has now been replaced by distant, more invisible forces. The new global economic system stretches beyond the reach of national regulation and accountability. Economic stability and security are threatened by unelected bureaucrats on the other side of the world. To be sure, the larger the economic system, the tougher it will be to keep it stable. A global economy is tougher to manage by multinational forces than several smaller national economies managed by their respective national governments, and is much less stable.

The American economy bears its allegiance to America, where the global economy bears its allegiance to no one country. Embracing the global economy means ignoring or discarding loyalties to the nation. A national economy values independence, patriotism and national pride. In a global economy, these concepts are of no value and are to be discouraged. If the American people are ever of the opinion that the American economy is beyond the control of their elected representatives, serious problems will lie ahead. How long can our government advocate a trade policy that has wrought so many crises and stagnated wages without significant populist resistance? Only time will tell.

Are we to continue to establish a "more perfect union" according to the Declaration of Independence, or a more perfect global economy according to the desire of free traders to lock us into an era of complete interdependence? One of the main problems with interdependence is that a nation cannot solve its own problems without creating problems for another. Are the gains of an independent heritage of America's past not worth protecting? America is a nation of laws, but a global economy seeks to produce where the fewest of those exist.

As America embraces the global economy, it must also simultaneously abandon such founding American virtues as independence, self-sufficiency, and self-reliance.

In a global economy, American workers are no longer seen as contributing stakeholders to company advancement and national prosperity, but as units of high labor-cost problems that need to be dealt with. And even though global markets may be increasingly beyond the control of the U.S. Government, they are not beyond the influence of the American consumer if we buy American.

"I cannot see the global system surviving. Political and financial instability are going to feed off each other in self-reinforcing fashion. In my opinion, we have entered a period of global disintegration only we are not yet aware of it."

George Soros

The global economy is a rather abstract concept, led by blind market forces. Markets aren't rational, and we often make bad policy judgments about the economy since these judgments are based on rational thinking. We would do well as a nation to put aside textbook economic theory and confront reality.

The reality of the 90's decade is that the global economy has turned many once-reliable theories into unreliable myths. The fall in the unemployment rate did not cause an increase in the inflation rate. Higher taxes did not lead us into recession. Increased productivity didn't always translate into higher wages. The theory of comparative advantage, which says that the U.S. will import goods from countries whose labor is low paid and low-skilled, didn't stop us from importing goods from countries with higher wage rates than our own, even when similar domestically produced alternatives were available. As globalization expands, even the jobs of white-collar workers are being transferred to low-wage countries.

Traditional economic theory also says that as a nation's currency becomes weaker, its exports become more competitive. For the United States, this should have meant that since the Japanese yen fell from 260 per U.S. dollar in 1980 to 100 per U.S. dollar in 1992, a smaller trade deficit should have been the result, but the weaker dollar had almost no effect. Trade deficits with Japan continued although a devalued dollar was supposed to make our goods cheaper in foreign markets. All we ended up with was a devalued dollar that signified decreased wealth compared to other countries. It's no wonder that China is following the protectionist Japanese model instead of the free trade model of the United States.

The table below shows fluctuation in the dollar's value compared to the Japanese yen between 1985 and 1995.

1 Dollar = 260 Yen in 1985
1 Dollar = 130 Yen in 1987
1 Dollar = 160 Yen in 1990
1 Dollar = 80 Yen in 1995

In 1981, the dollar could be exchanged for 4.25 French francs, but by 1985 the dollar could be exchanged for 10 French francs. In the span of four years, the exchange rate had more than doubled, meaning we had lost our comparative advantage. Should we have then abandoned all industries that were in direct competition with the French? If we had, in 1992, we would have had to recreate those same industries because $1 would again be exchanged for 4.80 French francs. This is why comparative advantage, if strictly followed as a reliable policy to dictate our trade policy in terms of what America should and should not produce, would result in sheer lunacy.

GDP (Gross Domestic Product) is increasingly a less reliable indicator of economic health. In his 1992 economic report, President Clinton stated that "Growth in real GNP or GDP does not ensure an increase in the standard of living. If real GDP grew less rapidly than the population, for example, real GDP per person would fall." Today, health care is 3.5% of GDP, so as more resources are needed to care for America's sick, GDP rises with the increased economic activity, and it is perceived that the country is more prosperous. It is projected that the cost of Medicare will eventually surpass spending on Social Security. The American legal system is 2% of GDP. The war on drugs is about 3% of GDP. The war on crime is about 2.5% of GDP. More prisons are built and more police are added to the federal payroll. Economic activity increases, and so does GDP. A higher GDP in America today is less impressive than it was several years ago before so many lawyers and social problems were as prevalent.

During the golden era of protectionism between 1871 and 1913, before Woodrow Wilson gave us the income tax and led us into WW I, GNP averaged 4.3% annually, which outpaced the average for the entire 20th century.

The example of rising productivity and falling wages is perhaps no better demonstrated than in the U.S. auto industry. According to the New York Times, workers employed by General Motors that were making $30,000 a year in 1992 were making $42,000 a decade earlier. No one can deny that the 1992 workers were more productive than those in 1982. It took 3100 people 54 months to develop the Chrysler K-Car, but it only took 700 people 33 months to develop the Dodge Neon.

More evidence that real wages for working Americans are directly affected by our governmental trade policies is shown as a result of President Lyndon B. Johnson's auto pact with Canada. America's trade surplus with Canada in the automotive sector turned into a deficit within one year after passage of the auto pact, and continued every year for the next 25 years except for one.

Perhaps we could look at the plight of the U.S farmer. At the heart of the uneasiness many Americans feel about the global economy is the farm crisis. Earlier I discussed the disconnect between rising productivity and rising wages, and the agriculture industry is no different. Although American farmers are continually more productive, higher living standards have not materialized. Each year it seems the government devises yet another bailout scheme to keep America's farmers farming. Still, foreclosures have skyrocketed. Financial lenders in North Dakota more than doubled the number of farms they foreclosed on for 1999 alone. Mediation services, which oversee disputes between farmers and their financial lenders, saw their cases more than double as well. The consequences are far-reaching. Taxpayer-funded guarantees from American universities are offered, along with government subsidies, but the foreclosures continue. The same universities offering grants to farmers have seen children from farming families quit college. Farmers in the Midwest struggle to find a crop that is profitable to grow, and farms that have been in the family for generations are being sold.

It is no surprise that the focus of many farmers in America has turned inward. Ranchers try to persuade congress for mandatory labels on meat stating country of origin. "Go Texan" commercials are aired featuring Tommy Lee Jones as consumers are given the choice of Canadian beef from over one million cattle that slaughterhouses in the U.S. buy each year. Other states create logos to help convince the American consumer to support the American farmer.

Cattle ranchers have a formidable case in urging the American consumer to buy local. Brazil has more cattle than both the United States and Argentina combined. As many export markets for U.S. beef remain closed, Brazil is always on the verge of prying open the U.S. market. Yet U.S. ranchers are barred from selling their beef to Europe, as that continent exercises its sovereign right to refuse agriculture imports that are not free of growth hormones. And despite NAFTA guarantees of free trade, barriers increase for American beef destined for Mexico.

Hog prices have plummeted to levels not seen since the Great Depression. As commodity prices sink, calls to mental-health hotlines soar. Since nearly 33% of all commodities of U.S. farmers are targeted for export, the Asian financial crisis of the late 1990's was particularly rough for America's farmers, as most of these exports are bound for Asian countries.

What are the answers? As in most industries, we should be protecting the American market for the American producer instead of surrendering our market for supposedly greener pastures that never seem to materialize.

The most-often proclaimed greener pasture is, of course, China. However, farm analysts had to significantly increase China's grain reserve estimates in 2001, which caused many who were once very optimistic toward China as an export market for U.S. grain to realize they had been overly optimistic. Many in the farm industry lobbied hard for China to be allowed into the WTO based on the theory that they would be one of the U.S.'s biggest export targets. Because of China's drought of 2000, many thought China would import large volumes of grain, and hopefully, most of it from America. But China, who has the world's largest grain-handling port, controls over 50% of the world's stockpile of grain, and represents 11% of the world's grain supply is now thought more in terms of a competitor rather than a potential customer.

The USDA claimed that its numbers just didn't make sense anymore. China considers its stockpile of grain reserves a state secret, and kept it off the radar screen. China witnessed famine before during the Mao Tse-tung era, and now equates national food supply to national independence.

As in every industry, America should not be making trade concessions to other countries based on estimates of important information that are purposely kept off the radar screen. America has too often been the victim of granting concrete concessions to other countries for promises from those countries that never materialize. China has a long history of breaking their promises to the U.S., and we clearly should have known better than to lobby for their accession into the WTO. China did not need to join the WTO to be a participator in the world economy. They already were. And Japan is sufficient proof that a country can still join the WTO and take advantage of open markets in the U.S. while their own markets remain closed to our exports. Joining the WTO certainly has not resulted in the end of protectionist policies for Japan, and it won't for China either.

Many advocates for full trade engagement with China, including President George W. Bush, have remarked that as we export our products to China, we also export our values. If this is true, it must also be true that China exports their values to the U.S. as well, which means that according to our multi-billion dollar trade deficit, we are importing far more communism from China than China is importing democracy from the United States.

Crafters of America's economic policy today are in uncharted waters, and America has no history books to use as a guide detailing how to steer a global economy through a recession that is technology-based. But there soon may be something very substantial to write about in the history books. The same global economic forces that ushered in the boom of the stock market of the 1990's are the same forces that caused the downturn that led us into recession in late 2001. To be fair, the tragic events of September 11 were no help, but even the most ardent of free trade economists agree that the writing was already on the wall for recession to take place. Items that normally point to a recession were already in place in the early months of 2001. Manufacturing had fallen 54% from January to February that year, which normally indicates that the entire economy, and not just certain sectors, has entered into recession. Despite claims that the recession of 2001 never took place, President George W. Bush has strongly argued that there was indeed a recession.

Even President Clinton lamented that the new economy may present insurmountable challenges to the nation.

"I came to this job committed to restoring the middle class and I did everything I knew to do. We lowered the deficit. We increased investment in education, in technology, in research and development. We expanded trade frontiers. We have seven million more jobs. We have a record number of millionaires. We have an all-time high stock market. We have more new businesses than ever before . . . . And most people are still working harder for lower pay than they were making the day I was sworn in as President. How did this happen? We're moving into a global economy, an information society. These income trends are huge, huge trends, huge, sweeping over two decades, fast international forces behind them, trillions of dollars of money moving across international borders working to find the lowest labor cost and pressing down, untold improvements in automation. So fast that you can't create enough high-wage jobs to overcome the ones that are being depressed in some sectors of the economy.

Bill Clinton, July, 1995 at Georgetown University.

The problem is that most of these jobs that were supposedly created are jobs that are funded by the U.S. taxpayer. In 2000, the health care sector was responsible for creating 45% of all new jobs that year, and was responsible for over 30% of GDP. By comparison, the much-admired housing sector was responsible for only 18% of the growth of the U.S. economy. And in a heavy blow to free traders, it was the government-subsidized housing market that kept the economy afloat before it fell into recession in March 2001—not any component of the so-called free market.

At least one senior Japanese official has displayed "utmost concern" that for U.S. economic expansion to continue, rising stock prices are crucial. He may be right.

In September of 1999, many Japanese policy makers and investors displayed cautious belief that the financial markets in the U.S. were a bubble that was running on borrowed time, not to mention borrowed cash. Japan, having experienced its own boom and bust cycle in the 1990's that contributed to a nearly continuous decade-long recession, have reason to be concerned. Japan's nervousness about America's soaring stock market and its sustainability is becoming more substantial. Stocks now make up nearly one-third of Americans' household wealth, and declining stock prices in 2000 caused household net worth to decrease for the first time since at least 1945, when the United States first started keeping track of this statistic.

Americans may need to be concerned about the nervousness of Japanese investors. Since during the boom of the 1990's, Americans borrowed heavily from foreigners, including the Japanese, to finance consumer spending and business investment. The percentage of U.S. debt that could be traced to foreign sources ran at 28% in 1998, as foreign assets increased to a record $6.2 trillion.

Luckily for the United States, foreigners are deciding to reinvest their earnings here rather than take them home, but if that trend reverses, America could be in for a serious change of lifestyle. Without huge foreign inflows of investment capital, our country would not be able to sustain economic activity at existing levels.

As long as America continues to consume more than it saves and runs budget deficits to maintain its debtor nation status instead of being a creditor nation as we were prior to 1985, it will continue to be dependent on foreign inflows of investment capital to maintain the status quo. Despite the recent recession, consumer confidence has remained fairly high, for a while, at least. Consumer optimism and consumption are being stimulated by the performance of the stock market, which also stimulates economic growth. It seems apparent we have reached a phase in America where we will both live by the stock market and die by the stock market.

Let us hope it doesn't end there, but rather let us hope we can return to a more stable system, once called the American system, of protection for the U.S. market and prosperity for all its citizens regardless of their chosen industry. Both our successful past of trade protection and our current system of an open U.S. market for foreign producers has demonstrated that, at least for the United States, protectionism equals prosperity and free trade equals failure.

Chapter 3

Foreign Investment— Good for America?

Foreign investment. To many it sounds like a natural good for America. But are foreign companies actually investing in America, or using America to invest in themselves?

One thing is for sure: foreign investment rapidly increased in the 1990's. But if Japanese companies, for example, increase their investment in manufacturing in America, have we stopped to think about who gets the return on that investment? America may supply the labor, but the profits will go back to Japan. If Japanese companies invest in manufacturing in America, we supply the labor and they get the return on investment, but if American companies invest in America, we supply the labor and America gets the return on the investment.

Foreign investors would not be investing in America if they could not redeem their investments for greater profit. Therefore, they are foreign redeemers of dollars that used to be ours. In the 1980's, ownership of America's land, factories and other assets by foreigners was seen as an American weakness, and a sign that Americans would take orders from distant masters that did not have America's best interest at heart. We would eventually forfeit control of our own destiny to those that were not primarily accountable to the American people or to American stockholders. As a result, foreign companies enhanced their political and economic power, and some stole sensitive military technology that took decades to develop in the interest of the national security and protection of the American people. Still, since 1980, the number of Americans working for foreign bosses has increased over $2\frac{1}{2}$ times. The debate over foreign investment has surfaced again simultaneously with the debate over free trade and the evidence of resulting job losses from such a trade policy. As more jobs are sacrificed in the name of free trade and the U.S. remains in recession, the economy will inevitably slide backward, demanding an even closer look into the advantages—if any—to foreign investment. Many Americans have forgotten about the massive Japanese foreign investment of the 1980's, but what if a similar economic invasion of our markets was to originate from Communist China? America's new-found patriotism since the September 11th tragedy may write a different chapter in history than if that catastrophic event had never taken place.

When foreigners assume ownership of U.S. land and factories, they become our landlords and holders of the mortgage on our national treasury. They dissipate wealth instead of creating it since their profits return to foreign lands and the taxes are paid to foreign governments.

Foreign owned companies pay fewer taxes to the United States government than comparable American owned companies. The more we support American owned companies, the stronger they will be financially and the less likely they will be to merge with or be taken over by foreign companies. Bill Archer, former Chairman of the House Ways and Means Committee, once argued that as American companies merge with foreign companies and move their headquarters overseas, they inevitably pay less money to the IRS. The biggest recent example of a former American company merging with a foreign company is when German-owned Daimler-Benz acquired Chrysler, the most successful automobile company in the 1990's (but not the biggest). Detroit and its workers will now take their orders—and layoff notices—from Stuttgart, Germany instead of Detroit, Michigan, and will have to fly across the Atlantic Ocean to protest corporate decisions.

When Daimler-Benz and Chrysler merged, Chrysler had a 44% stake in the newly formed company. By March of 1999, however, the percentage of American shareholders in DaimlerChrysler had dropped to 25%. Although the deal was passed off as a "merger of equals," it soon became obvious this was not to be the case. By June of 2000, Detroit could not keep up with the processing of resumes since so many former executives were leaving. Many of these same executives used to take pride in the fact that although Chrysler was the smallest American car company in the 1990's, it was still the most successful. "Fast is better than big" used to be the saying among Chrysler executives.

New CEO Jurgen Schremmp won and Chrysler lost. It would seem for a short time in the beginning that both would win, because at the time of the takeover, Chrysler was awash in profits. Differing from the initial announcement of a "merger of equals," Schremmp made Chrysler a mere subsidiary of the German auto maker. Almost every aspect of making Chryslers, from design to production, was to be controlled by Schremmp from the German headquarters.

After the ink on the deal was dry, Schremmp spent the night drinking it up with his new American colleagues, leading them in the singing of songs which included "Bye, Bye, Miss American Pie."

By January 2001, when it was evident that Chrysler was in deep financial trouble, Schremmp tried to put an American face on Chrysler, saying "I will not rest until this company—this American icon—is back where it belongs, at the top of the industry." But it was too late. Chrysler had been solidified as a German company. Most of the former American executive talent had left out of cultural differences, and the workers' morale wasn't faring too well either. In February 2001, within days of detailing plans to eliminate thousands of American jobs, Schremmp announced that German workers would be paid an 11% bonus. 140,000 hourly employees would get checks totaling nearly $1,500 each.

Any contribution Chrysler can make to DaimlerChrysler's bottom line will now further enable Airbus to compete with America's largest exporter—Boeing. Airbus is a heavily government-subsidized consortium of British Aerospace PLC, France's Aerospatiale Matra SA, Spain's Construcciones Aeronauticas SA, and the aerospace unit of DaimlerChrysler. In fact, Airbus won more orders than Boeing for the first time in history in 1999, the year after Chrysler merged with Daimler-Benz.

To be perfectly clear, the term "merger" can be deceiving. When a foreign company and an American company merge, the new company will either be American owned or foreign owned. If the newly-merged company is foreign owned, then the merger accounts to nothing more than foreign investment. There is no "merger of equals" or legitimate claim of having dual headquarters.

Despite the widely proclaimed positives of merger activity, most mergers fail to live up to their expectations. Several experts have estimated that 75% of all mergers fail to achieve their expected results. Over half of the merger deals between 1996 and 1998 actually reduced the stock prices of the companies involved, and over 80% of the merger deals saw stock prices stagnate. The year 2000 was the first in many years when, upon announcement of a merger, the majority of stock prices fell. Merging companies often underestimate the stress on the employees involved, whose concerns include their continued employment and potential cultural conflicts should they survive the merger. Cultural questions were at the heart of the DaimlerChrysler merger. In their uneasiness that Germany would become too much like America, German workers wondered how Americans could live on less than six weeks of vacation, and wanted to know why American university students had to pay their own way. Even though Germany's unemployment rate is still over 8%, many unemployed Germans live better than employed Americans who earn low wages. In Germany, every company must have an equal number of representatives for both shareholders and workers on the board.

The merger of British Petroleum and Amoco was trumpeted as a merger of equals as well, but Amoco's executives found out differently as soon as the ink was dry on the deal. British executives made it clear that Amoco was to be run by British Petroleum's structured management and culture, and anyone who felt uncomfortable about it could join the other 10,000 recently fired employees. Before the signing of the merger, it was estimated that only 6,000 jobs would be eliminated. Most of the newly-revised 10,000 job losses would come from Amoco's existing U.S. operations, which further documents why foreign investment is a job destroyer and not a job creator.

Foreign investors are already reaping more gains from their U.S. investments than Americans take home from foreign investments overseas. In the first nine months of 1999, foreign companies announced U.S. purchases of more than double the value of 1998's volume to $256 billion, which is four times the volume for all of 1997.

According to the latest data from the U.S. Commerce Department, of the $282 billion of foreign investment in 1999, only 3% was used to establish new operations, while 97% was used to acquire existing U.S. businesses. Although this may well have resulted in 500,000 more workers reporting to foreign bosses, it is doubtful this simple change of ownership created any new jobs. It is much more likely that such acquisitons led to layoffs in redundant job positions within the new foreign company. And according to the U.S. Department of Commerce, in the five years prior to 1992, foreign owned companies established 1,749 new U.S. plants. But according to IRS study in 1989, 72 percent of all foreign companies operating in the United States paid no U.S. taxes.

In 1995, the U.S. Commerce Department determined that foreign companies avoided paying one-half of their taxes due to the U.S. government. Foreign companies, despite their large investment in this country, create zero net jobs for Americans, because the overwhelming majority of Americans working with foreign bosses came through acquisitions of existing U.S. owned operations. And, when you take into account the layoffs that almost always accompany foreign acquisitions of existing U.S. companies, the number of jobs created by foreign investment may actually be negative.

Paul Craig Roberts, who helped President Reagan construct his tax cuts of the 1980's, says that "In 2000, 97 percent of direct investment by foreigners went for the purchase of existing U.S. assets," and that "We are not only losing our losing industrial jobs, we are losing ownership of our companies."

Foreign investment also makes us less independent, and gives us less of an authentic recent to celebrate Independence Day. As Charley Reese said in one of his syndicated columns, if you support interdependence instead of independence, stay home on the fourth. Independence Day is more than going to see fireworks displays. It is about celebrating our independence as a nation, including economically, from other nations.

"A free people . . . should promote such manufactories as tend to render them independent on others for essential, particularly military supplies," said George Washington in his first address to the U.S. Congress. Independence was likened to trade policy by our first president.

But with increased foreign investment, we become increasingly interdependent. Foreign companies, with so much investment in America, are no longer willing to take a passive interest in the make-up of our economy. With Honda and Toyota plants located in America, both companies feel that they should have a say in what a America's economic policy should be concerning the auto industry. Who could blame them? But should we grant concessions and tax breaks to companies of countries like Japan that discriminate against U.S. exports? Investing companies, foreign and domestic, want and expect to have a major voice in determining America's destiny, but we must be careful not to allow ourselves to reach the point where the majority of the American market is supplied by merely U.S. subsidiaries of foreign-owned companies. To the degree that this is true, it is to the same degree that we will have lost control of our own destiny.

Should we stop resisting foreign investment if the day comes that foreign companies did pay all the required taxes to the U.S. government, equaling the taxes paid by American companies? The answer is no. Both trade and economic independence are the reasons we should not.

Increasing foreign investment insures that our massive trade deficit will continue to expand. If we were to drastically reduce or eliminate foreign investment and resurrect substantial tariffs, we would both severly reduce bidding for jobs with public funds and collect more revenue at the same time—a double positive hit to the U.S. Treasury of the United States.

When we buy imports, we send our dollars to foreign lands. Foreigners use their new dollars (that used to be ours) to acquire our existing factories, land and banks. Then they get a seat at the table to tell us how our country and economy should be structured. Foreigners are doing this with dollars that used to belong to Americans!

Foreign companies also have a tendency to target their investment so they are geographically closer to each other in locations where the lowest wages in America are paid. According to company officials in the automotive industry, German companies, for instance, are likely to be located where they can help other German companies.

One in eight American workers in manufacturing is employed by a foreign owned U.S. subsidiary. Even with all the talk of the United States and other first world countries investing in third-world countries, we are still the largest recipient of foreign investment.

Wanting to limit foreign investment in my country should not be construed as isolationist. A common argument is that with so many screwdriver operations (U.S. assembly facilities ultimately owned by foreign companies,) someone has to buy these products. And the fact remains that no matter how strong the arguments in this book, there will always be Americans who will buy foreign owned companies' products simply because they are "made in the USA."

Almost every country has limits on foreign investment in one form or another, with the United States having one of the fewest. U.S. stock exchanges accept more listings of foreign companies than any other country's exchanges. Japan smartly prohibits foreign ownership or control of key manufacturing and high-technology sectors. China requires foreign investors to find a domestic partner and requires much of the factory production to be exported so as not to compete head-to-head with Chinese companies, thereby wisely securing the Chinese market for the Chinese producer. Singapore limits foreign investment in newspaper companies to 3%.

According to the U.S. Commerce Department, spending by foreign investors to establish or acquire existing U.S. businesses increased 17% in the year 2000 from the prior year to a record $320.9 billion. Until 1998, annual foreign investment in the United States had never surpassed the $80 billion mark.

Listed in Part III are 138 automobiles, where they are made, the ownership of the auto maker, and whether they are made with union or non-union labor. If you look through the entire list, you will notice that most foreign-owned auto makers use non-union labor. But regardless of how you may feel about the labor movement in general, the fact remains that foreign auto makers producing in the U.S. predominantly assemble their automobiles in low-wage states like Alabama and South Carolina, while American-owned auto makers (Ford and General Motors) predominantly produce in high-wage union states like Michigan and Ohio.

Every state deserves its fair share of jobs in our great country. We are all part of America and deserve jobs just like anyone else. The point is that this is one of many relatively unknown facts that give foreign-owned auto makers huge cost advantages over American-owned auto makers. Consider the following:

In 1997, the state of Alabama granted huge subsidies to Mercedes in exchange for a plant that would employ 1,500 people. What were the details of this huge incentive package? $300 million in tax breaks, $253 million in other direct incentives, $60 million in Alabama taxpayer money to send fellow Alabamans to Germany for training, and a promise to buy 2,500 of the new Mercedes SUV's at $30,000 each, representing another $210 million in guarantees. Based on just the initial $300 million grant alone, those 1,500 jobs will cost Alabama taxpayers $200,000 per job. Apparently Alabama, not Mercedes, will be paying those salaries for years to come. With deals like these, it's no wonder foreign auto makers have stepped up production in the U.S. We'll even pay their workers' salaries for them!

But it didn't stop there. DaimlerChrysler decided in August of 2000 to build a second plant next to their existing plant in Alabama. The German company will reportedly receive an additional $150 million in government incentives for the expansion.

The original deal Mercedes crafted with Alabama caused such a backlash from Alabama citizens that it cost then-Governor Jim Falson his reelection bid, since voters in that state did not appreciate commitments made to Mercedes that required school officials to raid education funds to the tune of $43 million. Education administrators refused to hand over the money, forcing Alabama to raid pension funds instead, and to secure financing at 9% interest to repay the borrowed funds.

The only difference between that financial shell game of tax incentives and the most recent deal of over $150 million in giveaways to Honda for their new plant in Alabama is that this deal is 30% less-costly than the former one. The announcement that Honda might hire 3,000 workers in the long run is reminiscent of trade concessions granted to China in exchange for promises that may never materialize in the future. Amazingly, Alabamans are receptive to the deal, even though it will take at least 20 years, according to the University of Alabama's Center for Business and Economic Research, before Alabama breaks even. And that depends on more Honda suppliers moving into the area. Since there are currently only 18 Honda dealers in the entire state, that realization is not probable unless more attractive financial giveaways are offered. Losses to be recovered include over $100 million in free land, site construction preparation and training for future employees. Honda will also receive in excess of $50 million in additional tax incentives. Although Alabama will supposedly not have to raid any education or pension funds this time around, it is still a case of bidding for jobs with public taxpayer funds. These funds could have been used for education, health care, or any number of state government programs to serve the social needs of Alabama citizens.

Depriving a state of adequate funds for education is a vicious cycle to initiate, as hindering academic achievement may eventually dampen efforts to attract new employers with well-trained workers in the future. The public school district in Toledo, Ohio is finding that out first hand. Tens of millions of dollars that could have worked for the benefit of over 38,000 students in the district went to grant various businesses tax abatements instead. Some of these companies are smaller and locally owned, and yet others are larger American-owned corporations. Owens Corning saves nearly $875,000 annually on school taxes, but German-owned DaimlerChrysler AG negotiated a $280 million incentive deal that will allow it to avoid paying $8 million in school taxes. Toledo is not an isolated case, however. Businesses surrounding the Memphis, Tennessee area have avoided paying so many taxes that would have funded public education that administrators are discussing eliminating programs such as high school athletics. Clearly, our schools and the communities they reside in will not improve with continued concessions like these.

But these large tax concessions did not start in the 1990's. Although Toyota did not start employing American workers until 1984, Toyota was given 1,500 acres of free land to construct an auto plant in 1987 in Georgetown, Kentucky. A Japanese steel company using Japanese steel built the auto plant. The U.S. government created a ''special trade zone'' so Toyota could import auto parts from Japan duty-free. Mitsui Bank of Japan handled financing. Total federal and state grants and incentives exceeded $100 million. These subsidies, of course, were courtesy of your tax dollars.

Tennessee gave Nissan $11,000 per job for their Smyrna plant built in 1980. South Carolina coughed up $79,000 per job to convince Germany's BMW to build their plant in Spartanburg in 1992. Were you aware that our government was using your money to create jobs? Or are these merely job announcements where you and I foot the bill? Job announcements do make for great rhetoric for state governors' re-election campaigns. How many years will it take each factory worker in Alabama to pay back the $200,000+ in tax money that the government gave away? A conservative answer would be ''several.''

This is not to say that American companies are not granted incentives to build plants here. Cadillac received $100 million in incentives to build their latest plant in Michigan. It is my opinion that we should not be imitating the Third World by using public money to bid for jobs, but when given the choice between foreign investment (Toyota, Mercedes, Nissan) and American investment (General Motors and Ford), American investment is much better for America.

According to Site Selection Magazine, of the top 10 biggest investment deals in the year 2000, eight resulted in American companies investing in America. One was an American company, Motorola, investing in Scotland. The other was Nissan investing in Mississippi—a traditional example of foreign companies avoiding high wage rates in America.

The deal Alabama gave Mercedes makes the deal Michigan gave GM seem rather frugal. The point here is that these huge incentives that are offered to foreign companies are rarely offered to our own companies here at home. Such incentives allow foreign companies to save hundreds or even thousands of dollars in costs per automobile. Since American companies acquire more of their parts from domestic sources, more jobs are supported and created in America's automotive parts industry when we support American owned companies.

Of the wages that are paid to Americans employed in the automotive industry, it is the American companies (General Motors and Ford) that pay the highest wages. Plants owned by General Motors and Ford are highly concentrated mostly in the higher-wage union states such as Michigan and Ohio, where transplant factories are mostly located in lower-wage, non-union states such as Alabama and South Carolina. So by supporting the home team, we also support higher wages. But of course to support the home team, we have to know who the home team is. GM and Ford are the only home team players left since Chrysler was acquired by German auto maker Daimler-Benz in 1999. The "big three" has now been reduced to the "big two."

One reason foreign auto companies locate plants in the United States is to squelch any possible uprising of protectionist or "Buy American" sentiment. Should Congress decide to raise tariffs on automobile imports, foreign companies would avoid part of the blow since they already have factories in the United States. And, contrary to claims of free traders, importing companies pay the tariff. Free traders would have you believe that the consumer always pays the tariff, but this is no more guaranteed than free trade is guaranteed to lower consumer prices. Do you really think that Nissan lowered the price of their Sentra after they moved their plant from Kentucky to Mexico in 1998?

Abraham Lincoln said on several occasions that the consumer usually is not the one who pays the tariff, as it is normally paid by the importer or foreign manufacturer.

So we see that it is not only American companies that move factories beyond our borders. The fact is that Ford and General Motors have nearly twice as many models made in America than all foreign auto makers, including Chrysler, combined.

To be fair, foreign auto makers don't always construct their plants in low-wage non-union States. Honda has one plant in Ohio—a state where higher union wages are present, although attempts to unionize the plant have failed. So consequently, Honda pays lower wage rates than GM in the same state. In fact, GM loses about $1,000 on every Cavalier they make in Ohio. And although Honda has a fraction of the factories in America that GM and Ford have, they claim they are taking a "huge risk" betting on America if the U.S. auto market were to experience a downturn. Apparently Chevrolet has accepted this "huge risk," even with the reality of losing money on some of their cars, while keeping production in the United States. Admittedly, GM and Ford have closed a number of factories over the last several years, but they still have far more factories in the U.S. than all foreign auto makers combined.

Some of the Hondas assembled in Ohio are actually exported back to Japan. This presents a potentially dangerous scenario because we are putting a greater and greater emphasis on our ability to reduce our burgeoning trade deficit into the hands of our competition.

As Charley Reese has said, "Toyota, public relations efforts notwithstanding, has its primary loyalty to Japan, as it should. If conditions arise in which Toyota must choose between what's in the best interest of its American subsidiaries and what's in the best interest of Japan, it will choose Japan. Anyone who loves his own country must necessarily respect others who love their countries."

If we love our country, and want to better be able to pay for the expense of preserving it, we should support not only the companies that produce in the United States, but also the ones headquartered here. They pay the taxes that fund the cost of government and make preservation of this great nation possible.

Foreign investment also has political influences that reach into the campaign finance reform issue. Foreign nationals are prohibited from contributing to our local, state and federal election process, but U.S. subsidiaries of foreign owned companies are not. So by supporting foreign-owned companies operating in the United States, we are enabling the increase of foreign influence in American politics.

We may not be able to stop foreign investment in America, but we can stop giving foreign companies the money with which to invest. America needs more American investment, not more foreign investment.

Chapter 4

Myths of the Smoot-Hawley Tariff

To be able to explain accurately the effects of the Smoot-Hawley Tariff of 1930, it is necessary first to rid ourselves of popular myths so that we can start with a clean slate and derive conclusions from fact, rather than from fantasy. I will list some common myths here, and then disprove them using facts according to history. The myths that prevail, even today, some 61 years after President Herbert Hoover signed the tariff bill, are as follows:

1. The Smoot-Hawley Tariff established the highest tariff rates in U.S. history, and the sharp rise in tariff rates caused countless nations to retaliate with tariffs of their own.

2. The Smoot-Hawley Tariff contributed to the instability of the stock market.

3. The Smoot-Hawley Tariff was responsible for causing the Great Depression.

Campaigning against Herbert Hoover for the presidency in 1932, Franklin D. Roosevelt saw the tariff as a way to get a leg up on his Republican opponent's incumbent bid. Even Republicans eventually began to mischaracterize their party's former president in later years, as well as the tariff bill he signed into law in 1930. Even Ronald Reagan said "The Smoot-Hawley Tariff helped bring on the Great Depression." Someone should have told President Reagan that the Smoot-Hawley Tariff was enacted over eight months *after* the Great Depression. Later, the former president said "the Smoot-Hawley tariff . . . made it virtually impossible for anyone to sell anything in America and . . . spread the Great Depression around the world." Someone should have told President Reagan that over two-thirds of the goods imported into the United

States entered duty-free, and that some nations actually increased exports to the United States after the Great Depression. There was actually a higher percentage of imports on the duty free list in 1930 than there was after Ronald Reagan left office. Al Gore fell for the same politically correct lie as Reagan in 1993 in his debate with Ross Perot, claiming the tariff "was one of the principle causes . . . of the Great Depression."

Even the Democrat Party Platform of 1928 proclaimed that tariffs were necessary to sustain "legitimate business and a high standard of wages for American labor." The platform also encouraged the equalization of the cost between production at home and abroad to "safeguard . . . the wage of the American laborer." Today, most Republicans and Democrats alike regard equalizing tariffs as extreme.

The confidence Hoover expressed in high tariffs in his re-election bid was echoed throughout the campaign. If the word of the day was that high tariffs had caused the Great Depression, Hoover's stance would have been obvious political suicide. Even FDR was unable entirely to avoid the call for high tariffs. On the campaign trail in October 1932, he proclaimed, "I favor . . . continued protection for American agriculture as well as American industry." The creation of the myth that the Smoot-Hawley tariff caused the Great Depression would have to wait.

Regardless of how one calculates tariff rates, either as a percentage of imports where tariffs are applied or as a percentage of all imports, duty-free or not, the Smoot-Hawley tariff did *not* have the highest rates in U.S. history. That claim belongs to the Tariff of Abominations of 1828, which caused neither a depression nor a recession. With the belief that high tariffs cause depressions and hamper economic growth, one has to wonder why there wasn't a Great Depression of 1830? The reason is that there are several factors that cause recessions and depressions. Some of these causes will be discussed in this chapter, and I will show that they were the cause of the Great Depression, not the Smoot-Hawley Tariff.

In their attempts to vilify Senator Smoot and Representative Hawley for supposedly proposing such extremely high tariff rates, many politicians, economists, and textbook writers seem to miss the fact that the 59.1 percent tariff rate only applied to one-third of all imports in 1932. The 59.1 percent rate is derived by using the most liberal method for calculating tariff percentages, and is actually higher than it should be. The reason the tariff was determined to be at such a falsely high level is because over 50 percent of U.S. imports were tariffed at a fixed rate. For example, if a particular good had a tariff rate of 25 cents per pound, and the product sold for a dollar, the tariff percentage was represented at 25 percent. However, with the prices falling for goods as the economy collapsed, the tariff rate would double if the value of the good decreased by one-half. So what was a 25 percent tariff rate before the depression instantly became a 50 percent tariff, although the consumer was actually getting the same product for less at the newly calculated higher tariff rate. In other words, a product that cost a dollar at a 25 percent tariff would cost $1.25. But if the price fell to 50 cents, the tariff was still 25 cents and the product now only cost 75 cents. The tariff rate, however, was now calculated to be 50 percent. The Smoot-Hawley tariff actually extended the list of imports that entered the country with no tariffs at all compared to the Fordney-McCumber tariff of 1922. What the Smoot-Hawley tariff did do was raise tariffs on particular import-sensitive goods, such as Canadian agriculture, that were already on the tariff list and increase the number of goods to which no tariffs were applied.

Free traders typically look at tariffs (indirect taxes) on imports as causing consumers to pay more while ignoring direct taxes on American consumers. There are few who will mention or acknowledge that President Hoover raised the top income tax rate from 25 percent to 65 percent in 1932. FDR continued this atrocious policy by further raising the rate to 79 percent! This insurmountable climb in the income tax rate heaped far more damage on the American consumer than any modest tariff increase on a select amount of import-sensitive items. Keep in mind that tariffs are a discretionary, indirect tax. The consumer can choose to buy the import or the domestic good, and therefore refuse to pay the tariff, but no consumer escapes direct income taxes. Everyone must pay. It's no wonder it took World War II to drag us out of the bottom of the economic barrel.

Was America the only nation to raise tariff rates before the depression? No. Many nations raised tariffs after World War I. France, Germany, Spain, Italy, Yugoslavia, Hungary, Czechoslovakia, Bulgaria, Romania, Belgium and Holland all raised their tariffs on imports to levels comparable to those before World War I. Even Britain, a free trade nation, declared that "new industries since 1915 would need careful nurturing and protection if foreign competition were not again to reduce Britain to a technological colony." The message was clear. Nations were rebuilding their industries after World War I and needed protection to re-develop them.

But what effect did the tariff have on the stock market? History shows that the crash was much more likely due to the inability of Congress to pass a tariff bill at all than because of the possibility that Congress might pass a high tariff bill. A business community and its nation perceived a lack of leadership, gridlock, and political maneuvering, rather than tending to the needs of the country. Records show that when Representative Hawley's bill passed the House Chamber five months before the stock market crashed, the Dow climbed over 5 points to 298.87. After Senator Smoot proposed an even more protectionist Senate version, the market peaked at 381 points. However, a republican Senator from Idaho, William Borah, formed a coalition of constituents to defeat the bill. On

October 3, the Dow lost 15 points. The front page of the New York Times stated: "Hoover Defeated on Flexible Tariff; Coalition in Senate, 47 to 42, Takes from President Duty-Fixing Power." The perception was that Hoover had no majority in Congress to pass the tariff bill. Democratic Senator George Norris tacked on an agricultural subsidies program, and Senator William Borah and his coalition of agrarian Republicans took charge of writing the tariff. The stock market did not crash out of fear of higher tariffs. If anything, it crashed due to the perception that Congress lacked the discipline and leadership to pass any tariff bill at all!

Prior to the crash, the National Association of Manufacturers complained to President Hoover of the inability of business to make decisions on industrial expansion, since the tariff bill had been haggled over for five months. The Bankers Trust director and former vice-president, Fred Kent, blamed the Democratic coalition, led by Senator George Norris, for their part in the stock market crash. "Industry cannot proceed, employ men, buy and process raw materials unless it can feel confident of markets," said Kent, and "there was a fear that if this [insurgent] bloc succeeded in rewriting the tariff bill in its own way, it might come to believe that it had the power to reduce tariffs." William Borah responded that if the fight of his coalition "shakes the Stock Exchange to the earth, let it go."

The volume of trade in respect to imports did drop off in 1930 after the passage of the Smoot-Hawley tariff, but what nation would not see a reduction in imports if the buying power of their citizens had just been cut in half or worse? One would think that out of the total volume of U.S. imports, during the deep depression years, import growth of non-dutiable goods would outpace those upon which duties were levied. However, this was not the case. From 1929 to 1931, the volume of both dutiable and non-dutiable imports declined almost equally at 52 percent. In fact, there were one hundred products that had higher tariffs applied to them that actually saw an increase in import volume. It is very interesting that despite the reduced buying power of Americans coupled with the fact higher import duties were being collected on some of these items, foreign producers did not eliminate their attemps to gain a greater share of the U.S. market. It is obvious that not only with the Smoot-Hawley tariff, but also with the preceding Fordney-McCumber Act of 1922, and basically since the first tariff in 1789, there was no decisive negative relationship between higher tariffs and import volumes.

Concerning the charge that nations enacted retaliatory tariffs against the United States for passing the Smoot-Hawley bill, historical documents do not support this view. Great Britain did not release any formal protests since it regarded the United States as a sovereign nation that did not look favorably upon other nations meddling in its affairs. Great Britain was also concerned that a formal protest might encourage still higher tariffs, which might work to the disadvantage of her exporters. Great Britain was one of America's leading trading partners, and avoided any formal protest. Sir Esme Howard, the British Ambassador to Washington at the time, informed London that "official representations . . . against the proposed tariff increases . . . [would be] a mistake."

Foreign diplomats generally avoided specific threats of retaliation against the United States, since any such language would be considered an infringement upon national sovereignty, and it was not the place of foreign governments to protest the Constitutionally enacted laws of the United States. Furthermore, the word "protest" during the time of the Great Depression did not automatically express dissatisfaction with U.S. trade policy. The word "protest" usually represented the argument that treaty rights of a foreign nation had been violated.

Canada briefly discussed retaliation in 1929 with U.S. Secretary of State Frank Kellogg. Canada warned Kellogg that raised tariff rates might result in a high probability for retaliation. Canadian Minister Vincent Massey was encouraged to release an official statement representing Canada's position, but none was ever written. Canada did not want to antagonize high tariff legislators in Congress. Instead, Massey decided to go a more discreet route via the American press. After meeting with the editor of the New York World, Massey was "impressed" by the position of the editor "that Canada will never be taken seriously by the United States . . . until she is prepared to strike back." I would suppose that a similar opinion is shared by the Chinese about the United States today. The United States repeatedly languishes over its huge trade deficit with China, but our market remains open to their goods while their market is virtually closed to ours. China will never take the United States seriously until we have the courage to take a stand and apply higher tariffs on Chinese goods like the Chinese have applied to our goods!

Many nations of that time embraced the idea that retaliation would be counterproductive. They feared antagonizing Congress or a grass roots brushfire of nationalistic patriotism among U.S. citizens that might lead to discrimination of their imported goods. Historical records show that the Smoot-Hawley tariff did little to encourage foreign countries to retaliate with high tariffs of their own. In May 1931, the State Department report found that "by far the largest number of countries do not discriminate against the commerce of the United States in any way." Data from the U.S. Commerce Department show that the reason for the severe drop in exports in almost every American export industry was because of economic problems related to the depression, not foreign retaliation for higher U.S. tariffs. Some U.S. exports, however, did see significant gains in foreign market share. Exports of apples, pears and grapefruits increased. Exports of prunes went up 31 percent, and exports of dried apricots soared higher by 72 percent. Exports of raw materials such as cotton and rayon held steady. Exports of American films increased 49 percent, and exports of false teeth rose 24 percent.

The assertion that the Smoot-Hawley tariff was responsible for the Great Depression is a myth based on ignorance of historical facts in favor of pursuing free-trade economic textbook theory. The Smoot-Hawley tariff post-dated the stock market crash, and therefore could not have caused it. There is no convincing evidence that it made the Great Depression more severe, or was responsible for significant retaliation by foreign countries. There are no reputable claims of evidence that point to the Smoot-Hawley tariff of 1930 as a contributor to the second world war which occurred several years later. I have never heard or read about any German blaming America's Smoot-Hawley tariff for urging Hitler's aggression. In this case, only America blames America.

Senator John Heinz III, who died tragically in a plane crash in 1991, had developed a national reputation for his expertise in international commerce. During his years of serving in Congress, Senator Heinz III was appointed to the Chairmanship of the Subcommittee on International Finance and Monetary Policies. He had this to say about the Smoot-Hawley myth in 1985:

"It gravely concerns me that every time someone in this administration or the Congress gives a speech about a more aggressive trade policy, or the need to confront our trading partners with their subsidies, barriers to imports and other unfair practices, others in Congress immediately react with speeches on the return of the Smoot-Hawley Tariff Act of 1930, and the dark days of blatant protectionism and depression . . . It seems that for many of us that Smoot-Hawley has become a code word for protectionism and, in turn, a code word for the depression. Yet, when one recalls that Smoot-Hawley was not enacted until more than 8 months after the October, 1929 economic collapse, it is hard to conceive how it could have led to the Great Depression . . . the changes supposedly wrought by this single bill in 1930 appear fantastic."

It is interesting that many political writers today blame the Great Depression on the Smoot-Hawley tariff, but not all of them do. When Robert Kuttner, an editor for BusinessWeek magazine, wrote about the recent Enron scandal, he likened it to the "pyramid schemes" of the electric utilities industry of the 1920's, which, like Enron, ended up burning investors who believed in their companies. The investors got "soaked" when it was too late to realize that the companies were operating beyond the grasp of government regulation, which led to their collapse, and helped bring on the Great Depression. Milton Friedman has consistently maintained that the Great Depression occurred when the money supply contracted in the early 1930's. A March 2001 issue of the Wall Street Journal claimed that the Great Depression was the result of overspeculation of stock market prices by the Fed and too little attention given to the domestic economy. In July of 2001, another Wall Street Journal column claimed that the excess capacity of world production was responsible. With the exception of these brave writers and their editorials, the majority of today's economic thinkers lay the blame squarely and solely on Representative Hawley and Senator Smoot.

However, most writers who engaged the issue closer to that era—the ones who actually lived through it—had a completely different opinion. Even after Smoot lost his Senate seat at the age of seventy to a man twenty years younger, the *New York Times* had much good to say about him, calling him "a statesman of the highest type." Unfortunately, with Smoot's loss, the protectionist era, America's policy since the first tariff in 1789, had ended. Speaking before the American Bankers Association in 1931, the ABA President remarked, "We, the men in this hall, who control the economic destiny of the nation, knew in 1927 that this terrible depression was coming and we did nothing about it."

Such a statement suggests that there were conditions far and above minor tweaking in U.S. trade policy that led to the Great Depression. That is why President Franklin D. Roosevelt took steps to completely restructure both America's currency and banking system by creating the Federal Deposit Insurance Corporation (FDIC) to support the national economy solely upon "the full faith and credit of the United States Government." The practice of converting U.S. currency into gold was prohibited, and gold could only be used by businesses when it was absolutely necessary for the manufacture of goods. Although the Trade Agreements Act of 1934 did allow President Roosevelt to lower tariffs, the reduction represented less than 6/100th of 1 percent of our GNP. It would therefore take an extreme stretch of the imagination to believe that this minor reduction in tariffs, in the light of all the major banking and currency reforms initiated by FDR, played a significant role in America's economic recovery.

Further analysis of the economy during the depression years reveals that nearly two-thirds of the drop in imports between 1929 and 1933 occurred *prior* to the Smoot-Hawley tariff.

Free traders also like to point to the writings of Adam Smith, author of "The Wealth of Nations," whose work expressed his theories on international trade in 1776. But Smith emerges as a protectionist when one reads the following quote from his book: "Every individual endeavors to employ his capital as near home as he can, and consequently as much as he can in support of domestic industry."

In summary, we continue to fail to recognize the dilemma that sits before us by ignoring the wisdom of our founding fathers. We are on another unsustainable path, but we have refused to learn from history. However, this time, when it becomes obvious that the path we are on is unsustainable, America will not be able to blame a policy of domestic

protection. Free trade and free-running global commerce will be the unde-
niable culprit. I remain confident that America will someday have no
choice but to return to a policy of protection for domestic industries. It
is sad to also believe it will take a national or global economic crisis for
the U.S. Government to wake up and confront this issue.

Part III

American Made/Union Made— General Products

Just because a Union made product is made in the USA doesn't mean that it is made by an American company. Profits made by foreign companies are repatriated to the foreign country, and the taxes on those profits are paid to foreign governments, not to the U.S. government. Now more than ever, especially since the war on terrorism has prompted our elected officials to put 20,000 workers on the federal payroll for air security, America is in danger of losing its national tax surplus. We should be supporting the American companies that make things in the USA, so American owned companies will make the profits, and the U.S. government will be paid the taxes.

A United Auto Workers study found that over 500,000 jobs have vanished because of foreign "transplant" factories. The tax breaks and subsidies offered to transplanted foreign manufacturers are rarely offered to Ford and GM. Yet, they allow foreign-owned producers operating in the United States to save hundreds or even thousands of dollars per vehicle in production costs. These subsidies are paid for by your tax dollars.

America needs American investment, not foreign investment. A recent study found that foreign companies—even those that produce here—pay less than 1% of their profits in taxes to America. Only American workers and American companies pay taxes to fund the cost of government. They deserve our patriotic support. It is because of these and many other reasons documented in this book that I endorse only the American-owned products on the following two lists.

The following Union Made/American Made lists are the result of a joint effort by the Union Label & Service Trades Department of the AFL-CIO and myself. The Union Label & Service Trades Department provided the union made information and I researched the ownership information for all the products and services. It should be understood that the Union Made/American Made information is the latest data available, and the manufacturing location for some of the products may have moved outside the United States since the research was completed. The related ownership information, however, is current.

Brand	Category	Nationality
3M	Adhesive Tape	American
Scotch	Adhesive Tape	American
Curtis	Air Compressors	American
Dresser-Rand	Air Compressors	American
Comfort Maker	Air Conditioners	American
Day N' Night	Air Conditioners	American
Emerson	Air Conditioners	American
Fedders	Air Conditioners	American
Frigidaire	Air Conditioners	Sweden
Heil	Air Conditioners	American
Payne	Air Conditioners	American
Tempstar	Air Conditioners	American
Trane	Air Conditioners	American
Armstrong	Air Conditioning/Heating Equipment	American
Bryant	Air Conditioning/Heating Equipment	American
Carrier	Air Conditioning/Heating Equipment	American
Coleman/Evcon	Air Conditioning/Heating Equipment	American
Lennox	Air Conditioning/Heating Equipment	American
Rheem	Air Conditioning/Heating Equipment	England
Sears	Air Conditioning/Heating Equipment	American
York International	Air Conditioning/Heating Equipment	American
Airborne Express	Air Courier Services	American
DHL	Air Courier Services	American
Air Wisconsin	Airlines	American
Alaska	Airlines	American
Allegheny Commuter	Airlines	American
American	Airlines	American
American Eagle	Airlines	American
Comair	Airlines	American
Continental	Airlines	American
Continental Express	Airlines	American
Delta	Airlines	American
Executive	Airlines	American
Flagship	Airlines	American
Flagship Express	Airlines	American
Horizon Air	Airlines	American
KLM	Airlines	American
Northwest	Airlines	American
Simmons	Airlines	American
Southwest	Airlines	American
TWA	Airlines	American
TWA Express	Airlines	American
United	Airlines	American
USAir	Airlines	American
USAir Shuttle	Airlines	American

Wings West	Airlines	American
Altes	Ale	American
Ballantine	Ale	American
Heilman	Ale	American
Miller Genuine Draft	Ale	South Africa
Miller High Life	Ale	South Africa
Miller Ice	Ale	South Africa
Miller Reserve	Ale	South Africa
Weinhard's	Ale	American
Alcan	Aluminum Foil	Canada
Diamond Foil	Aluminum Foil	American
Reynolds	Aluminum Foil	American
Reynolds Wrap	Aluminum Foil	American
Prestone	Anti-Freeze	American
5 Brother	Apparel	American
Alexander Julian	Apparel	American
Allyn St. Georges	Apparel	American
Arctic Cat	Apparel	American
Austin Reed of Regent Street	Apparel	American
Barrier Jackets	Apparel	American
Bike	Apparel	American
Bridal Originals	Apparel	American
Brittania	Apparel	American
Calvin Klein Formal Wear	Apparel	American
Cambridge Tailoring	Apparel	American
Carhartt	Apparel	American
Carhartt's	Apparel	American
Chaps	Apparel	American
Chaps Formal Wear	Apparel	American
Christian Dior	Apparel	American
Damon Neckties	Apparel	American
Demtre Ski Sweaters	Apparel	American
Don Alleson	Apparel	American
Emily Rose	Apparel	American
Enro Neckties	Apparel	American
Evan Picone	Apparel	American
Five Brother	Apparel	American
Foxcroft Neckties	Apparel	American
Gant	Apparel	Sweden
Garan	Apparel	American
Hathaway	Apparel	American
Hickey Freeman Formal Wear	Apparel	American
Jaymar Ruby Formal Wear	Apparel	American
Joseph A. Bank Clothiers Formal Wear	Apparel	American
King Louie	Apparel	American
L.L. Bean	Apparel	American

L.L. Bean Leather Gloves	Apparel	American
McGregor	Apparel	American
Men's 505	Apparel	American
Men's 517	Apparel	American
Mighty Mac	Apparel	American
Nadine	Apparel	American
Nicole Miller	Apparel	American
Oscar De La Renta Formal Wear	Apparel	American
Oshkosh B'Kosh	Apparel	American
Palm Beach	Apparel	American
Perry Ellis	Apparel	American
Pierre Cardin	Apparel	American
Private Label Formal Wear	Apparel	American
Ralph Lauren Formal Wear	Apparel	American
Rare Edition	Apparel	American
Rawlings	Apparel	American
Roffe Ski Wear	Apparel	American
Southwick Formal Wear	Apparel	American
Sylvia	Apparel	American
Ultimax Socks	Apparel	American
Wigwam Socks	Apparel	American
Dixon	Art Supplies	American
Goldrite	Art Supplies	American
Jon Gnagy	Art Supplies	American
Permalba	Art Supplies	American
Webber	Art Supplies	American
AC Delco	Auto Parts	American
AC Delco Air Filters	Auto Parts	American
Akro Floor Mats	Auto Parts	American
Allied Signal	Auto Parts	American
Amoco Auto Batteries	Auto Parts	England
Autolite	Auto Parts	American
Casite	Auto Parts	American
Champion Auto Batteries	Auto Parts	American
Champion Spark Plugs	Auto Parts	American
Flex-Vent	Auto Parts	American
General Motors Replacement Tail Lights	Auto Parts	American
Goodyear Rubber Products	Auto Parts	American
Hastings	Auto Parts	American
Motorcraft Auto Batteries	Auto Parts	American
Motorhoney	Auto Parts	American
Powerflex	Auto Parts	American
Price-Costco Auto Batteries	Auto Parts	American
RPG Landshield Gloss	Auto Parts	American
Trico	Auto Parts	England
Tuffy Mufflers	Auto Parts	American

United Technologies	Auto Parts	American
Wal-Mart Auto Batteries	Auto Parts	American
Gerber	Baby Food/Formula	Sweden
Nature Lock	Baby Food/Formula	Sweden
Tender Harvest	Baby Food/Formula	Sweden
Arm & Hammer	Baking Goods	American
Kroger	Baking Goods	American
Lucky Leaf Pie Filling	Baking Goods	American
Multifoods	Baking Goods	Canada
Royal Pie Mixes	Baking Goods	American
White House Pie Filling	Baking Goods	American
Weber-Stephen	Barbecue Grills	American
Bryon's	Barbecue Sauce	American
Heinz	Barbecue Sauce	American
Alpha Keri	Bath Soap	American
Dial	Bath Soap	American
Dove	Bath Soap	Unilever*
Irish Spring	Bath Soap	American
Lifebuoy	Bath Soap	Unilever*
Shield	Bath Soap	Unilever*
Action Pak	Batteries	American
C & D Power	Batteries	American
Delco Freedom	Batteries	American
Energizer	Batteries	American
Everready	Batteries	American
Exide	Batteries	American
K-Mart	Batteries	American
Ray-O-Vac	Batteries	American
Shell	Batteries	Netherlands
Hanover	Beans	American
Ranch Style Beans	Beans	American
Altes	Beer	American
Ballantine	Beer	American
Budweiser	Beer	American
Busch	Beer	American
Falstaff	Beer	American
Heilman	Beer	American
King Cobra	Beer	American
L.A. Beer	Beer	American
Labatt Blue	Beer	Belgium
Labatt Lite	Beer	Belgium
Lone Star	Beer	American
Michelob	Beer	American
Miller Genuine Draft	Beer	South Africa
Miller High Life	Beer	South Africa
Miller Ice	Beer	South Africa
Miller Lite	Beer	South Africa

Miller Reserve	Beer	South Africa
Miller Special Dark	Beer	South Africa
Old German	Beer	American
Pearl	Beer	American
Pearl Lite	Beer	American
Red Dog	Beer	American
Schlitz	Beer	American
Schlitz Light	Beer	American
Schlitz Malt Liquor	Beer	American
Sharp's	Beer	American
Weinhard's	Beer	American
Culligan	Bottled Water	France
Poland Spring	Bottled Water	Swiss
Barton	Bourbon	American
Ancient Age	Bourbon Whiskey	American
Benchmark	Bourbon Whiskey	American
Blanton	Bourbon Whiskey	American
Kentucky Tavern	Bourbon Whiskey	American
Old Fitzgerald	Bourbon Whiskey	American
Wild Turkey	Bourbon Whiskey	France
Freihofer	Bread	Canada
Merita	Bread	American
Federal Signal	Burglar Alarms	American
Aurora	Burial Caskets	American
Batesville	Burial Caskets	American
Greyhound	Bus Coach Service	Canada
Blue Bonnet	Butter/Margarine	American
Fleischmanns	Butter/Margarine	American
Imperial	Butter/Margarine	Unilever*
Land O'Lakes	Butter/Margarine	American
Coleman	Camping/Travel Trailers	American
Canadian Host	Canadian Whiskey	American
Canadian Supreme	Canadian Whiskey	American
Will & Baumer	Candles	American
Lifesavers	Candy	American
Nestle	Candy	Swiss
Russell Stover	Candy	American
Sees	Candy	American
American Olean	Ceramic Tile	American
Cap'n Crunch	Cereal	American
Grainfield's	Cereal	England
Life	Cereal	American
Nabisco Cereal (Hot)	Cereal	American
Purina	Cereal	Swiss
Bacardi Breezers	Champagne	Bermuda
Carlo Rossi	Champagne	American
Chase-Limoge	Champagne	American

Cooks	Champagne	American
Cribari	Champagne	American
Dunnewood	Champagne	American
Eden Roc	Champagne	American
Inglenook	Champagne	American
Mumm	Champagne	American
Bloodhound	Chewing Tobacco	England
Lancaster Limited Reserve	Chewing Tobacco	American
Skoal	Chewing Tobacco	American
Brooks Foods	Chili	American
Brooks Foods Chili Mix	Chili	American
Hormel	Chili	American
Quaker Oats	Chili	American
Heinz	Chili Sauce	American
Hall	China	American
Lenox	China	American
Delaware Ribbons & Bows	Christmas Decorations	American
Bel Air	Cigarettes	England
Benson & Hedges	Cigarettes	England
Capri	Cigarettes	England
Carlton	Cigarettes	England
GPC	Cigarettes	England
Kool	Cigarettes	England
L & M	Cigarettes	American
Lark	Cigarettes	American
Marboro	Cigarettes	American
Merit	Cigarettes	American
Newport	Cigarettes	American
Pyramid	Cigarettes	American
Richmond	Cigarettes	England
Bances	Cigars	American
Elgin	Clocks	American
Chock Full O'Nuts	Coffee	American
K-Mart	Coffee	American
Maxwell House	Coffee	American
Superior	Coffee	American
Walgreens	Coffee	American
Rubber Queen	Console Cup Holders	American
Pittsburgh Corning	Consumer Fiberglass	American
Heinz	Cookies	American
Ripon	Cookies	American
Toroware	Cooking Utensils	American
Corelle Ware	Cookware	American
Ekco Oven Secret	Cookware	American
General Housewares	Cookware	American
Mirro	Cookware	American
Pyrex	Cookware	American

Regal Ware	Cookware	American
Revere Foil Containers	Cookware	American
Revereware Independence	Cookware	American
Wearever	Cookware	American
Revlon Age Defying	Cosmetics	American
Enjoli	Cosmetics	American
Sunshine Cheese	Crackers	American
Camillus	Cutlery	American
Carvel Hill	Cutlery	American
Carnation	Dairy Products	American
Cool Whip	Dairy Products	American
Kemps	Dairy Products	Netherlands
Ryan Milk	Dairy Products	American
Sani-Dairy	Dairy Products	American
Steffans Sour Cream	Dairy Products	American
Yoplait	Dairy Products	American
Arrid XX	Deodorant	American
Beyond	Deodorant	American
FDS	Deodorant	American
Huggies	Diapers	American
Fosteria	Dinnerware	American
Lancaster	Dinnerware	American
Electrasol	Dishwasher Detergent	England
Jet-Dry	Dishwasher Detergent	England
Amana Perfect Balance	Dishwashers	American
Caloric	Dishwashers	American
General Electric	Dishwashers	American
Hotpoint	Dishwashers	American
Pencrest	Dishwashers	American
Speed Queen	Dishwashers	American
Chaps	Dress Shirts	American
Christian Dior	Dress Shirts	American
Enro	Dress Shirts	American
Foxcroft	Dress Shirts	American
Snuggle	Fabric Softener	Unilever*
Agco	Farm Equipment	American
Badger	Farm Equipment	American
Mayline	Filing Cabinets	American
Bactine	First Aid	Germany
Gorham	Flatware	American
Lenox	Flatware	American
Rubber Queen	Floor Mats	American
Congoleum	Floor Tile	American
Rubbermaid	Food Storage	American
Saran Wrap	Food Storage	American
Tupperware Plastic Kitchenware	Food Storage	American
Air Step	Footwear	American

Buster Brown	Footwear	American
Cantilever	Footwear	American
Connie	Footwear	American
Danner	Footwear	American
Fan Fare	Footwear	American
Florsheim	Footwear	American
Hush Puppies	Footwear	American
Hy-Test	Footwear	American
Irish Setter	Footwear	American
Lady Red Wing	Footwear	American
Life Stride	Footwear	American
Mason Shoe, B.A. Mason	Footwear	American
Night Life	Footwear	American
Nunn-Bush	Footwear	American
Red Wing	Footwear	American
Sperry	Footwear	American
Stacy-Adams	Footwear	American
Stride Rite	Footwear	American
Thoroghgood	Footwear	American
Tingley	Footwear	American
Tiny Steps	Footwear	American
Trimkids	Footwear	American
Wee Kids	Footwear	American
Weyenberg	Footwear	American
Wood-N-Stream	Footwear	American
Ambush	Fragrances	American
Canoe	Fragrances	American
Canoe Sport	Fragrances	American
Tabu	Fragrances	American
Amana	Freezers	American
Caloric	Freezers	American
Electrolux	Freezers	Sweden
Frigidaire	Freezers	Sweden
GE	Freezers	American
GE Monogram	Freezers	American
General Electric	Freezers	American
Gibson	Freezers	Sweden
Hotpoint	Freezers	American
Kelvinator	Freezers	Sweden
KitchenAid	Freezers	American
Maytag	Freezers	American
Pencrest	Freezers	American
Speed Queen	Freezers	American
Whirlpool	Freezers	American
White-Westinghouse	Freezers	Sweden
Banquet	Frozen Food	American
Banquet Cheese Nuggets	Frozen Food	American

Banquet Chicken Nuggets	Frozen Food	American
Banquet Cream Pies	Frozen Food	American
Banquet Southern Fried Breast Tenders	Frozen Food	American
Birdseye	Frozen Food	American
Downy Flake	Frozen Food	American
Empire Turkey Pies	Frozen Food	American
Gorton's Seafood	Frozen Food	Unilever*
Hormel Chicken Pies	Frozen Food	American
Hormel Light N' Lean	Frozen Food	American
Hungry Jack	Frozen Food	American
Jeno's	Frozen Food	American
Kemps Ice Cream	Frozen Food	Netherlands
Le Menu	Frozen Food	American
Morton's	Frozen Food	American
Mrs. Paul's	Frozen Food	American
On-Cor	Frozen Food	American
Ore-Ida	Frozen Food	American
Pappalos	Frozen Food	American
Swanson	Frozen Food	American
Totino's	Frozen Food	American
Weight Watchers	Frozen Food	American
American Seating (office)	Furniture	American
Bentson (office)	Furniture	American
Brown Jordan (patio)	Furniture	American
DMI Furniture (office)	Furniture	American
Hufcor	Furniture	American
International Tables (wood)	Furniture	American
La-Z-Boy	Furniture	American
La-Z-Boy (office)	Furniture	American
La-Z-Boy Recliners	Furniture	American
La-Z-Boy Rockers	Furniture	American
Marvel (office)	Furniture	American
Mayline	Furniture	American
Meadowcraft	Furniture	American
Pennsylvania House (wood)	Furniture	American
Plantation Patterns	Furniture	American
Samsonite	Furniture	American
Schnadig (wood)	Furniture	American
Shelby Williams (office)	Furniture	American
Sunbeam (outdoor)	Furniture	American
United Chair (office)	Furniture	American
Kleen Guard	Furniture Polish	American
Brown & Bigelow Playing Cards	Games	American
Golden Books	Games	American
Golden Books Puzzles	Games	American
Genie	Garage Door Openers	Japan

Stanley	Garage Door Openers	Bermuda
Sinkmaster	Garbage Disposals	American
Waste King	Garbage Disposals	American
Appletime Apple Sauce	General Food Products	American
Armour Turkey Bacon	General Food Products	American
Campbell's Pork & Beans	General Food Products	American
Chef Boyardee	General Food Products	American
Chun King	General Food Products	American
Cool Whip	General Food Products	American
Country Skillet Catfish	General Food Products	American
Cream of Rice	General Food Products	American
Dinty Moore	General Food Products	American
Dinty Moore Chicken Stew	General Food Products	American
Dominick's Ice	General Food Products	American
Festal Tendersweet Canned Vegetables	General Food Products	American
Food Club Olives	General Food Products	American
Food Club Tacos	General Food Products	American
Food Club Turkey & Gravy Dinners	General Food Products	American
French's Mustard	General Food Products	England
French's Worcestershire Sauce	General Food Products	England
Gebhart Refried Beans	General Food Products	American
Goya Olives	General Food Products	American
Goya Salsa	General Food Products	American
Grecian	General Food Products	American
Hanover Canned Vegetables	General Food Products	American
Heinz Gravy	General Food Products	American
Heinz Ketchup	General Food Products	American
Hidden Valley Ranch	General Food Products	American
Hormel Chunk Turkey	General Food Products	American
Hormel Corned Beef Hash	General Food Products	American
Hormel Scalloped Potatoes & Ham	General Food Products	American
Hormel Turkey Burgers	General Food Products	American
IGA Olives	General Food Products	American
Kingston Tacos	General Food Products	American
La Victoria Salsa & Sauces	General Food Products	American
Lenders Bagels	General Food Products	American
Longmont Turkey Breast	General Food Products	American
Manwich	General Food Products	American
Monterey Mushrooms	General Food Products	American
Morningstar Farms	General Food Products	American
Old El Paso	General Food Products	American
Peter Piper's Pickles	General Food Products	American
Prairie Farm Cottage Cheese	General Food Products	American
Red Star Yeast	General Food Products	American

Rosarita Tacos	General Food Products	American
Schweigert	General Food Products	American
Sealtest Sour Cream Dip	General Food Products	American
Singleton Shrimp	General Food Products	American
Sizzlean Turkey Bacon	General Food Products	American
Steffans Cottage Cheese	General Food Products	American
Stokely Canned Vegetables	General Food Products	American
Swanson Broth	General Food Products	American
Sweet Sue Chicken & Dumplings	General Food Products	American
Sweet Sue Chicken Stew	General Food Products	American
Van Camp's Pork & Beans	General Food Products	American
Vlasic	General Food Products	American
Vlasic Olives	General Food Products	American
Vlasic Pickle Relish	General Food Products	American
Vlasic Sauerkraut	General Food Products	American
Weight Watchers	General Food Products	American
Welch's Jam/Jelly	General Food Products	American
White House	General Food Products	American
White House Applesauce	General Food Products	American
Worthington Foods	General Food Products	American
Yoplait Yogurt	General Food Products	American
Onan	Generators	American
Anchor Glass	Glassware	American
Steuben	Glassware	American
Super Glue	Glue	Germany
Kingsford Match Light Charcoal Briquettes	Grill Accessories	American
Ace Combs	Hair Care Products	American
Adorn	Hair Care Products	American
Consort	Hair Care Products	American
Mink	Hair Care Products	American
Tame	Hair Care Products	American
TCB	Hair Care Products	American
Tresemme	Hair Care Products	American
V05	Hair Care Products	American
White Rain Shampoo	Hair Care Products	American
Dobbs	Hats	American
L.L. Bean	Hats	American
Resistol	Hats	American
Stetson	Hats	American
Patton	Heaters	American
Freightliner	Heavy Trucks	Germany
Kenworth	Heavy Trucks	American
Mack	Heavy Trucks	France
Volvo	Heavy Trucks	Sweden
Eckrich	Hot Dogs	American

Frank 'N Stuff	Hot Dogs	American
Hebrew National	Hot Dogs	American
Hormel	Hot Dogs	American
Ohse	Hot Dogs	American
Oscar Mayer	Hot Dogs	American
Seitz	Hot Dogs	American
Swift-Eckrich	Hot Dogs	American
Wranglers	Hot Dogs	American
Lysol	Household Cleaners	England
Pine-Sol	Household Cleaners	American
Hunter	Household Fans	American
Lasko	Household Fans	England
Patton	Household Fans	American
Phillips	Household Fans	England
84 Lumber Bathroom Tubs & Shower Bases	Household Furnishings	American
Buckhorn Storage & Files	Household Furnishings	American
Kohler Bath Tubs	Household Furnishings	American
Kohler Plumbing Fixtures	Household Furnishings	American
Kohler Shower Doors	Household Furnishings	American
Kohler Toilets	Household Furnishings	American
Lady Pepperell	Household Furnishings	American
Pillowtex Bedspreads	Household Furnishings	American
Pillowtex Pillowcases	Household Furnishings	American
Pillowtex Sheets	Household Furnishings	American
Sears Bathroom Tubs & Shower Bases	Household Furnishings	American
Bionaire	Humidifiers	American
Combat	Insecticides	American
Armstrong	Insulation	American
Arizona	Jeans	American
Brittania	Jeans	American
Canyon River Blues	Jeans	American
County Seat	Jeans	American
Dakota	Jeans	American
John Henry	Jeans	American
Kids R Us	Jeans	American
L.L. Bean	Jeans	American
Lee	Jeans	American
Levis 532	Jeans	American
McGregor	Jeans	American
Men's 505	Jeans	American
Men's 517	Jeans	American
Mighty Mac	Jeans	American
Appletime	Juice	American
Lucky Leaf Cider	Juice	American
Nature's Own	Juice	American

Pure Tropics	Juice	American
Season's Best	Juice	American
Sunkist	Juice	American
Tropicana	Juice	American
Welch's	Juice	American
Polar Ware	Kitchen Sinks	American
Louisville Ladder	Ladders	American
Anchor Hocking	Lamps & Lighting	American
Ajax	Laundry Detergent	American
All	Laundry Detergent	Unilever*
Arm & Hammer	Laundry Detergent	American
Fab	Laundry Detergent	American
Purex	Laundry Detergent	American
Ralphs	Laundry Detergent	American
Sure	Laundry Detergent	Unilever*
Surf	Laundry Detergent	Unilever*
Vons	Laundry Detergent	American
Wisk	Laundry Detergent	Unilever*
Gilmour Garden Hoses	Lawn & Garden	American
Green Gold	Lawn & Garden	American
Greenview	Lawn & Garden	American
Lebanon	Lawn & Garden	American
Koret Handbags	Leather Goods	American
Bic	Lighters	France
Ronii Refillable	Lighters	American
Aireloom	Mattresses	American
Eastman House	Mattresses	American
King Koil	Mattresses	American
Perfect Sleeper	Mattresses	American
Sealy	Mattresses	American
Serta	Mattresses	American
Simmons	Mattresses	American
Heinz	Mayonnaise	American
Hellman's	Mayonnaise	Unilever*
Armour Bacon	Meats	American
Armour Genoa	Meats	American
Armour Salami	Meats	American
Armour Sausage	Meats	American
Armour Smokies	Meats	American
Black Label	Meats	American
Black Label Bacon	Meats	American
Boar's Head Ham	Meats	American
Boar's Head Salami	Meats	American
Boar's Head Sausage	Meats	American
Bryan Family Recipe	Meats	American
Carl Buddig Lunch Meat	Meats	American
Country Pride	Meats	American

Country Pride of Delmarva	Meats	American
Decker Bacon	Meats	American
Di Lusso	Meats	American
Eckrich Bacon	Meats	American
Eckrich Sausage	Meats	American
Empire Poultry	Meats	American
Falls Bacon	Meats	American
Fast N' Easy Bacon	Meats	American
Gallo Salami	Meats	American
Hillshire Farms Bacon	Meats	American
Hillshire Farms Lunch Meat	Meats	American
Hillshire Poultry	Meats	American
Homeland	Meats	American
Hormel	Meats	American
Hormel Bacon	Meats	American
Hormel Pork Chops	Meats	American
Hormel Sausage	Meats	American
Jimmy Dean Sausage	Meats	American
Kahn's Bacon	Meats	American
Kahn's Ham	Meats	American
Layout Pack Bacon	Meats	American
Messina	Meats	American
Miss Goldie Chicken	Meats	American
Ohse Lunch Meat	Meats	American
Old Smokehouse Sausage	Meats	American
Omaha Steaks	Meats	American
Oscar Mayer Bacon	Meats	American
Oscar Mayer Lunch Meat	Meats	American
Rosa Grande	Meats	American
Sara Lee Bacon	Meats	American
Sara Lee Ham	Meats	American
Schweigert Lunch Meat	Meats	American
Sizzlean Bacon	Meats	American
Spam	Meats	American
Sugardale	Meats	American
Sugardale Bacon	Meats	American
Swift Bacon	Meats	American
Swift Brown 'N Serve Sausage	Meats	American
Swift Sausage	Meats	American
Tennessee Pride Sausage	Meats	American
Thorn Apple Valley Bacon	Meats	American
Tyson's Poultry	Meats	American
Waynes Farms Chicken	Meats	American
Wranglers	Meats	American
Southwestern Bell Wireless	Mobile Telephone Services	American
Pennzoil	Motor Oil	Netherlands
Unocal	Motor Oil	American

Harley-Davidson	Motorcycles	American
Listerine	Mouthwash	American
Mayflower	Moving Services	American
Bach	Musical Instruments	American
Baldwin Pianos	Musical Instruments	American
Selmer	Musical Instruments	American
Steinway Pianos	Musical Instruments	American
Yamaha	Musical Instruments	Japan
Independent Nail	Nails	American
Vision Ease	Optical Lenses	American
Actifed	OTC Medications	American
Alka-Seltzer	OTC Medications	Germany
Ammens Medicated Powder	OTC Medications	American
Bayer Aspirin	OTC Medications	Germany
Haley's M-O	OTC Medications	Germany
Head & Chest	OTC Medications	American
Lubriderm	OTC Medications	American
Neo-Synephrine	OTC Medications	Germany
Norwich Aspirin	OTC Medications	American
Pepto Bismol	OTC Medications	American
Polysporin	OTC Medications	American
Riopan	OTC Medications	American
Rolaids	OTC Medications	American
American Lacquer	Paint	American
Glidden	Paint	England
PPG	Paint	American
Red Spot	Paint	American
Sherwin Williams	Paint	American
Dixie Cups	Paper Products	American
Skinner	Pasta	American
Shoprite	Pasta	American
Prince	Pasta	American
American Beauty	Pasta	American
Dominick's	Pasta Sauce	American
Prego	Pasta Sauce	American
Prince	Pasta Sauce	American
Shoprite	Pasta Sauce	American
Jif	Peanut Butter	American
Skippy	Peanut Butter	Unilever*
Parker Pen	Pens/Pencils	American
Sheaffer	Pens/Pencils	France
Trojan Condoms	Personal Care	American
9-Lives	Pet Food	American
Alpo	Pet Food	Swiss
Alpo Protein Plus	Pet Food	Swiss
Gravy Train	Pet Food	American
Kal Kan	Pet Food	American

Ken-L Ration	Pet Food	American
Meijer	Pet Food	American
Skippy	Pet Food	American
Kite	Pipe Tobacco	England
Sir Walter Raleigh	Pipe Tobacco	England
Kroger	Pizza	American
Natalina	Pizza	American
American Standard	Plumbing Fixtures	American
Eljer	Plumbing Fixtures	American
Speakman	Plumbing Fixtures	American
Jiffy Pop	Popcorn	American
Orville Redenbacher	Popcorn	American
Wise	Popcorn	American
Amana	Ranges	American
Caloric	Ranges	American
Kenmore	Ranges	American
Magic Chef	Ranges	American
Roper	Ranges	American
Speed Queen	Ranges	American
Whirlpool	Ranges	American
White-Westinghouse	Ranges	Sweden
Bic	Razors	France
Norelco	Razors	Netherlands
Personna	Razors	American
Trac I	Razors	American
Amana	Refrigerators	American
Caloric	Refrigerators	American
Electrolux	Refrigerators	Sweden
Frigidaire	Refrigerators	Sweden
GE	Refrigerators	American
GE Monogram	Refrigerators	American
General Electric	Refrigerators	American
Gibson	Refrigerators	Sweden
Hotpoint	Refrigerators	American
Kelvinator	Refrigerators	Sweden
KitchenAid	Refrigerators	American
Maytag	Refrigerators	American
Pencrest	Refrigerators	American
Roper	Refrigerators	American
Speed Queen	Refrigerators	American
Whirlpool	Refrigerators	American
White-Westinghouse	Refrigerators	Sweden
Congoleum	Rugs	American
First Alert	Safes	American
Hellman's	Salad Dressings	Unilever*
Kraft	Salad Dressings	American
Barton	Scotch	American

Foamy	Shaving Cream	American
Nivea	Skin Care	Germany
Revlon Age Defying	Skin Care	American
Empire	Small Appliances	American
Farberware	Small Appliances	American
Genie	Small Appliances	Japan
Hamilton Beach Coffee Makers	Small Appliances	American
Nesco	Small Appliances	American
Open Country Campware	Small Appliances	American
Pollenex	Small Appliances	American
Presto	Small Appliances	American
Proctor-Silex Coffee Makers	Small Appliances	American
Regal Ware	Small Appliances	American
Rival	Small Appliances	American
Simer	Small Appliances	American
Ademco	Smoke Detectors	American
First Alert	Smoke Detectors	American
Crunch N' Munch	Snacks	American
Frito's	Snacks	American
Hunt's Snack Packs	Snacks	American
Kellogg's Pop-Tarts	Snacks	American
Lay's Potato Chips	Snacks	American
Lunch Makers	Snacks	American
Nutrigrain Bars	Snacks	American
Planters	Snacks	American
Super Pretzel	Snacks	American
Tender Delite Corn Chips	Snacks	American
Wise Potato Chips	Snacks	American
Campbell's	Soup	American
Lipton	Soup	Unilever*
Progresso	Soup	American
Diamond Crystal Table Salt	Spices/Seasonings	American
Durkee - French	Spices/Seasonings	England
Mortons Salt	Spices/Seasonings	American
Mrs. Dash	Spices/Seasonings	American
Red Cross Table Salt	Spices/Seasonings	American
Sterling Halite Salt	Spices/Seasonings	American
Sterling Salt	Spices/Seasonings	American
Sysco Salt	Spices/Seasonings	American
Browning Firearms	Sports Equipment	Belgium
Brunswick	Sports Equipment	American
Callaway	Sports Equipment	American
Don Alleson	Sports Equipment	American
Eagle Basketballs	Sports Equipment	American
Eagle Golf Balls	Sports Equipment	American
Everlast	Sports Equipment	American
Louisville Hockey Sticks	Sports Equipment	American

Louisville Slugger	Sports Equipment	American
Louisville Slugger Baseball Hats	Sports Equipment	American
Muskin Swimming Pools	Sports Equipment	France
NordicTrack	Sports Equipment	American
Penn	Sports Equipment	Austria
Powerbilt	Sports Equipment	American
Rawlings	Sports Equipment	American
Spalding	Sports Equipment	American
Titleist	Sports Equipment	American
Top Flite	Sports Equipment	American
Top-Flite	Sports Equipment	American
Wilson	Sports Equipment	Finland
Jensen	Stereo Speakers	American
Rubbermaid	Storage Products	American
Crystal	Sugar	American
Dixie Crystal	Sugar	American
Great Western	Sugar	England
Holly	Sugar	American
IGA	Sugar	American
Jewel	Sugar	American
Sysco	Sugar	American
Fosteria	Tableware	American
Lancaster	Tableware	American
Superior	Tea	American
Tetley	Tea	England
Toshiba	Televisions	Japan
Sharp	Televisions	Japan
Cooper	Tires	American
Goodyear	Tires	American
Lander	Toiletries	American
Armstrong	Tools	American
Black & Decker Hand Saws	Tools	American
Blue Point	Tools	American
Channellock	Tools	American
Huck	Tools	American
Mac Tools	Tools	American
Porter Cable	Tools	American
Rotor	Tools	American
Snap-On	Tools	American
Stanley	Tools	Bermuda
Vermont American	Tools	American
Lionel Trains	Toys	American
Jensen	Turntables	American
Hoover	Vacuum Cleaners	American
Lucky Leaf	Vinegar	American
White House	Vinegar	American
Alcoa	Vinyl Siding	American

Armstrong	Vinyl Tile	American
Nafco	Vinyl Tile	France
Centrum	Vitamins	American
Geritol	Vitamins	England
One-A-Day	Vitamins	Germany
Amana	Washers & Dryers	American
Amana Perfect Balance	Washers & Dryers	American
Caloric	Washers & Dryers	American
Electrolux	Washers & Dryers	Sweden
Frigidaire	Washers & Dryers	Sweden
General Electric	Washers & Dryers	American
Gibson	Washers & Dryers	Sweden
Hotpoint	Washers & Dryers	American
Kelvinator	Washers & Dryers	Sweden
KitchenAid	Washers & Dryers	American
Maytag	Washers & Dryers	American
Pencrest	Washers & Dryers	American
Speed Queen	Washers & Dryers	American
Westinghouse	Washers & Dryers	Sweden
Whirlpool	Washers & Dryers	American
White-Westinghouse	Washers & Dryers	Sweden
American Time	Watches	American
Bartles & James	Wine	American
Beringer	Wine	Swiss
Boone's Farm	Wine	American
C.K. Mondavi	Wine	American
Charles Krug	Wine	American
Chase-Limoge	Wine	American
Chateau St. Michelle	Wine	American
Cooks	Wine	American
Cribari	Wine	American
Dunnewood	Wine	American
E & J Brandy	Wine	American
Eden Roc	Wine	American
Franzia	Wine	American
Gallo	Wine	American
Inglenook	Wine	American
Krug	Wine	American
Mumm	Wine	American
Saddle Mountain	Wine	American
Weibel	Wine	American

American Made/Union Made— Automobiles

General Motors—American Company

Make and Model	Labor	Location of Manufacture
AM General Hummer	Union	U.S.
Buick Century	Union	Canada
Buick LeSabre	Union	U.S.
Buick Park Avenue	Union	U.S.
Buick Regal	Union	Canada
Buick Rendezvous	unclear	Mexico
Cadillac Deville	Union	U.S.
Cadillac Eldorado	Union	U.S.
Cadillac Escalade	Union	U.S.
Cadillac Seville	Union	U.S.
Chevrolet Astro	Union	U.S.
Chevrolet Avalanche	unclear	Mexico
Chevrolet Blazer	Union	U.S.
Chevrolet Camaro	Union	Canada
Chevrolet Cavalier	Union	U.S./Mexico
Chevrolet Corvette	Union	U.S.
Chevrolet Express	Union	U.S.
Chevrolet Impala	Union	Canada
Chevrolet Lumina	Union	Canada
Chevrolet Malibu	Union	U.S.
Chevrolet Monte Carlo	Union	Canada
Chevrolet Prizm	Union	U.S.
Chevrolet S-10	Union	U.S.
Chevrolet Silverado	Union	U.S./Canada/Mexico
Chevrolet Suburban	Union	U.S./Mexico
Chevrolet Tahoe	Union	U.S./Mexico
Chevrolet Tracker	Union	U.S./Canada
Chevrolet Trailblazer	Union	U.S.
Chevrolet Trailblazer XL	Union	U.S.
Chevrolet Venture	Union	U.S.
GMC Envoy	Union	U.S.
GMC Jimmy	Union	U.S.
GMC Safari	Union	U.S.
GMC Savana	Union	U.S.
GMC Sierra	Union	U.S./Canada
GMC Sonoma	Union	U.S.
GMC Yukon XL	Union	U.S./Mexico
GMC Yukon/Denali	Union	U.S.
Oldsmobile Alero	Union	U.S.

Oldsmobile Aurora	Union	U.S.
Oldsmobile Bravada	Union	U.S.
Oldsmobile Intrigue	Union	U.S.
Oldsmobile Silhouette	Union	U.S.
Pontiac Aztek	unclear	Mexico
Pontiac Bonneville	Union	U.S.
Pontiac Grand Am	Union	U.S.
Pontiac Grand Prix	Union	U.S.
Pontiac Montana	Union	U.S.
Pontiac Sunfire	Union	U.S./Mexico
Pontiac Trans Sport	Union	U.S.
Pontiac Vibe	Union	U.S.
Saturn EV1	Union	U.S.
Saturn LS	Union	U.S.
Saturn S	Union	U.S.

Ford—American Company

Ford Contour	Union	U.S./Mexico
Ford Crown Victoria	Union	Canada
Ford Econoline/Club Wagon	Union	U.S.
Ford Escape	Union	U.S.
Ford Escort	unclear	Mexico
Ford Excursion	Union	U.S.
Ford Expedition	Union	U.S.
Ford Explorer	Union	U.S.
Ford Explorer Sport Trac	Union	U.S.
Ford F-Series Pickup	Union	U.S./Canada/Mexico
Ford Focus	Union	U.S.
Ford Mustang	Union	U.S.
Ford Ranger	Union	U.S.
Ford Taurus	Union	U.S.
Ford Thunderbird	Union	U.S.
Ford Windstar	Union	Canada
Lincoln Blackwood	Union	U.S.
Lincoln Continental	Union	U.S.
Lincoln LS	Union	U.S.
Lincoln Navigator	Union	U.S.
Lincoln Town Car	Union	U.S.
Mercury Cougar	Union	U.S.
Mercury Grand Marquis	Union	Canada
Mercury Mountaineer	Union	U.S.
Mercury Mystique	Union	U.S./Mexico
Mercury Sable	Union	U.S.
Mercury Villager	Union	U.S.

DaimlerChrysler—German Company

Chrysler 300M	Union	Canada
Chrysler Cirrus	Union	U.S.
Chrysler Concorde	Union	Canada
Chrysler LHS	Union	Canada
Chrysler Prowler	Union	U.S.
Chrysler Sebring Coupe/Sedan	Union	U.S.
Chrysler Sebring Convertible	Union	U.S./Mexico
Chrysler Town & Country	Union	U.S./Canada
Dodge Avenger	Union	U.S.
Dodge Caravan/Grand Caravan	Union	U.S./Canada
Dodge Dakota	Union	U.S.
Dodge Durango	Union	U.S.
Dodge Intrepid	Union	Canada
Dodge Neon	Union	U.S.
Dodge Ram Pickup	Union	U.S./Mexico
Dodge Ram Van/Wagon	Union	Canada
Dodge Stratus	Union	U.S.
Dodge Viper	Union	U.S.
Jeep Cherokee	Union	U.S.
Jeep Grand Cherokee	Union	U.S.
Jeep Wrangler	Union	U.S.
Mercedes M-Class Utility	Non-Union	U.S.
Plymouth Breeze	Union	U.S.
Plymouth Neon	Union	U.S.
Plymouth PT Cruiser	unclear	Mexico
Plymouth Voyager/Grand Voyager	Union	U.S./Canada

BMW—German Company

X-5 Utility	Non-Union	U.S.

Honda—Japanese Company

Acura CL	Non-Union	U.S.
Acura TL	Non-Union	U.S.
Acura MD-X	Non-Union	U.S./Canada
Honda Accord	Non-Union	U.S./Mexico/ Japan
Honda Civic	Non-Union	U.S./Canada/ Japan
Honda Odyssey	Non-Union	U.S./Canada
Honda Passport	Non-Union	U.S.

Isuzu—Japanese Company

Isuzu Amigo	Non-Union	U.S.
Isuzu Hombre	Union	U.S.
Isuzu Rodeo	Non-Union	U.S.

Mazda—Japanese Company

Mazda 626	Union	U.S.
Mazda B-Series Pickup	Union	U.S.
Mazda Tribute Utility	Union	U.S.

Mitsubishi—Japanese Company

Mitsubishi Eclipse	Union	U.S.
Mitsubishi Galant	Union	U.S.

Nissan—Japanese Company

Nissan Frontier	Non-Union	U.S.
Nissan Quest	Non-Union	U.S.
Nissan Sentra	unclear	Mexico
Nissan Xterra	Non-Union	U.S.

Subaru—Japanese Company

Subaru Legacy/Outback	Non-Union	U.S.

Suzuki—Japanese Company

Suzuki Swift	Union	Canada
Suzuki Vitara	Union (Canada)	Canada/Japan

Toyota—Japanese Company

Toyota Avalon	Non-Union	U.S.
Toyota Camry	Non-Union	U.S./Japan
Toyota Corolla	Union–on–Union	U.S./Canada
Toyota Sequoia	Non-Union	U.S.
Toyota Sienna	Non-Union	U.S.
Toyota Solara	Non-Union	Canada
Toyota Tacoma	Union	U.S.
Toyota Tundra	Non-Union	U.S.

Bibliography

Business Week, The McGraw-Hill Companies, New York, NY, Various issues.

Consumer Reports, Consumers Union of U.S., Inc., Yonkers, NY, Various issues.

Directory of Chain Restaurant Operators 2001, Chain Store Guide, Tampa FL

Directory of Corporate Affiliations LexisNexis Group 2000, 2001 New Providence, NJ

Directory of Department Stores 2000, Chain Store Guide, Tampa FL

Directory of Drug Store and HBC Chains 2001, Chain Store Guide, Tampa FL

Directory of Discount & General Merchandise Stores 2001, Chain Store Guide, Tampa FL

Directory of Home Center Operators & Hardware Chains 2001, Chain Store Guide, Tampa FL

Directory of Supermarket, Grocery & Convenience Store Chains 2001, Chain Store Guide, Tampa FL

Batra, Dr. Ravi, *The Myth of Free Trade,* Simon & Schuster, New York, 1993

Buchanan, Patrick J., *The Great Betrayal,* Little Brown and Company, Boston, 1998

Choate, Pat, *Agents of Influence,* Simon & Schuster, New York. 1990

Donoho, Annette, *Buy American.* Waikoloa, HI, 1991

Eckes, Alfred E. Jr., *Opening America's Market,* The University of North Carolina Press, Chapel Hill,1995

Fingleton, Eamon, *In Praise of Hard Industries,* Houghton Mifflin Company, Boston, 1999

Frank, Dana, *Buy American,* Beacon Press, Boston, 1999

Goldsmith, Sir James, *The Trap,* Carroll & Graf Publishers, New York, 1993

Greider, William, *One World, Ready or Not,* Simon & Shuster, New York, 1997

Kennedy, Allan A., *The End of Shareholder Value,* Perseus Publishing, Cambridge, 2000

Longworth, Richard C., *Global Squeeze,* Contemporary Books, Chicago, 1998

Norman, Al, *Slam-Dunking Wal-Mart!,* Raphel Marketing, Atlantic City,1999

Stelzer, Gus R., *The Nightmare of Camelot,* Peanut Butter Publishing, Seattle, 1994

The Wall Street Journal, Dow Jones & Company, Inc., New York, Various issues

Index

Chapter 5 - Health & Beauty Aids

Chapter 6 - Clothing & Accessories

Chapter 7 - Electronics

Book Order Form

Please send me _____ copies of How Americans Can Buy American @$24.95 each. Add $4.00 postage and handling for the first book and $2.00 for each additional book.

Name: _____

Address: _____

City: _____ State: _____ Zip: _____

Payment is accepted by check, money order or credit card.

Credit card: Visa Master Card AMEX Discovery (circle one)

Card number: _____

Name on card: _____ Exp. date: _____

Website orders: www.howtobuyamerican.com

Phone orders: 1-888-US OWNED (1-888-876-9633)